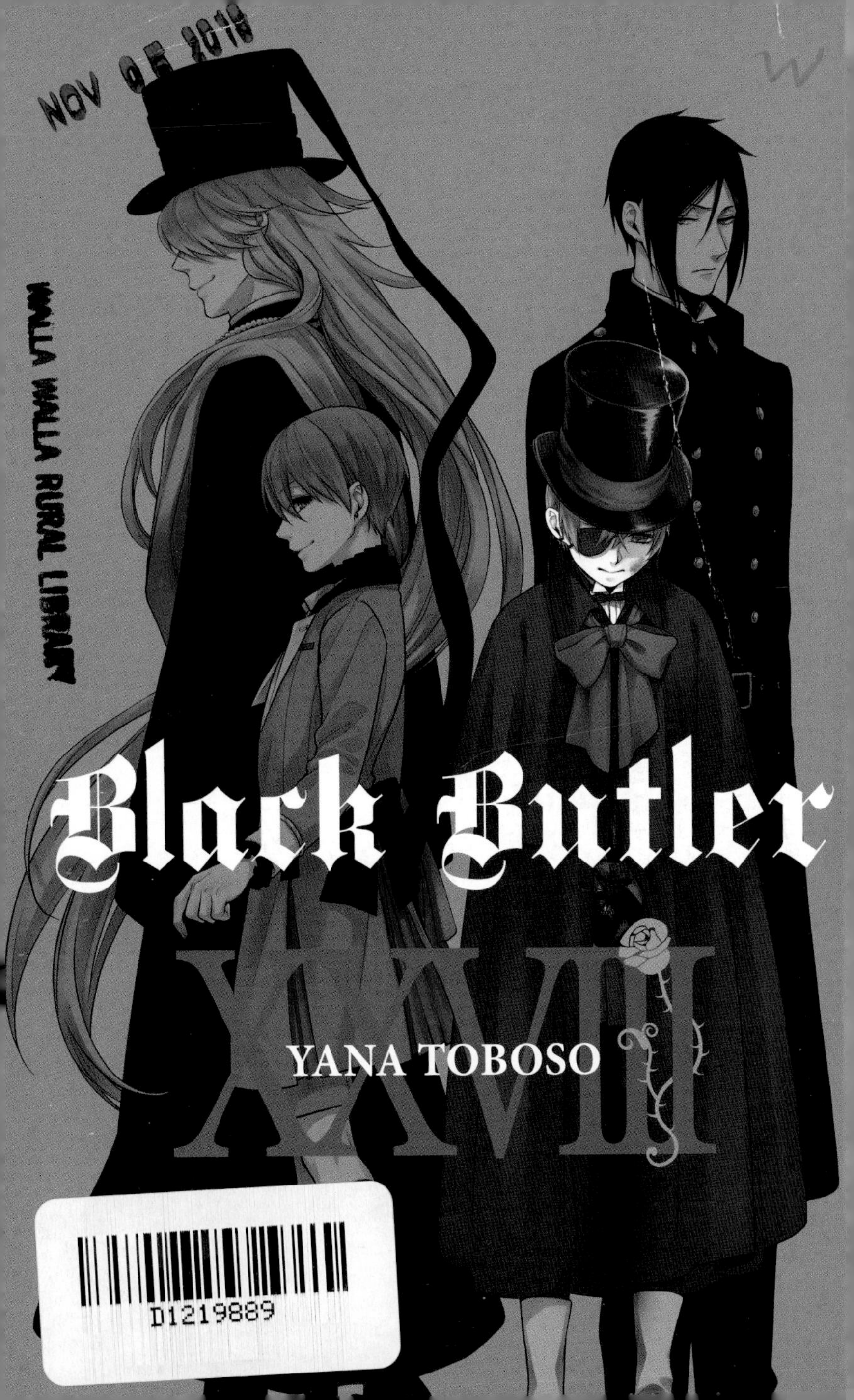

Black Butler

XXVII

YANA TOBOSO

Contents

Chapter 140
At dawn : The Butler, Asserting

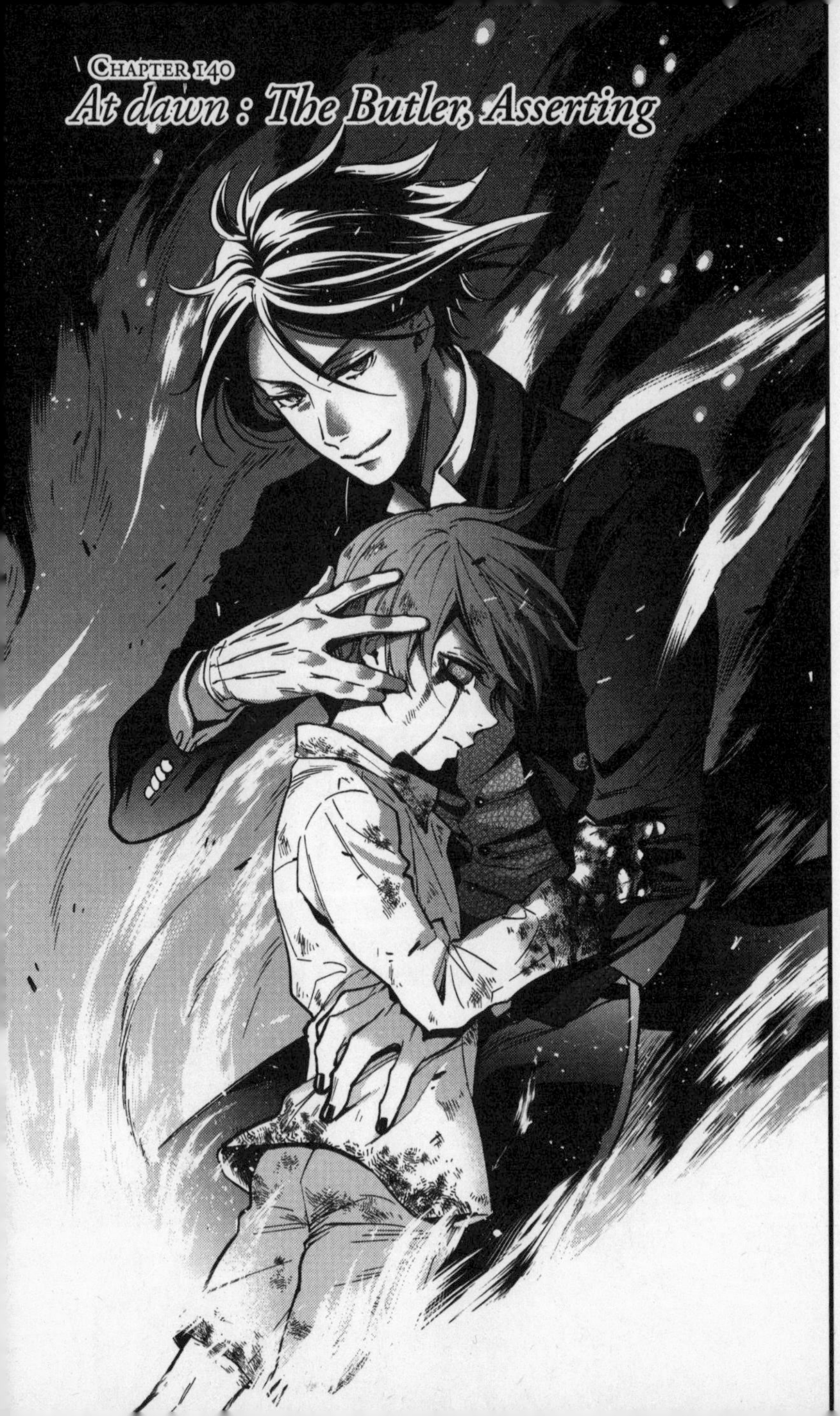

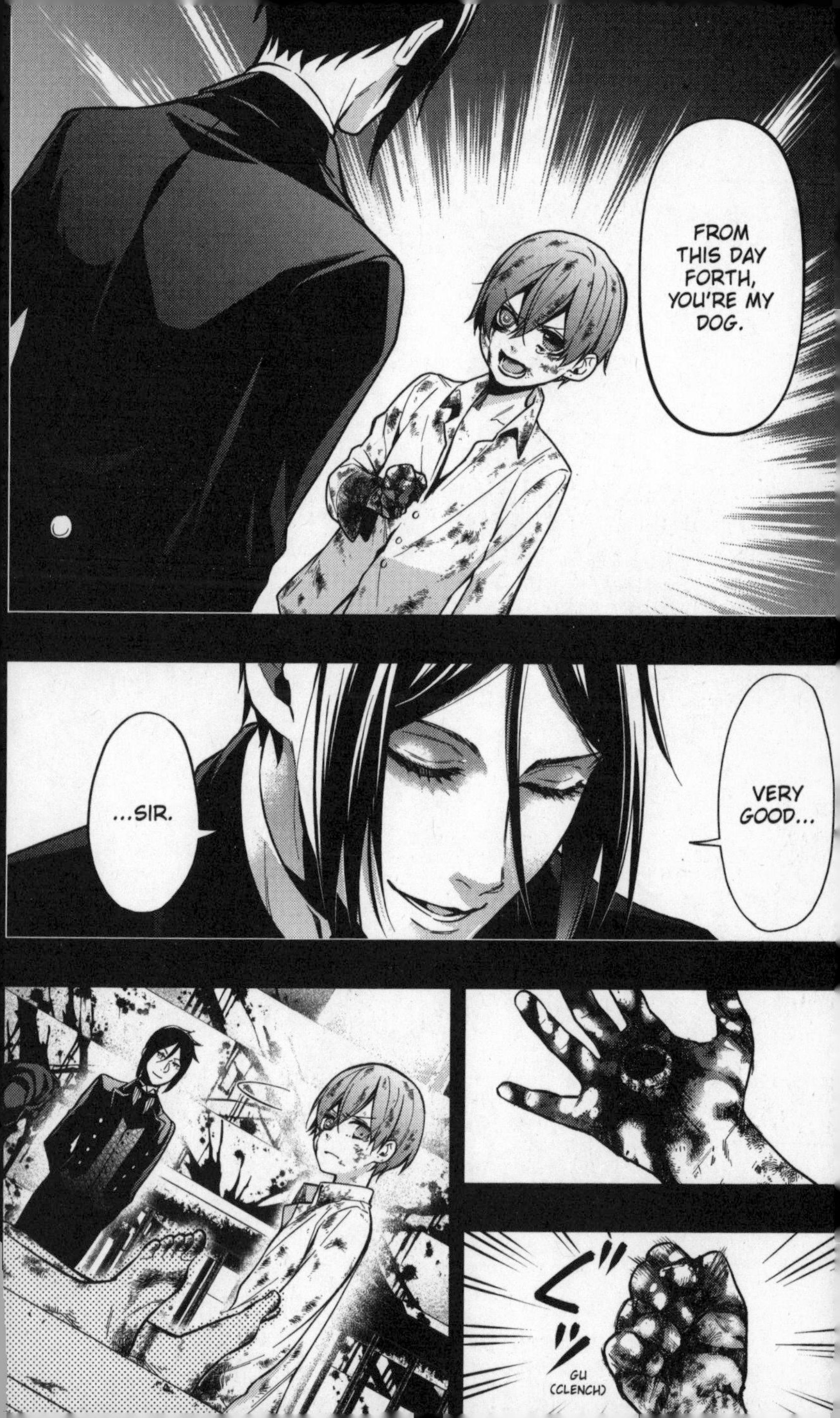
FROM THIS DAY FORTH, YOU'RE MY DOG.
VERY GOOD...
...SIR.
GU (CLENCH)

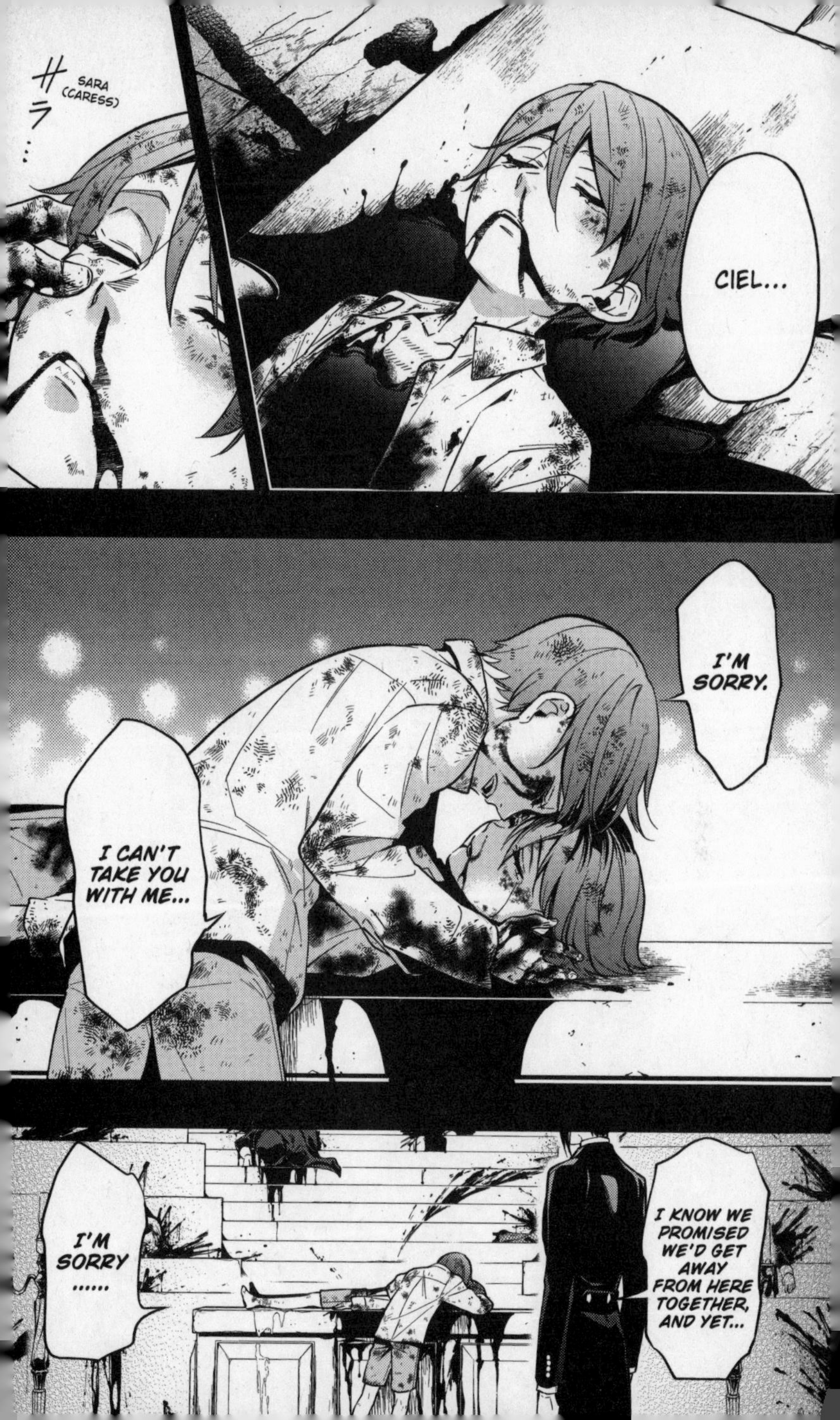
CIEL...
サラ…
SARA (CARESS)
I'M SORRY.
I CAN'T TAKE YOU WITH ME...
I KNOW WE PROMISED WE'D GET AWAY FROM HERE TOGETHER, AND YET...
I'M SORRY ......

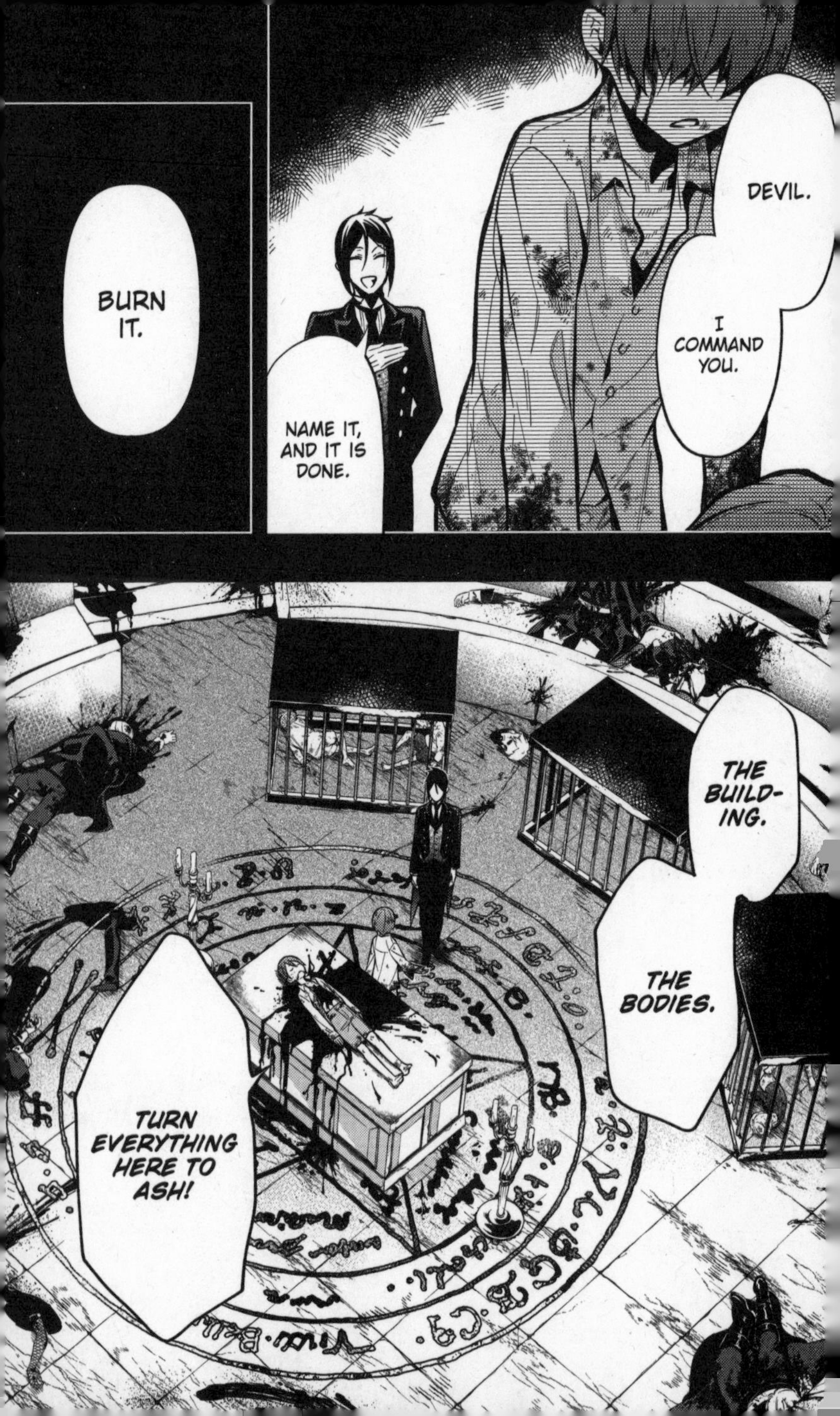
DEVIL.
I COMMAND YOU.
NAME IT, AND IT IS DONE.
BURN IT.
THE BUILDING.
THE BODIES.
TURN EVERYTHING HERE TO ASH!

...YOUR LIE GROWS EVER CLOSER TO BEING PERFECT.

IF YOU DESTROY THE EVI-DENCE...

JUST AS I EX-PECTED FROM YOU, MY LORD!

A WISE DECISION.

PACHIN (SNAP)

(GLARE)

—ALL RIGHT, THEN.

ENOUGH OF YOUR CHATTER. GET TO IT!

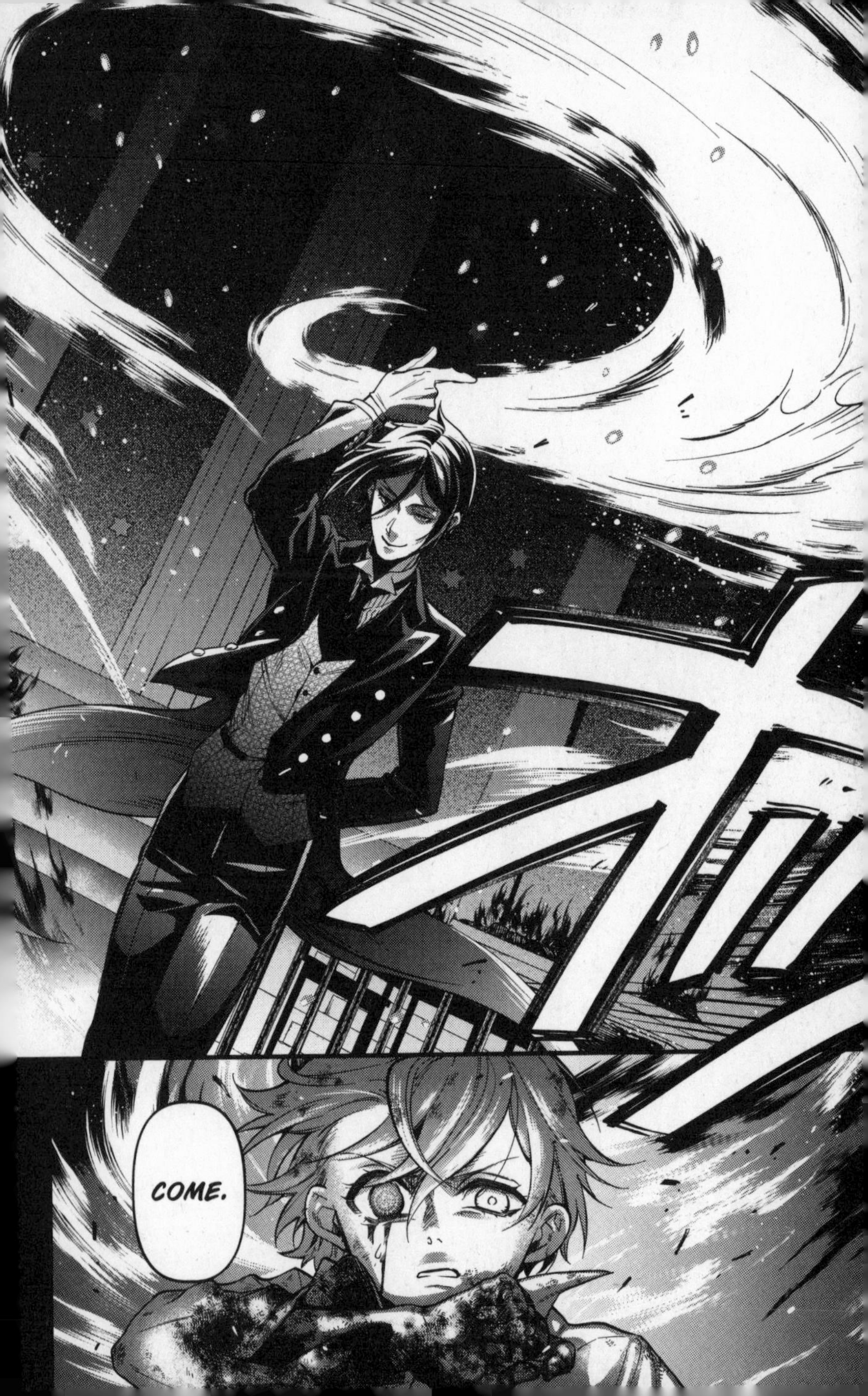
COME.

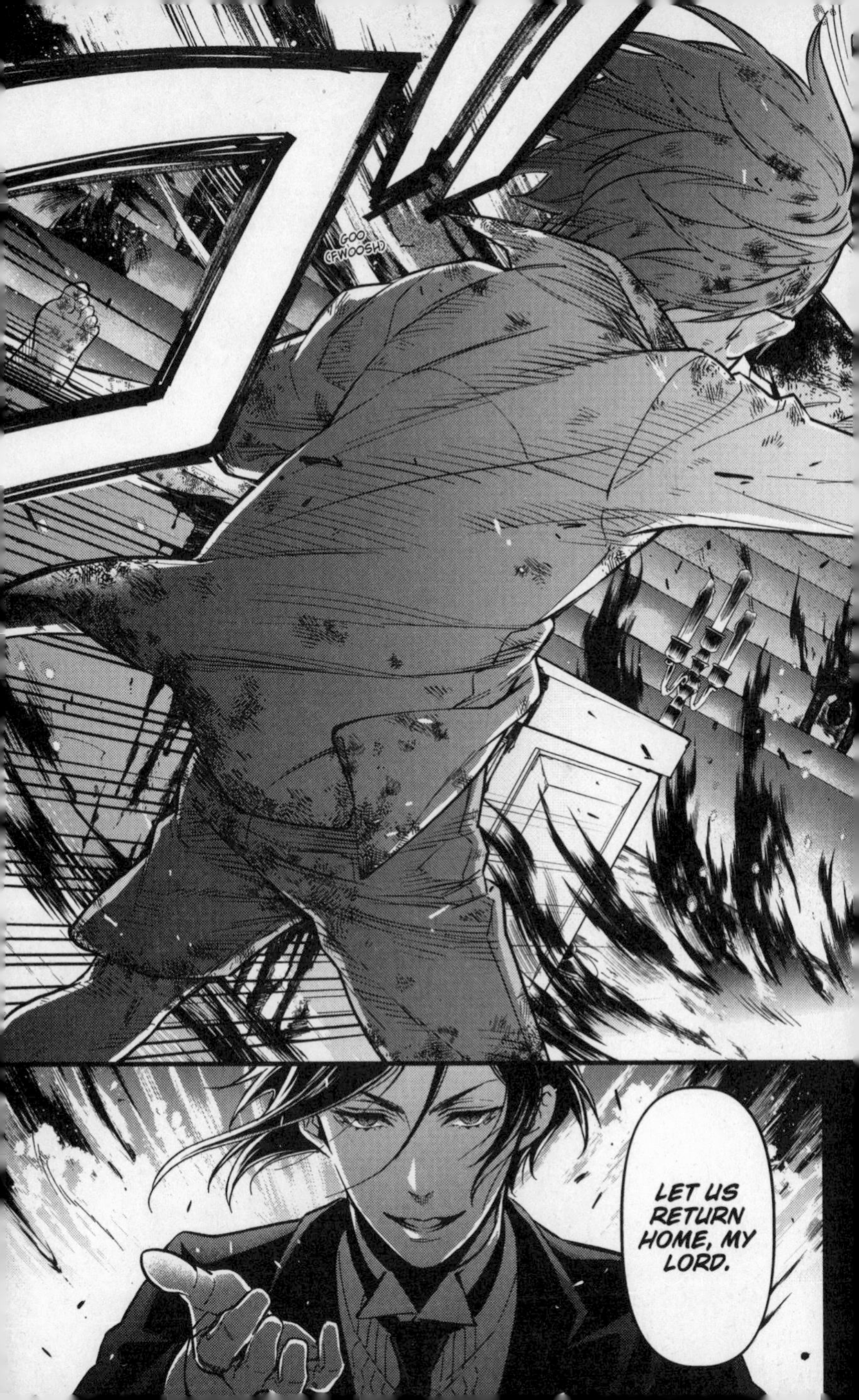
GOO (FWOOSH)
LET US RETURN HOME, MY LORD.

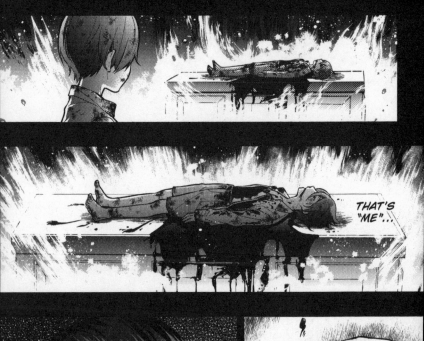

THAT'S "ME"...

THE SURVIVOR...

...IS THE STRONG AND COURAGEOUS "HEIR TO EARL PHANTOMHIVE."

...THE COWARDLY, CRYBABY SPARE.

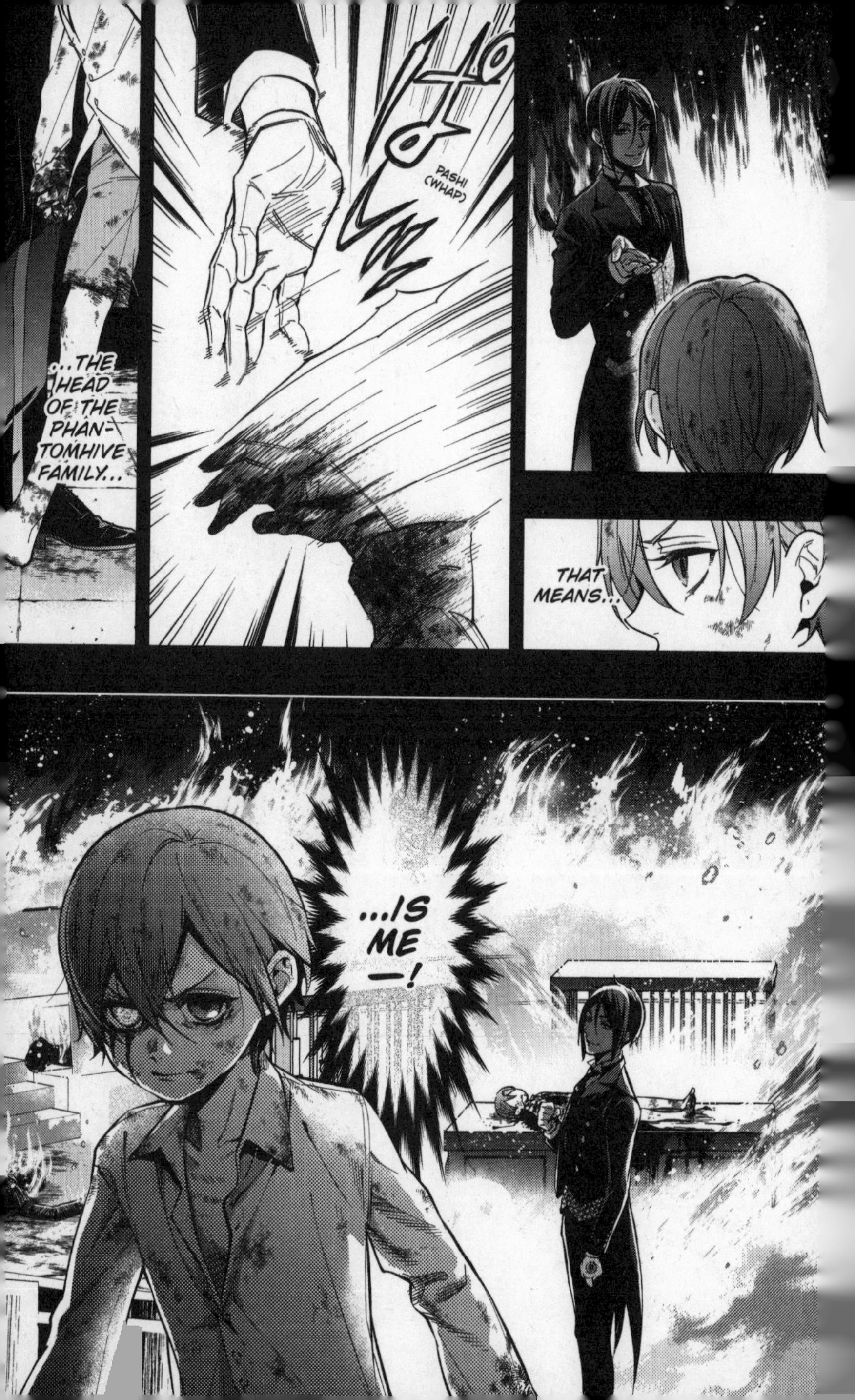
THAT MEANS...
PASHI (WHAP)
...THE HEAD OF THE PHAN-TOMHIVE FAMILY...
...IS ME—!

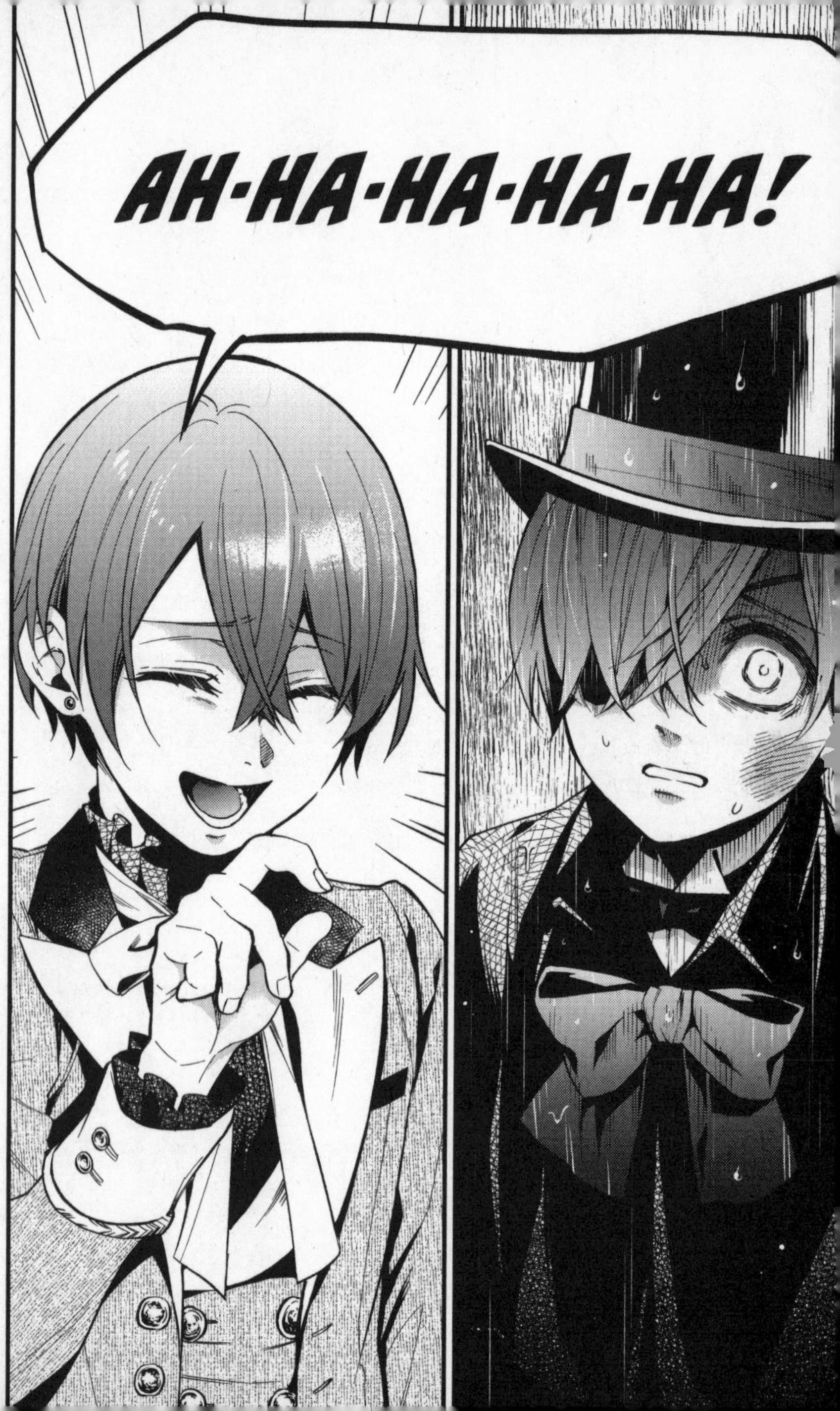
AH-HA-HA-HA-HA-HA!

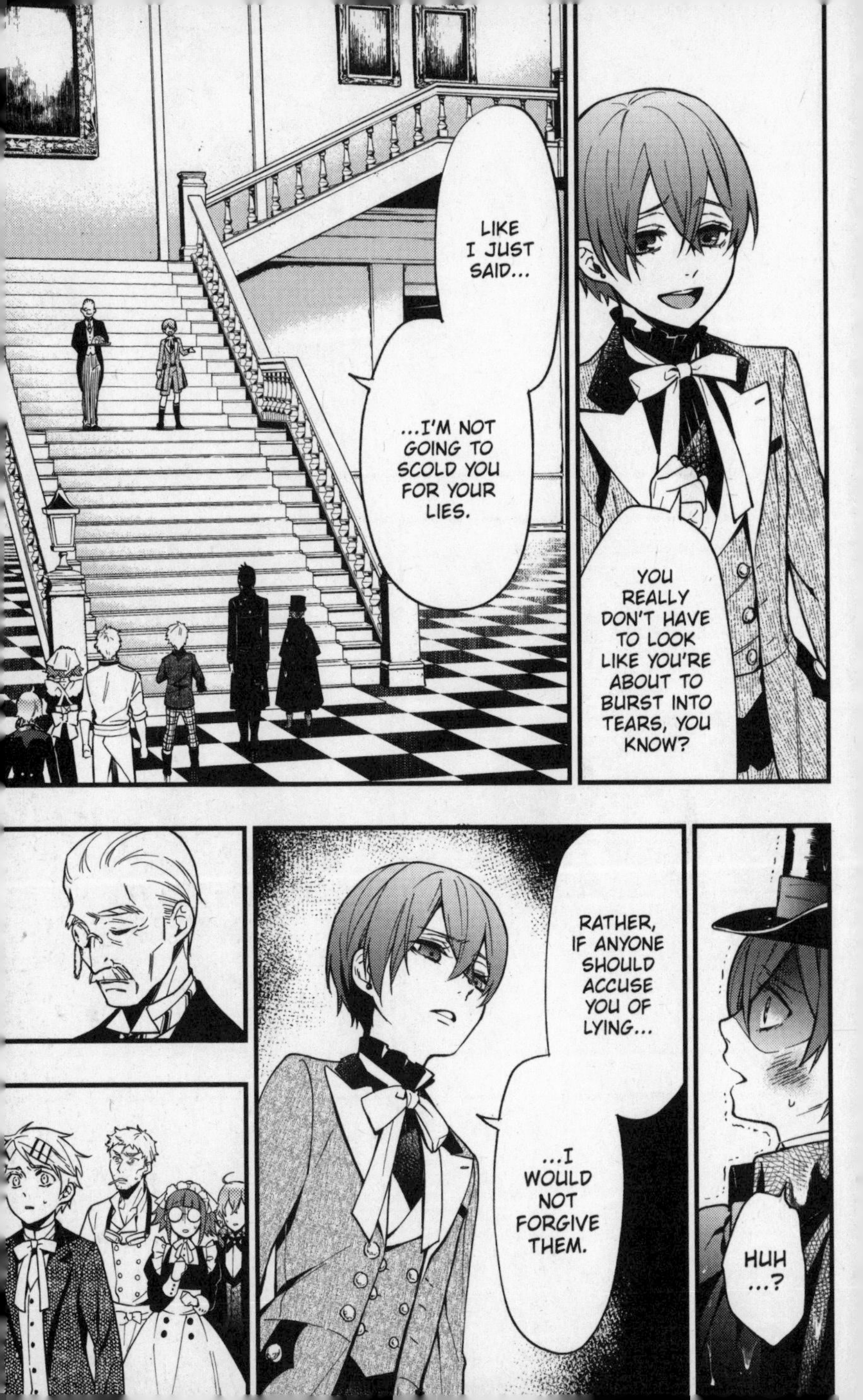
LIKE I JUST SAID...
...I'M NOT GOING TO SCOLD YOU FOR YOUR LIES.
YOU REALLY DON'T HAVE TO LOOK LIKE YOU'RE ABOUT TO BURST INTO TEARS, YOU KNOW?
RATHER, IF ANYONE SHOULD ACCUSE YOU OF LYING...
...I WOULD NOT FORGIVE THEM.
HUH ...?

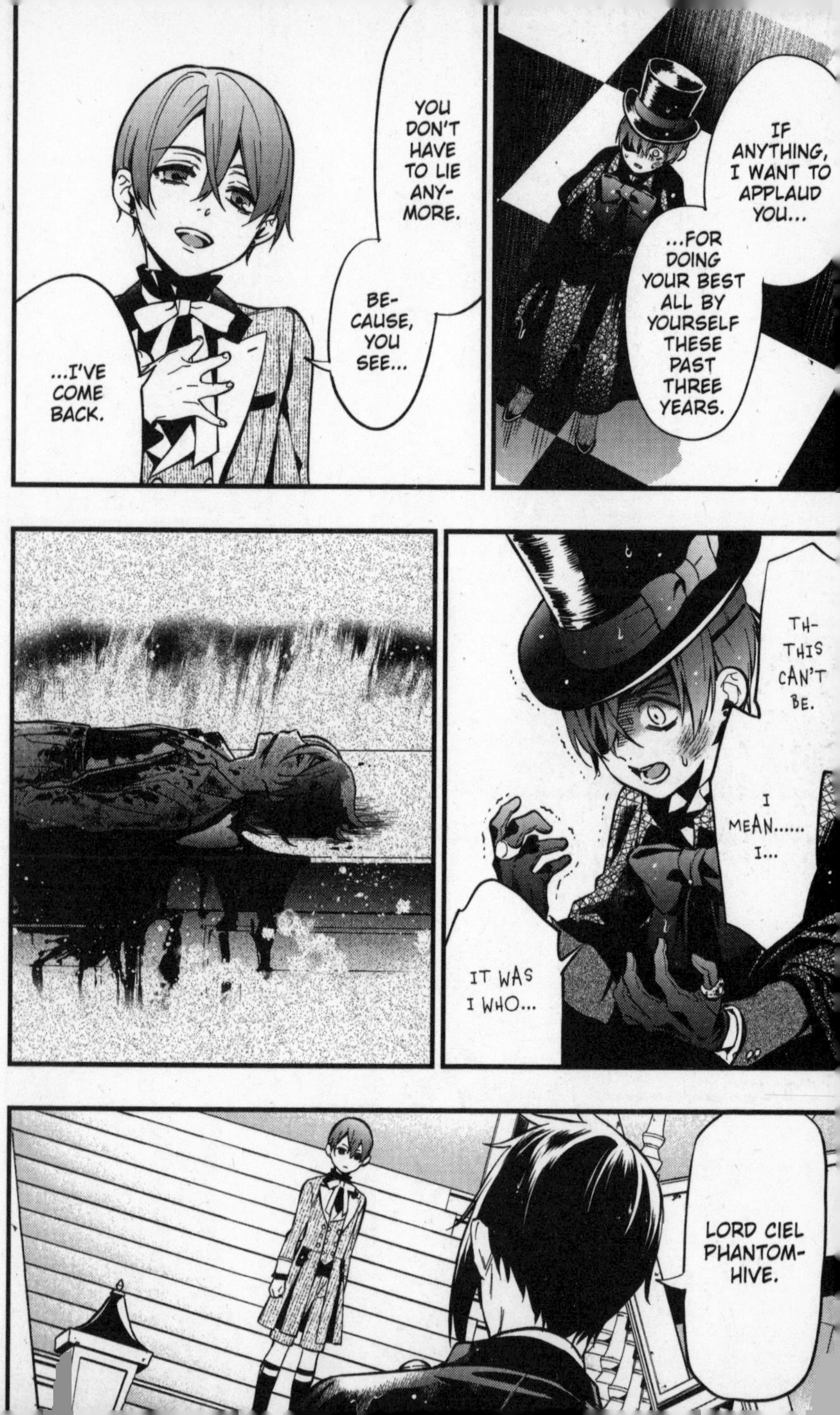
IF ANYTHING, I WANT TO APPLAUD YOU...
...FOR DOING YOUR BEST ALL BY YOURSELF THESE PAST THREE YEARS.
YOU DON'T HAVE TO LIE ANY-MORE.
BE-CAUSE, YOU SEE...
...I'VE COME BACK.
TH-THIS CAN'T BE.
I MEAN...... I...
IT WAS I WHO...
LORD CIEL PHANTOM-HIVE.

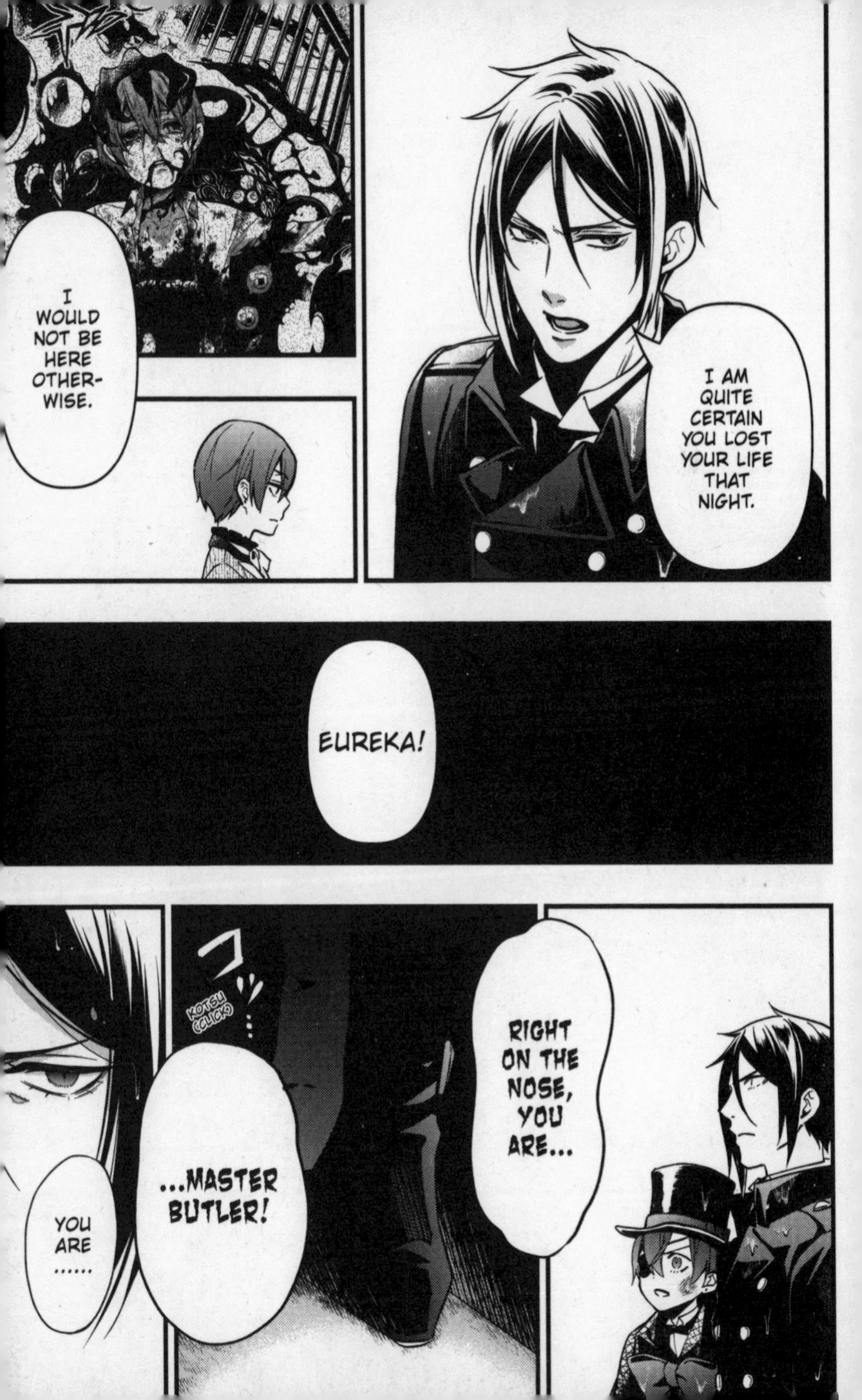
I AM QUITE CERTAIN YOU LOST YOUR LIFE THAT NIGHT.
I WOULD NOT BE HERE OTHER-WISE.
EUREKA!
RIGHT ON THE NOSE, YOU ARE...
KOTSU (CLICK)
...MASTER BUTLER!
YOU ARE ......

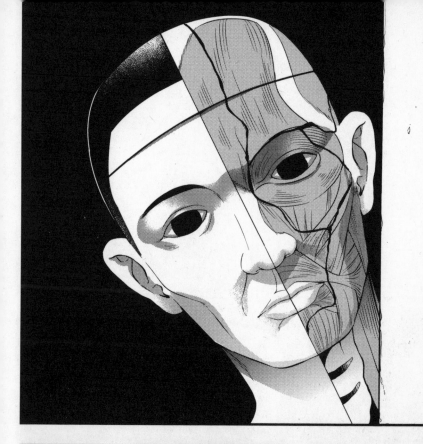

WHO IS THAT?

HEE! HEE...

NU (POP)

?

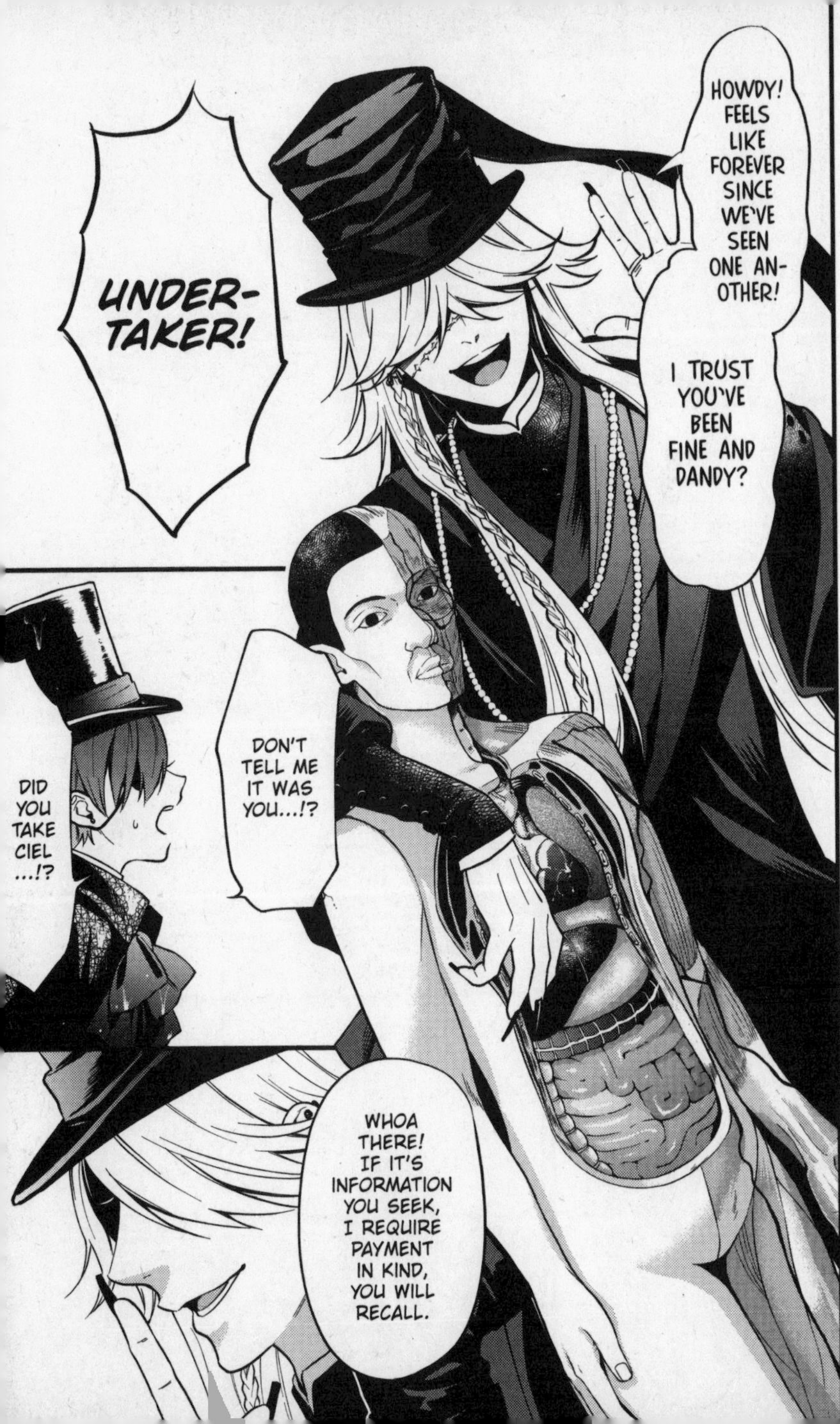
HOWDY! FEELS LIKE FOREVER SINCE WE'VE SEEN ONE AN-OTHER!
I TRUST YOU'VE BEEN FINE AND DANDY?
UNDER-TAKER!
DON'T TELL ME IT WAS YOU...!?
DID YOU TAKE CIEL ...!?
WHOA THERE! IF IT'S INFORMATION YOU SEEK, I REQUIRE PAYMENT IN KIND, YOU WILL RECALL.

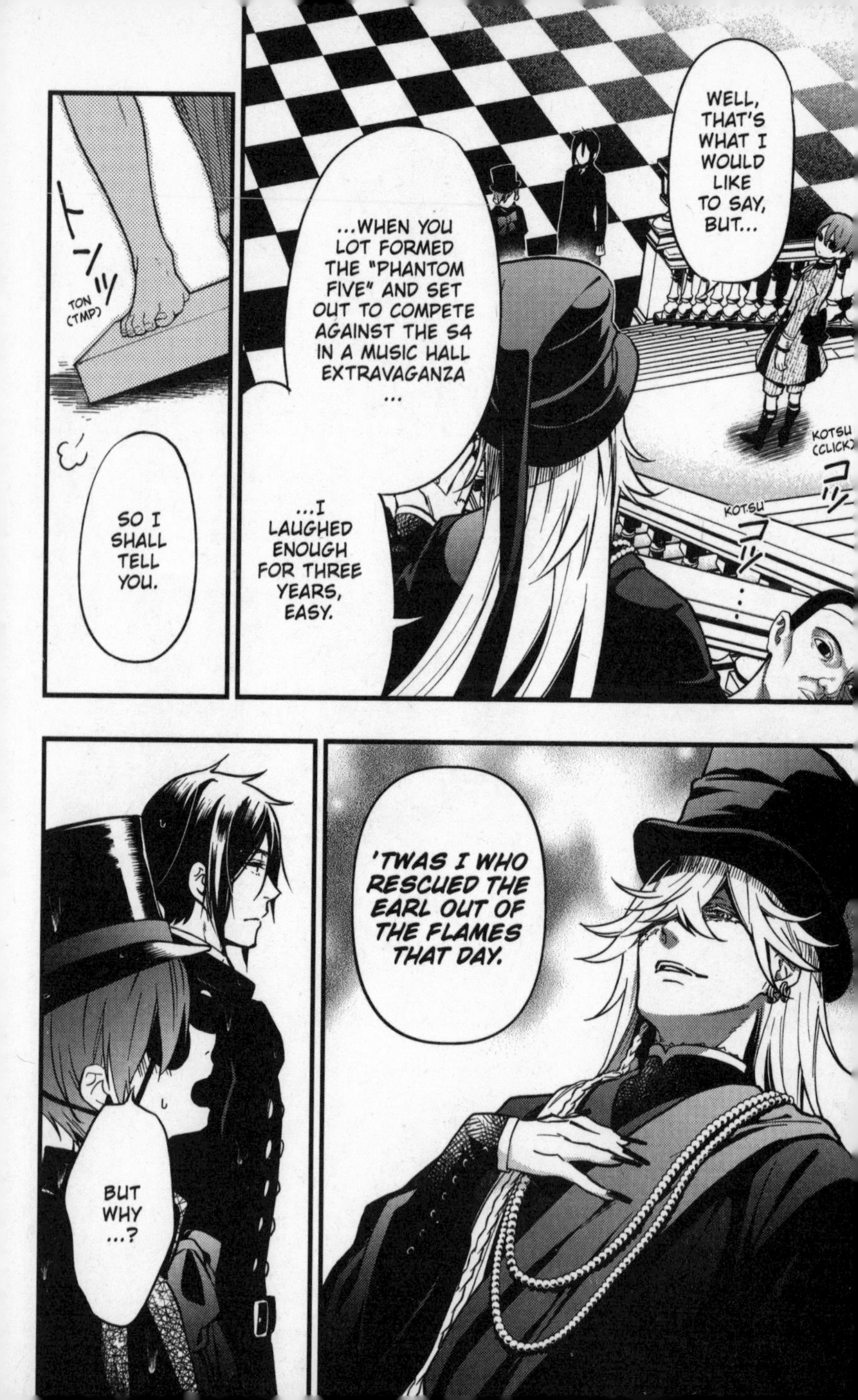
WELL, THAT'S WHAT I WOULD LIKE TO SAY, BUT...
...WHEN YOU LOT FORMED THE "PHANTOM FIVE" AND SET OUT TO COMPETE AGAINST THE S4 IN A MUSIC HALL EXTRAVAGANZA...
KOTSU (CLICK)
KOTSU
...I LAUGHED ENOUGH FOR THREE YEARS, EASY.
TON (TMP)
SO I SHALL TELL YOU.
'TWAS I WHO RESCUED THE EARL OUT OF THE FLAMES THAT DAY.
BUT WHY...?

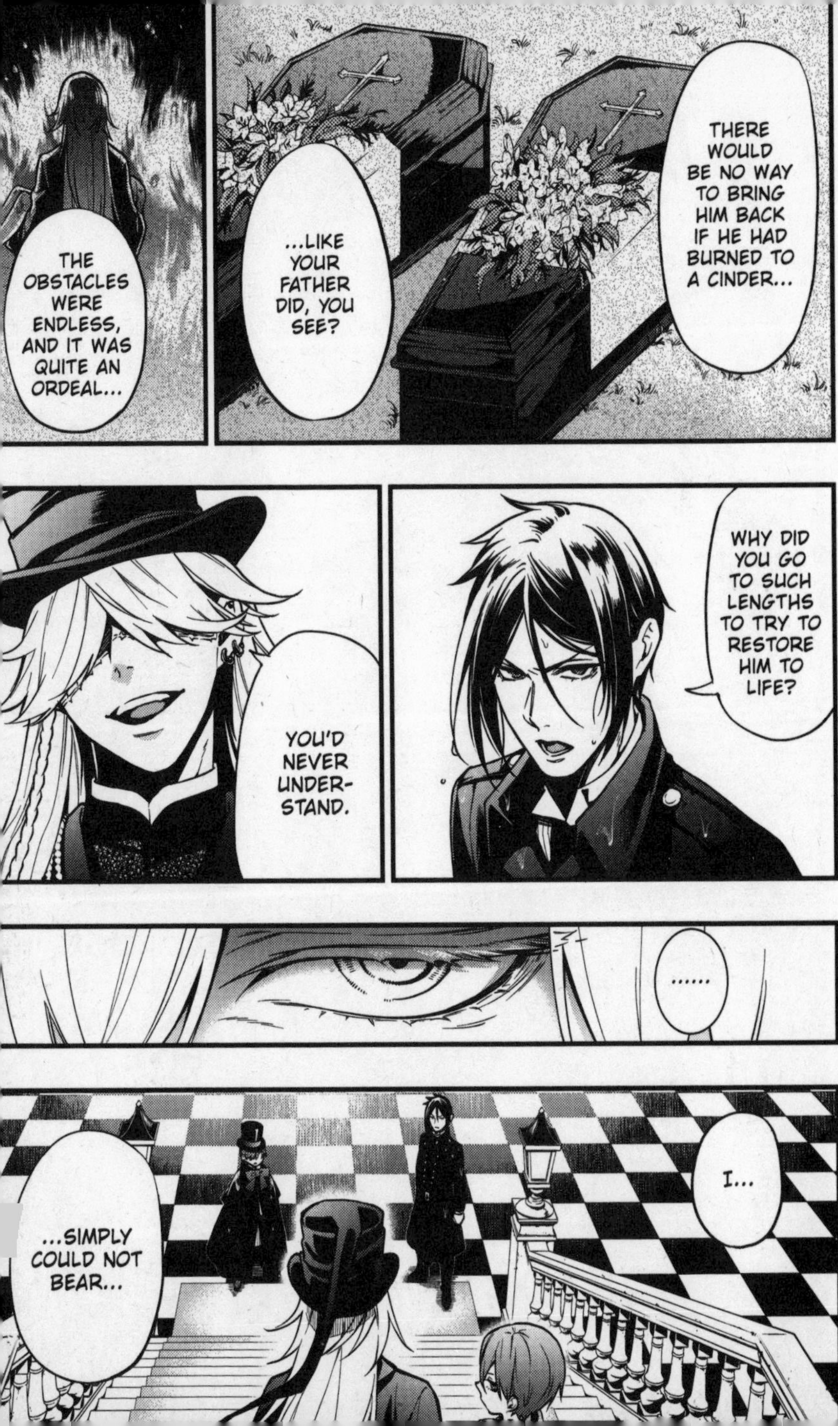
THERE WOULD BE NO WAY TO BRING HIM BACK IF HE HAD BURNED TO A CINDER...
...LIKE YOUR FATHER DID, YOU SEE?
THE OBSTACLES WERE ENDLESS, AND IT WAS QUITE AN ORDEAL...
WHY DID YOU GO TO SUCH LENGTHS TO TRY TO RESTORE HIM TO LIFE?
YOU'D NEVER UNDER-STAND.
......
I...
...SIMPLY COULD NOT BEAR...

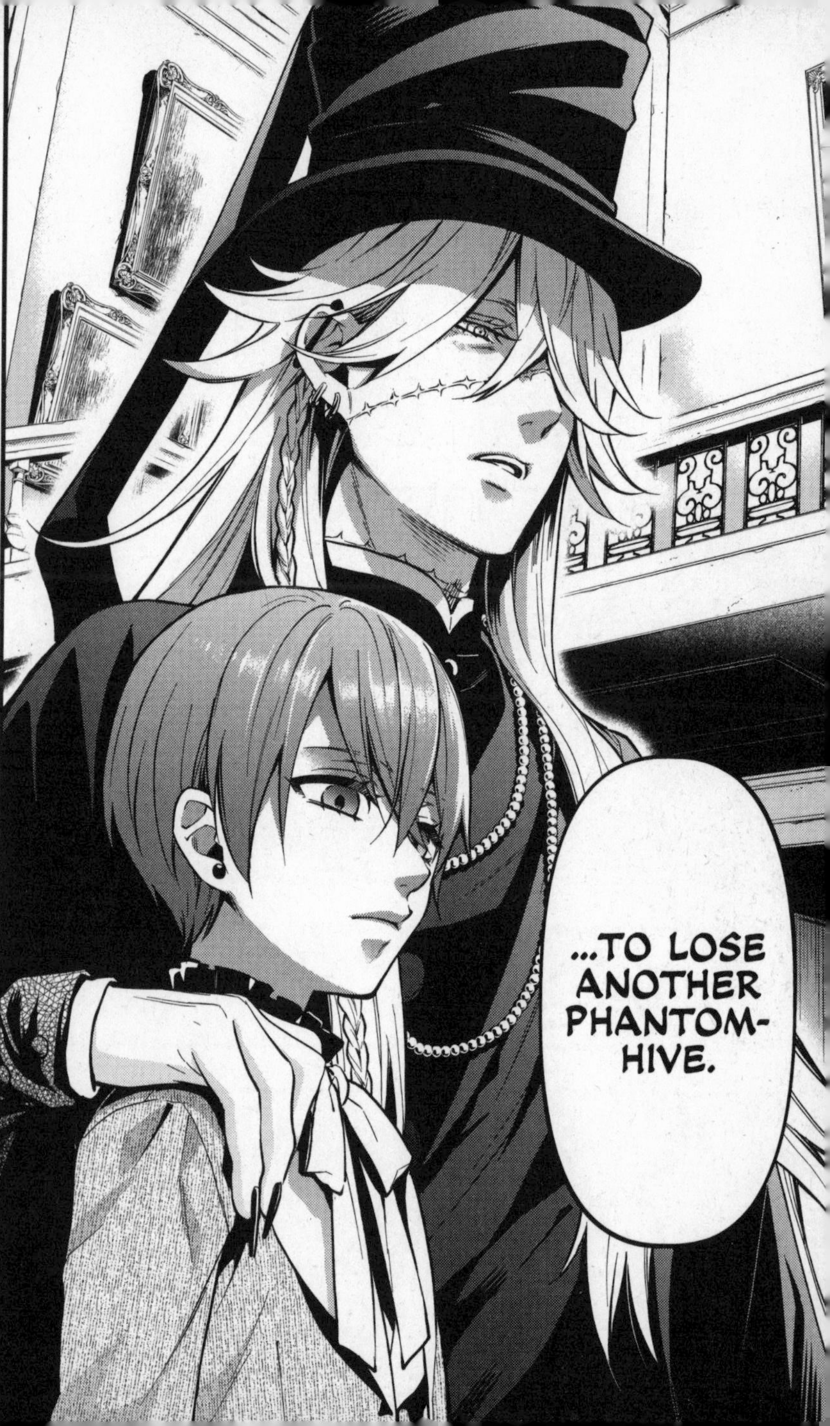
...TO LOSE ANOTHER PHANTOM-HIVE.

Black Butler

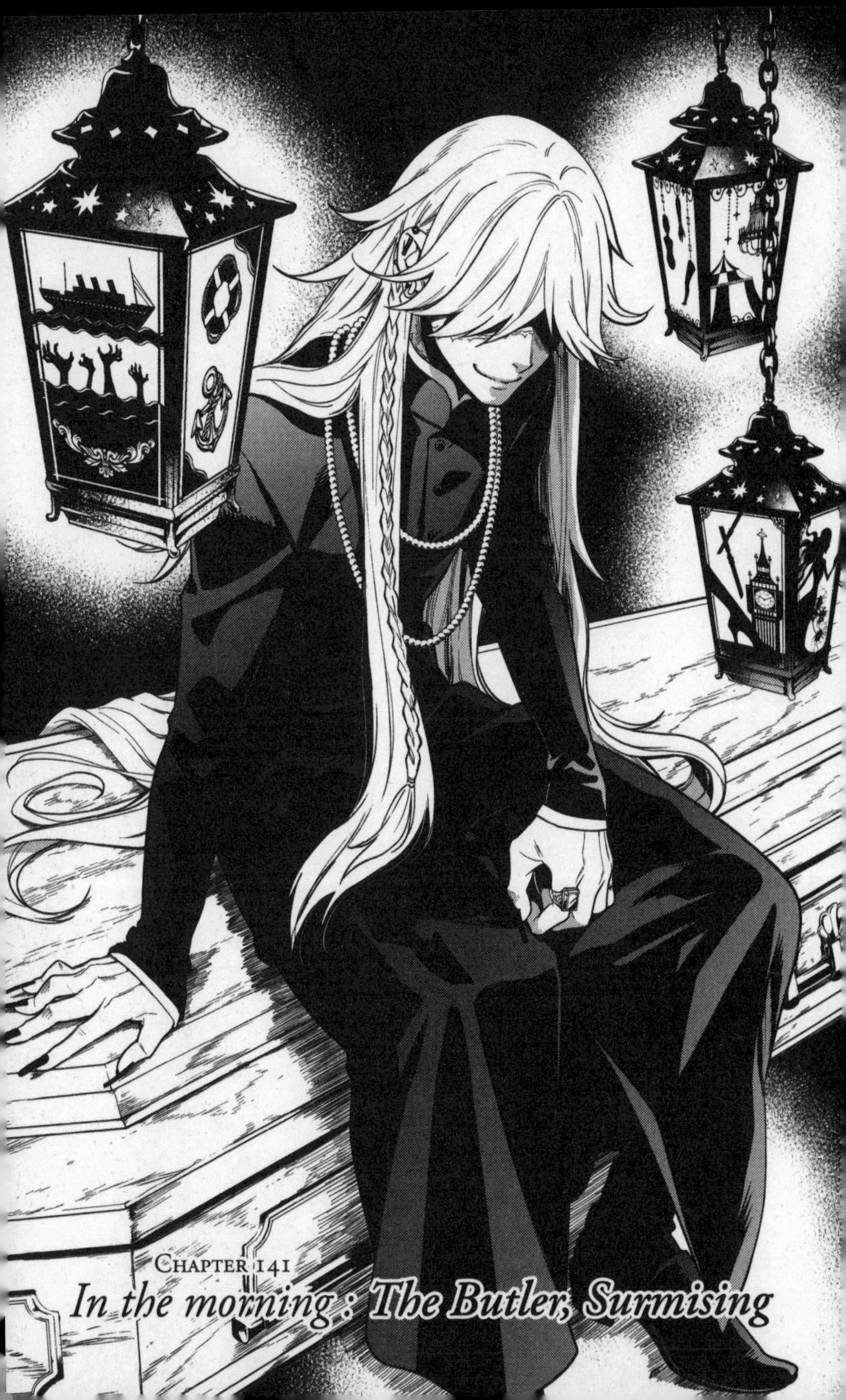

Chapter 141
In the morning : The Butler, Surmising

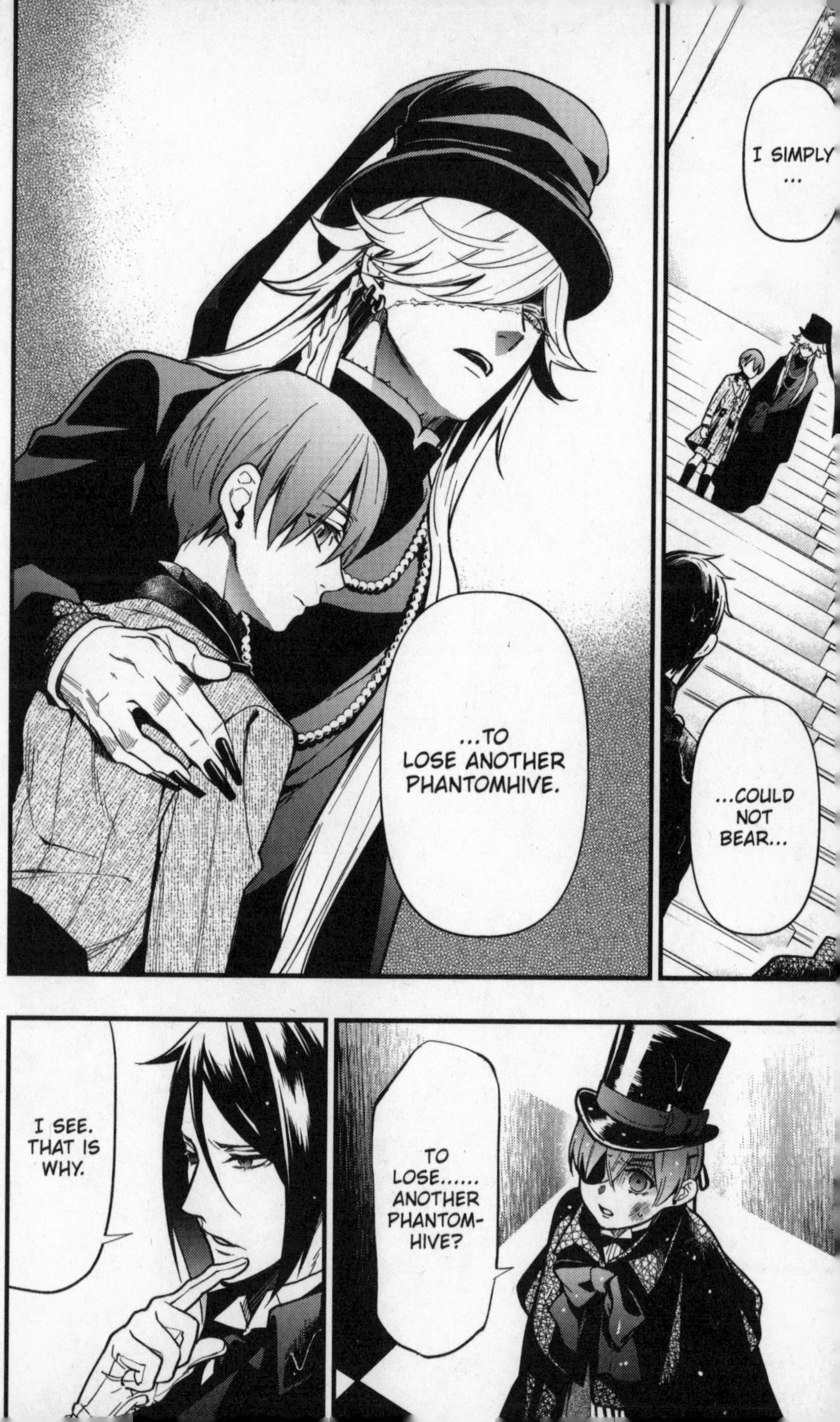
I SIMPLY ...
...COULD NOT BEAR...
...TO LOSE ANOTHER PHANTOMHIVE.
TO LOSE...... ANOTHER PHANTOM-HIVE?
I SEE. THAT IS WHY.

THAT CHAIN OF MOURNING LOCKETS YOU DROPPED ABOARD THE *CAMPANIA*...

SINCE CONFIRMING ONE AMONGST THEM WAS FOR THE YOUNG MASTER'S GRANDMOTHER, I HAVE HAD AN INKLING, BUT...

MEDICAL CERTI

Cloudia Phan

...IT APPEARS YOUR ATTACHMENT TO THE PHANTOMHIVE HOUSE GOES FAR DEEPER THAN WHAT I HAD SURMISED.

I LEAVE THAT TO YOUR IMAGINATION.

EXACTLY WHAT RELATIONSHIP DOES A GRIM REAPER LIKE YOU HAVE TO THIS HOUSE?

FIRST OF ALL—

EVEN IF HE WERE TO TELL YOU, IT'S NO CONCERN OF YOURS.

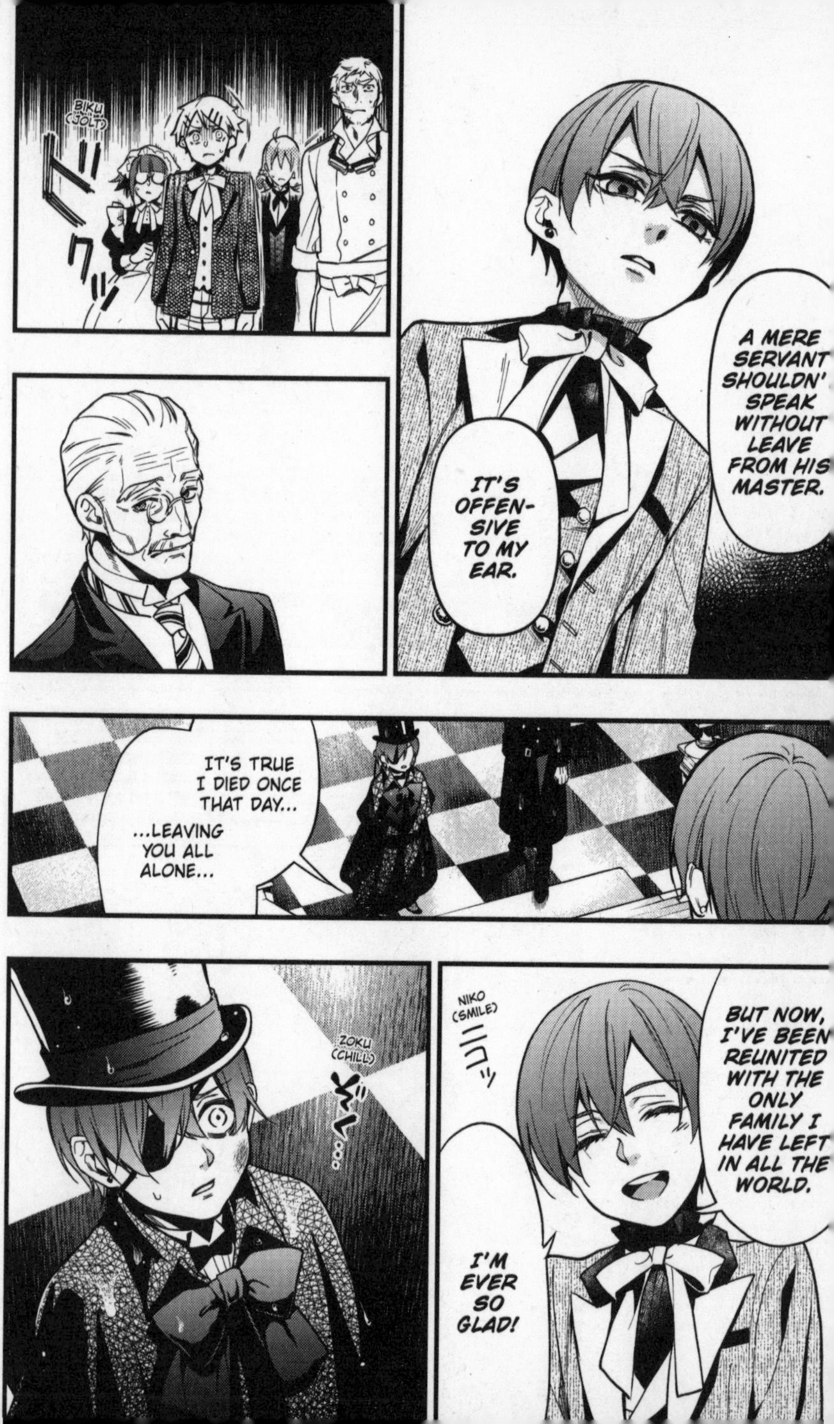
A MERE SERVANT SHOULDN' SPEAK WITHOUT LEAVE FROM HIS MASTER.
IT'S OFFEN-SIVE TO MY EAR.
BIKU (JOLT)
IT'S TRUE I DIED ONCE THAT DAY...
...LEAVING YOU ALL ALONE...
NIKO (SMILE)
BUT NOW, I'VE BEEN REUNITED WITH THE ONLY FAMILY I HAVE LEFT IN ALL THE WORLD.
I'M EVER SO GLAD!
ZOKU (CHILL)

AREN'T YOU HAPPY...

...TO SEE YOUR ELDER BROTHER AFTER ALL THIS TIME?

DEAR, DEAR.

WHAT DOES IT MATTER IF HE'S ALIVE OR DEAD?

...... BRINGING THE DEAD BACK TO LIFE—

IT'S PURE MAD-NESS ...!

HE WAS CHOCK-FULL OF EPISODES ...

...BUT MY REANIMATION SKILLS WEREN'T QUITE UP TO SNUFF, SO...

...IT WAS, UNFORTU-NATELY, A TIME-CONSUMING PROCESS.

THAT'S ...

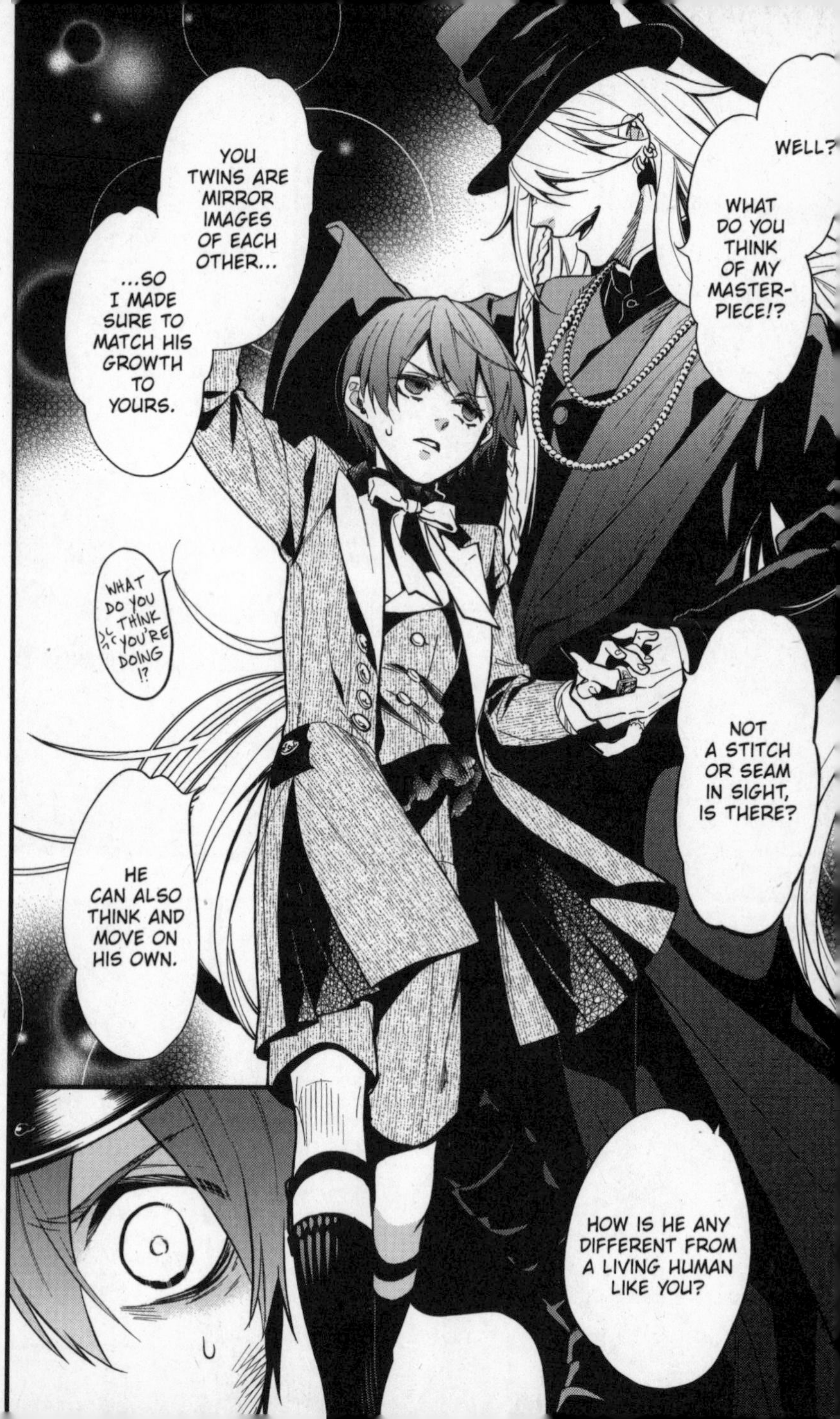
WELL?
WHAT DO YOU THINK OF MY MASTER-PIECE!?
YOU TWINS ARE MIRROR IMAGES OF EACH OTHER...
...SO I MADE SURE TO MATCH HIS GROWTH TO YOURS.
WHAT DO YOU THINK YOU'RE DOING!?
NOT A STITCH OR SEAM IN SIGHT, IS THERE?
HE CAN ALSO THINK AND MOVE ON HIS OWN.
HOW IS HE ANY DIFFERENT FROM A LIVING HUMAN LIKE YOU?

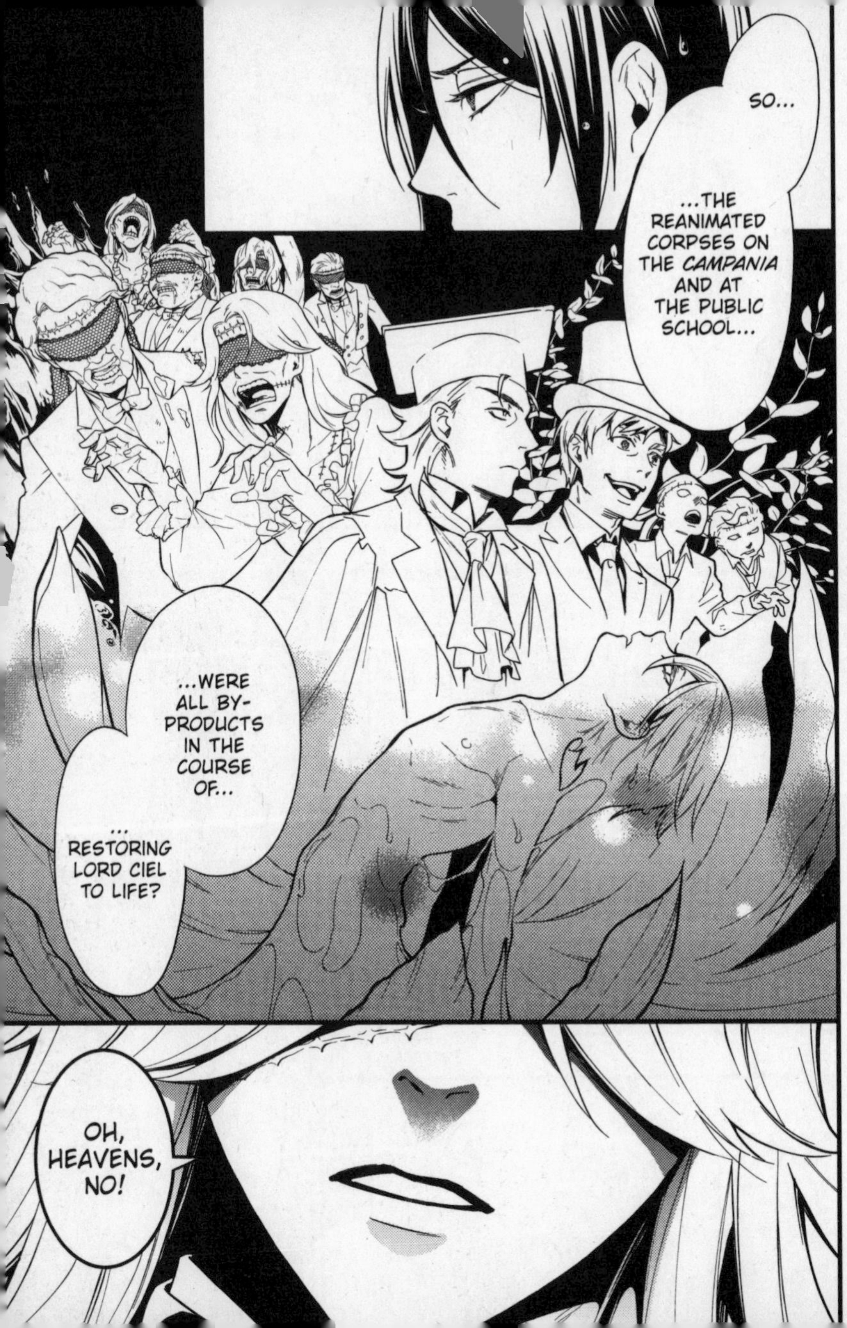
SO...
...THE REANIMATED CORPSES ON THE *CAMPANIA* AND AT THE PUBLIC SCHOOL...
...WERE ALL BY-PRODUCTS IN THE COURSE OF...
...RESTORING LORD CIEL TO LIFE?
OH, HEAVENS, NO!

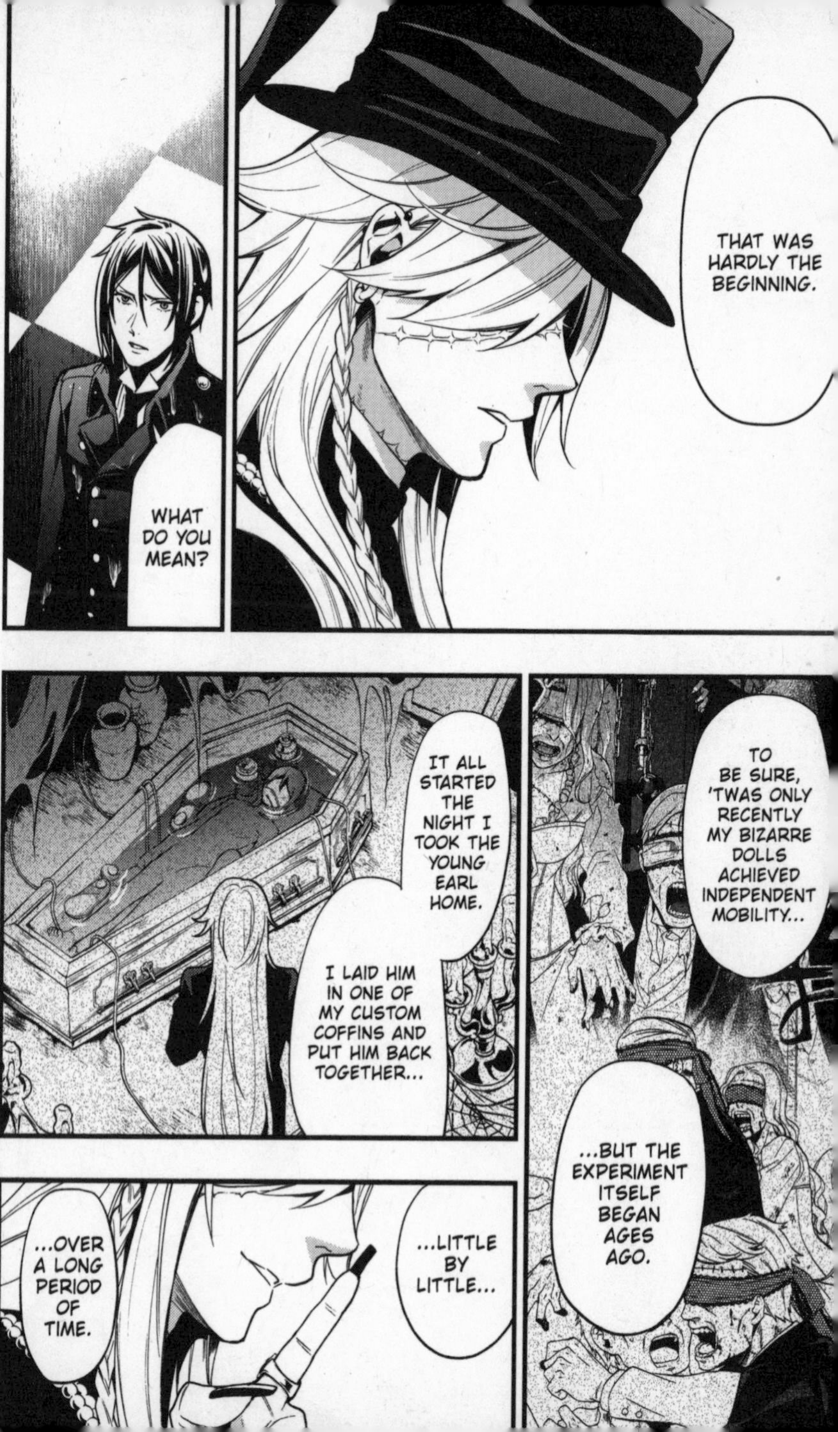
THAT WAS HARDLY THE BEGINNING.
WHAT DO YOU MEAN?
TO BE SURE, 'TWAS ONLY RECENTLY MY BIZARRE DOLLS ACHIEVED INDEPENDENT MOBILITY...
...BUT THE EXPERIMENT ITSELF BEGAN AGES AGO.
IT ALL STARTED THE NIGHT I TOOK THE YOUNG EARL HOME.
I LAID HIM IN ONE OF MY CUSTOM COFFINS AND PUT HIM BACK TOGETHER...
...LITTLE BY LITTLE...
...OVER A LONG PERIOD OF TIME.

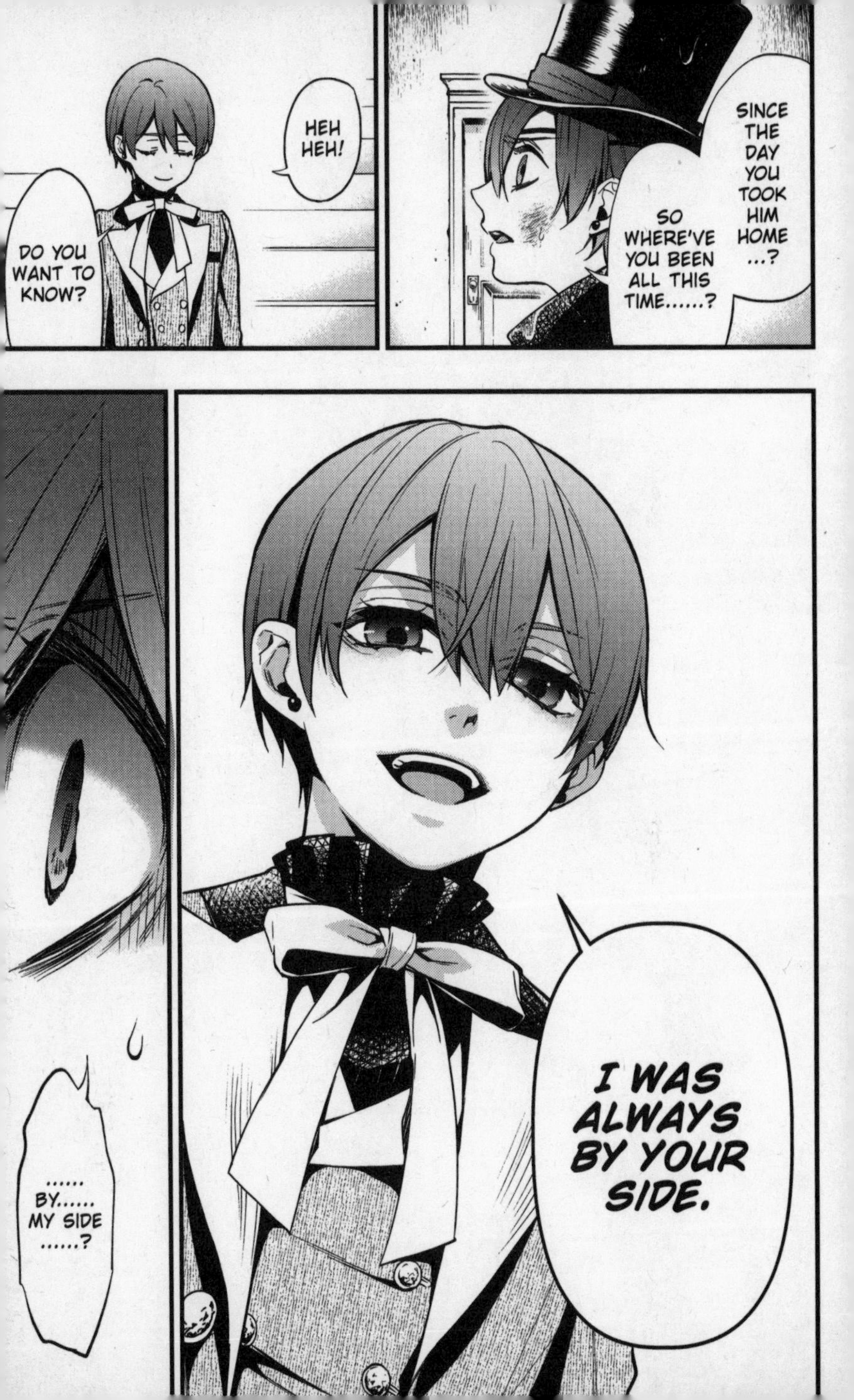
SINCE THE DAY YOU TOOK HIM HOME ...?
SO WHERE'VE YOU BEEN ALL THIS TIME......?
HEH HEH!
DO YOU WANT TO KNOW?
I WAS ALWAYS BY YOUR SIDE.
...... BY...... MY SIDE ......?

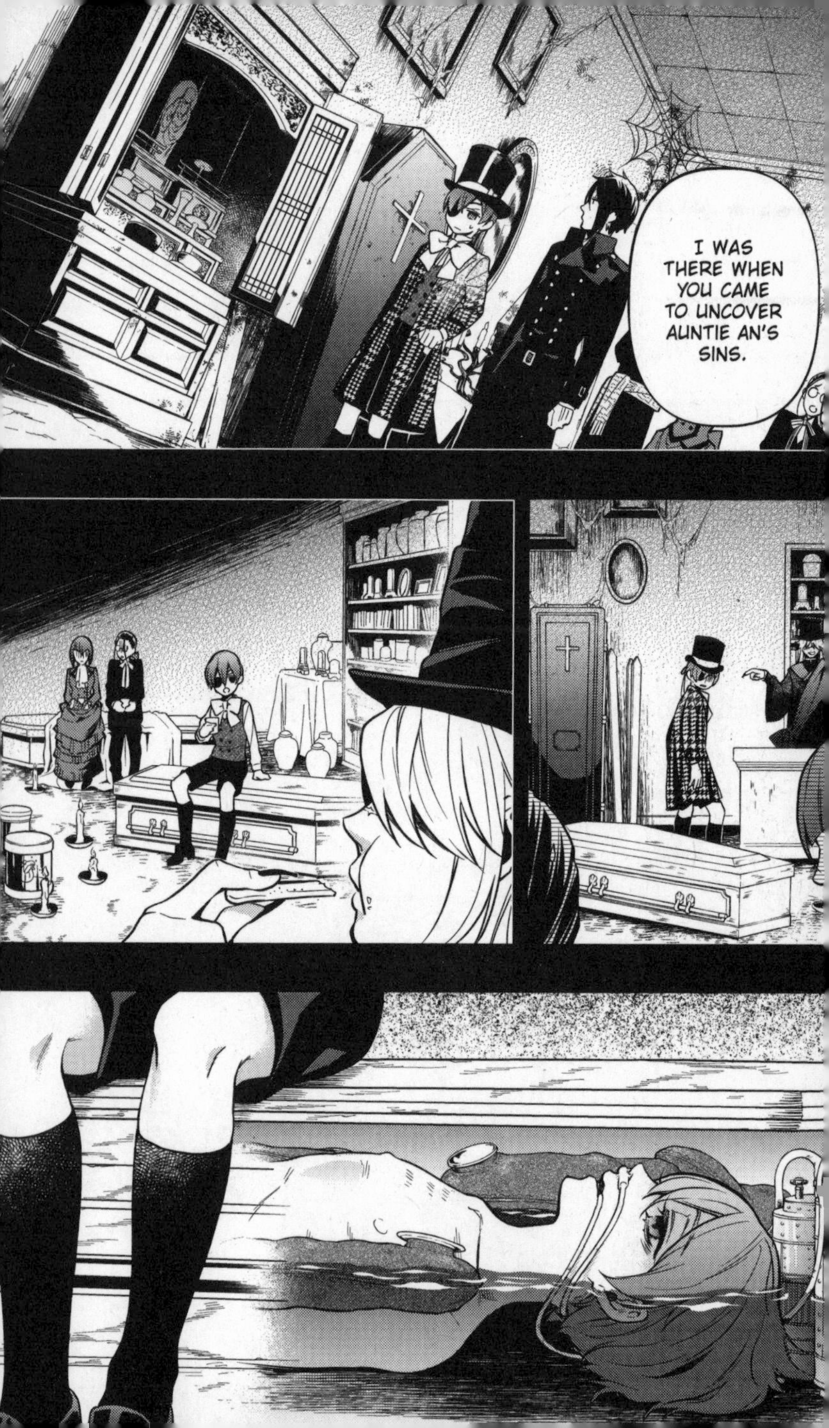
I WAS THERE WHEN YOU CAME TO UNCOVER AUNTIE AN'S SINS.

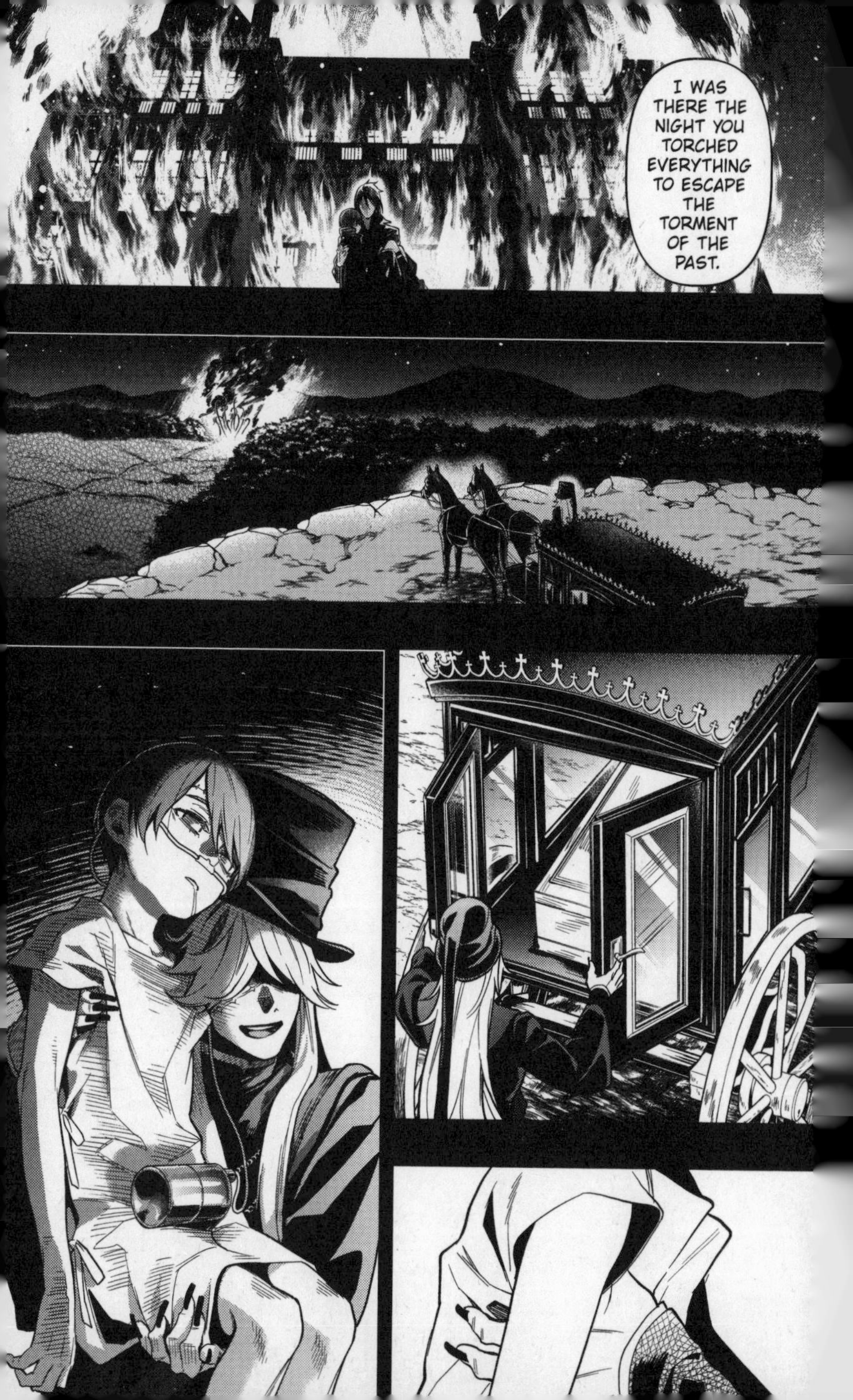
I WAS THERE THE NIGHT YOU TORCHED EVERYTHING TO ESCAPE THE TORMENT OF THE PAST.

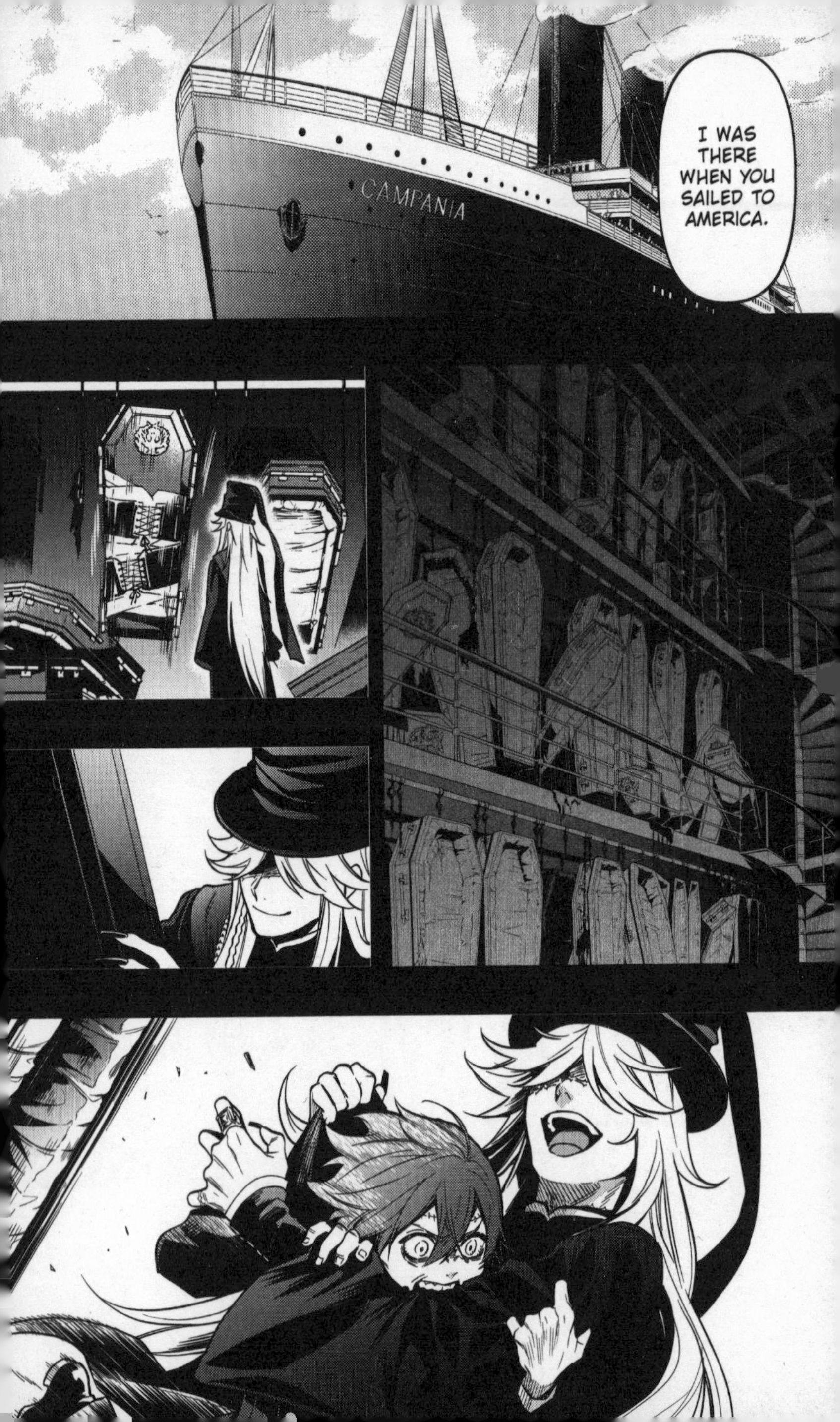
I WAS THERE WHEN YOU SAILED TO AMERICA.
CAMPANIA

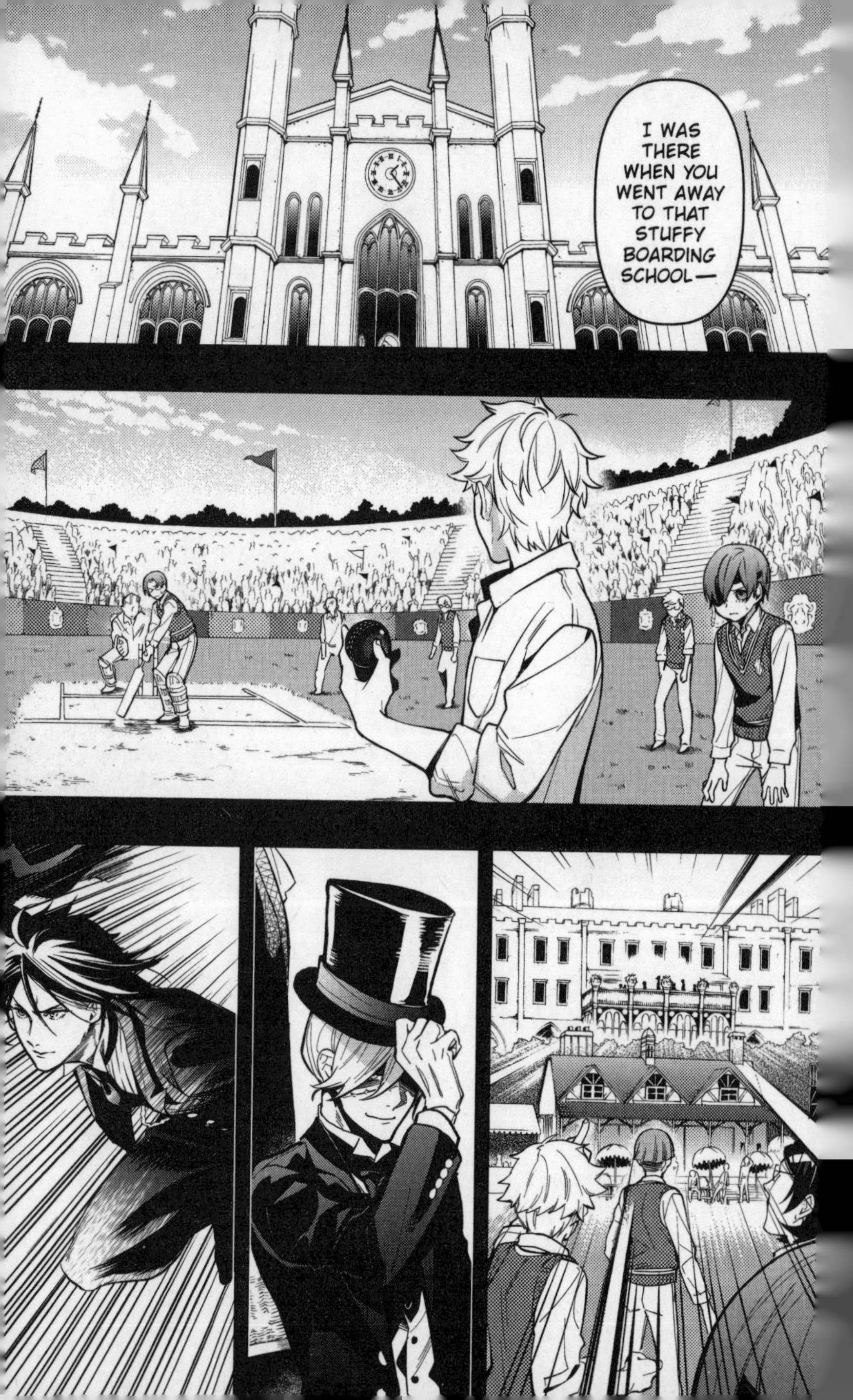
I WAS THERE WHEN YOU WENT AWAY TO THAT STUFFY BOARDING SCHOOL—

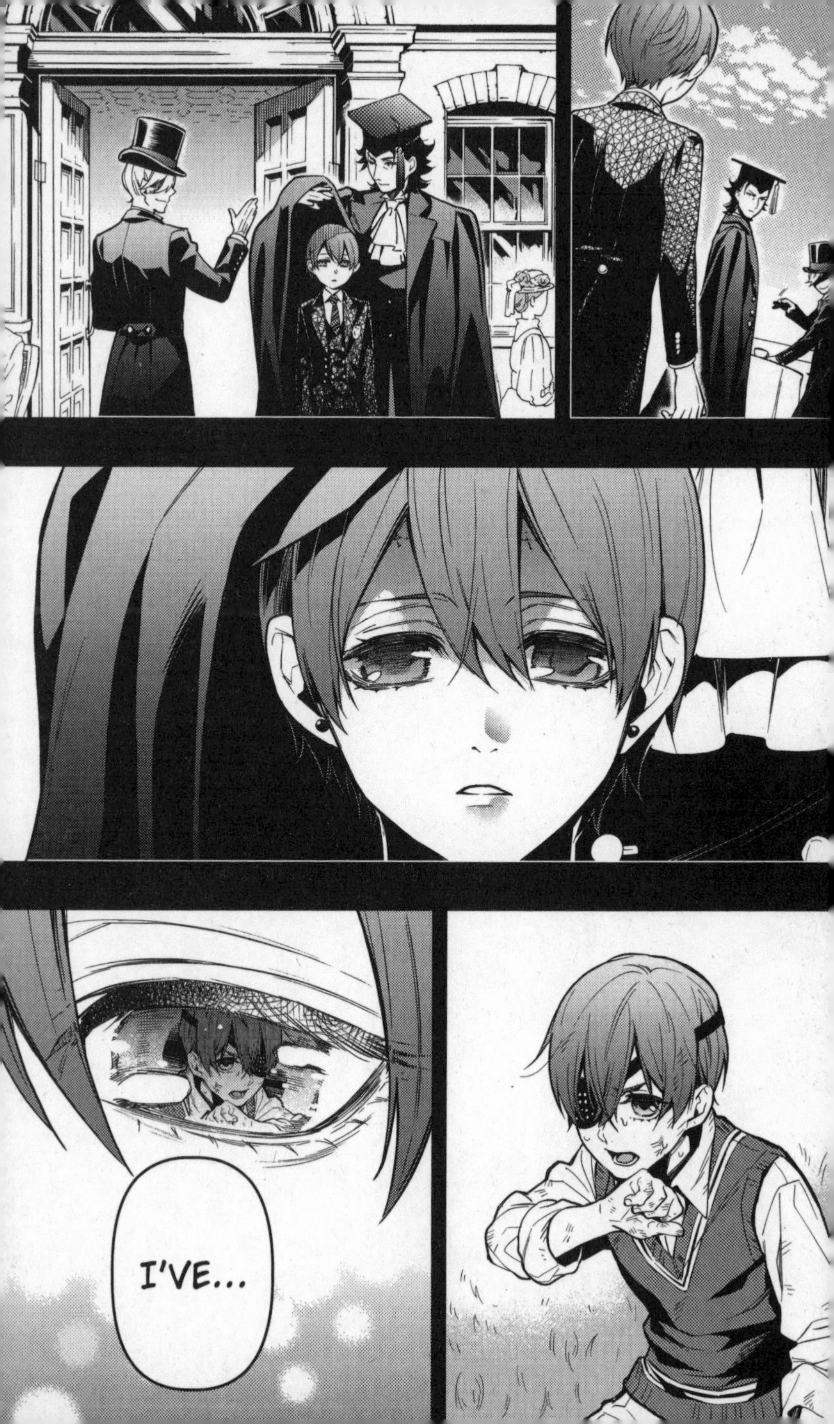
I'VE...

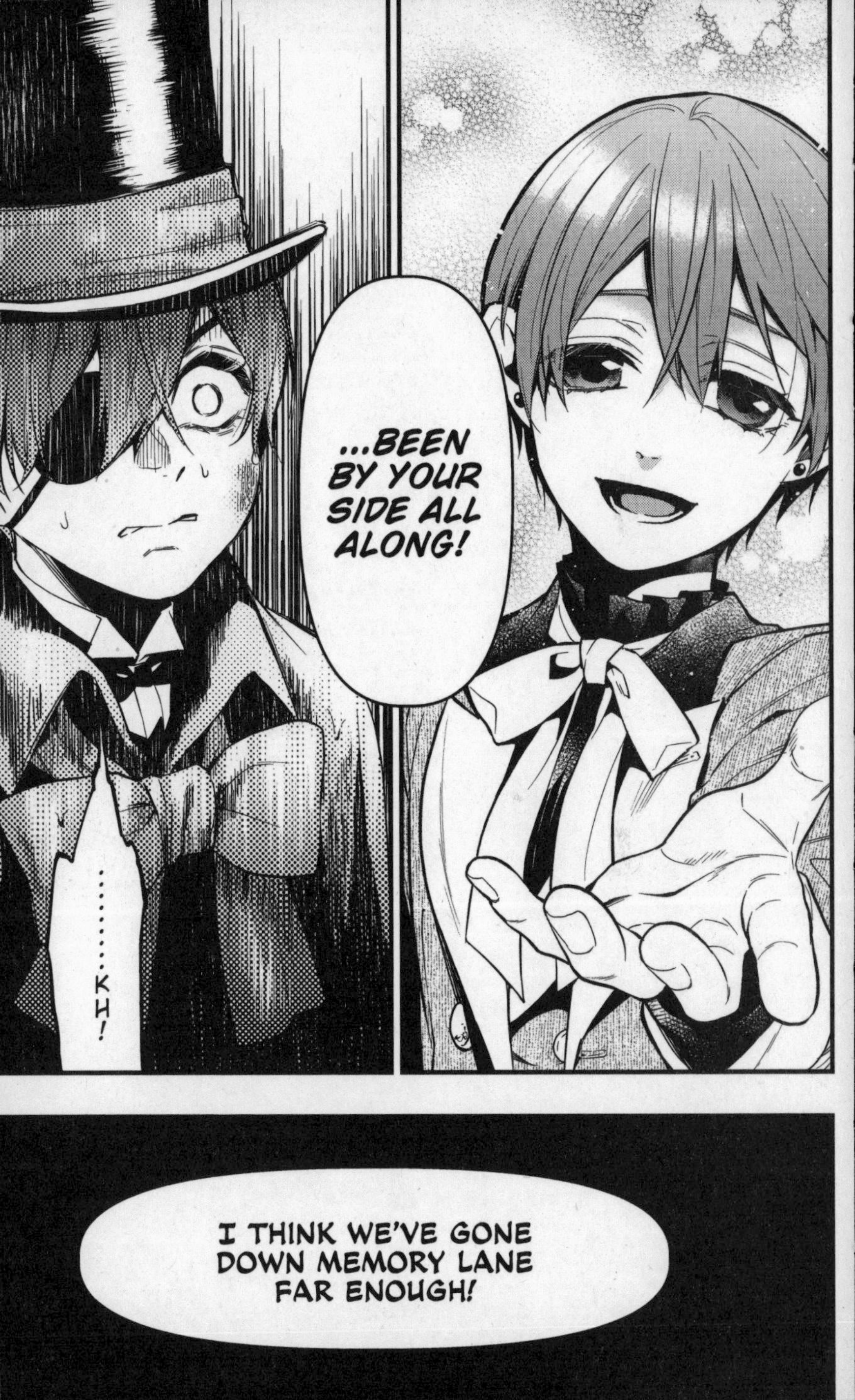
...BEEN BY YOUR SIDE ALL ALONG!
......KH!
I THINK WE'VE GONE DOWN MEMORY LANE FAR ENOUGH!

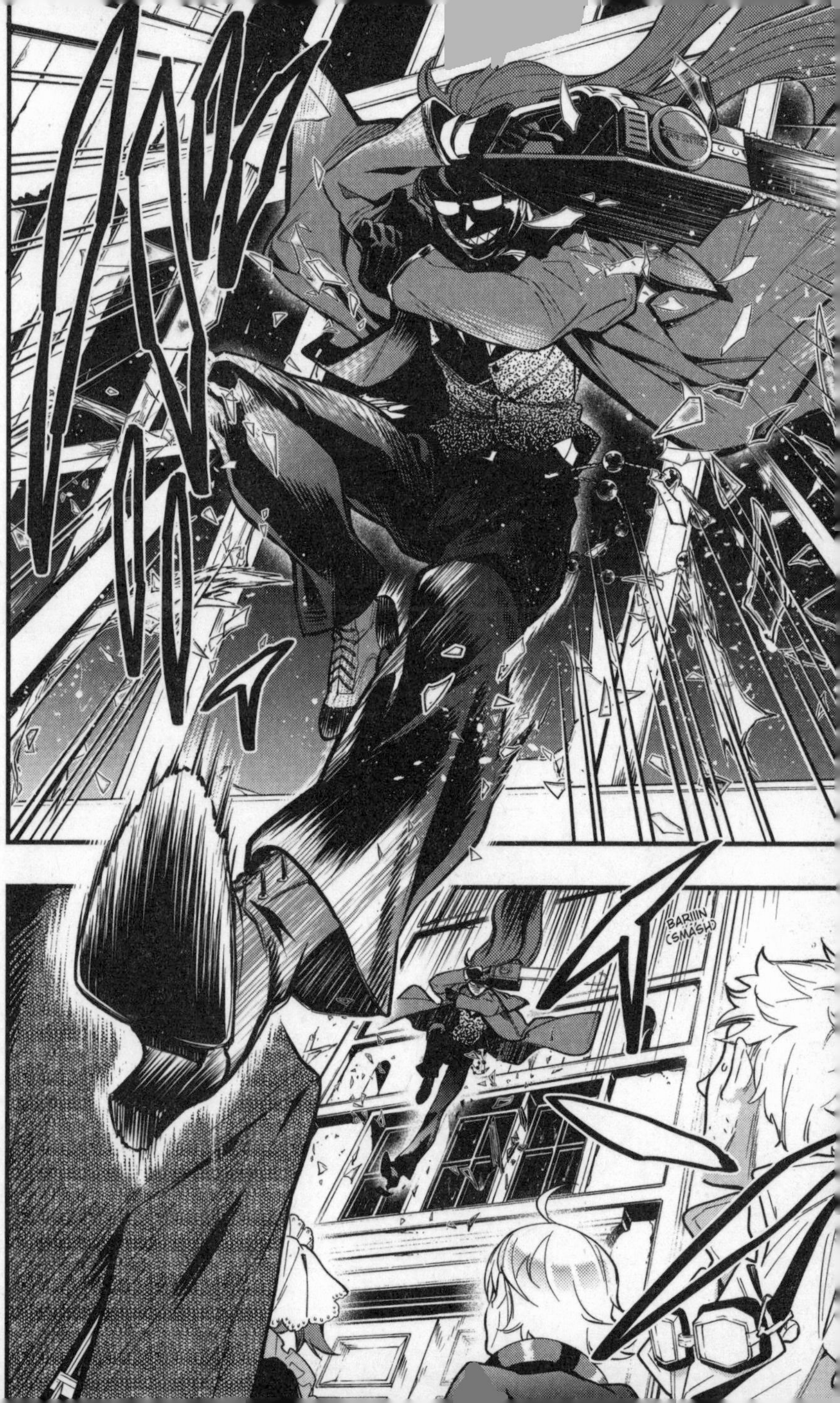
BARIIIN
(SMASH)

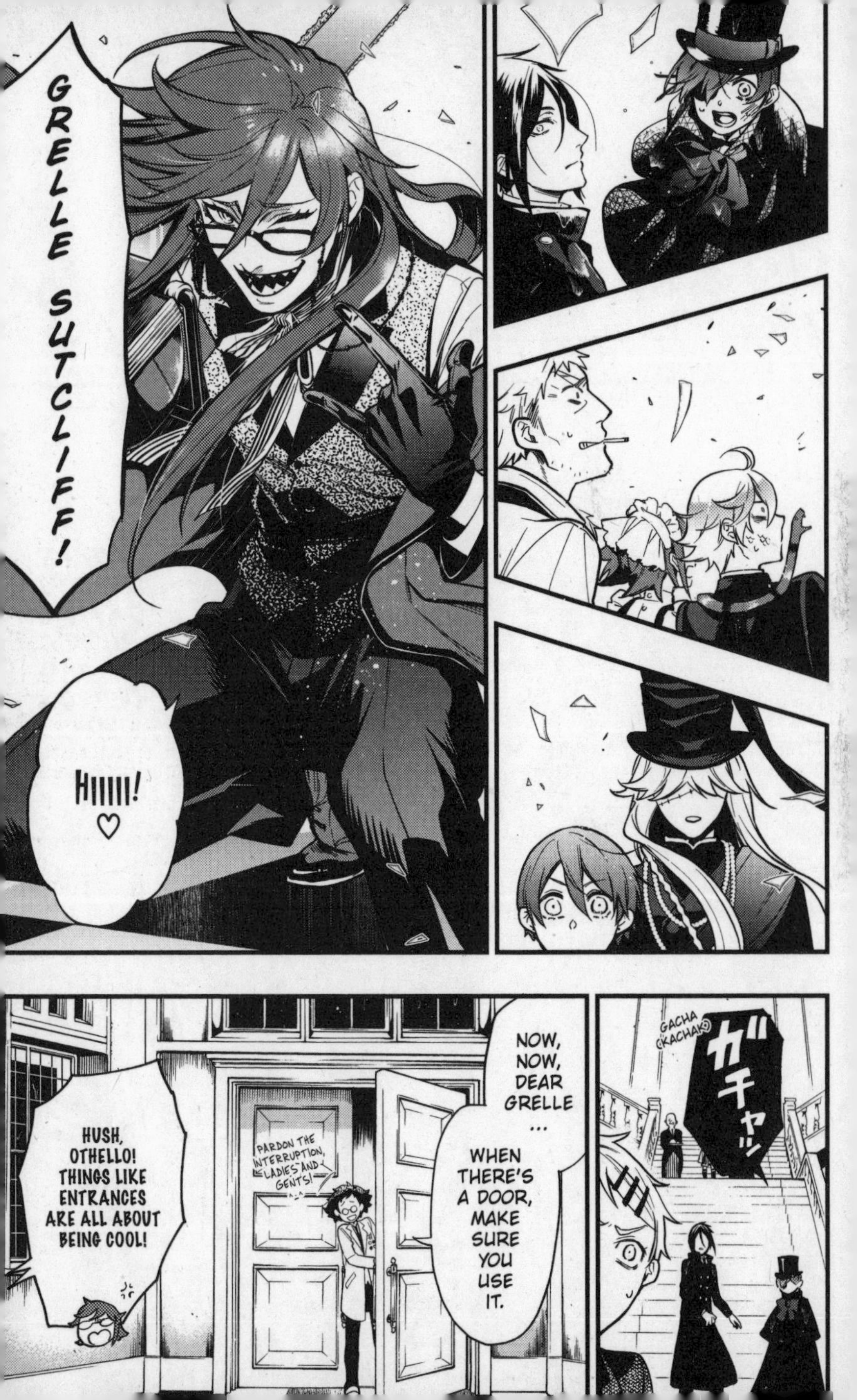
GRELLE SUTCLIFF!
HIIIII! ♡
GACHA KACHAK
ガチャッ
NOW, NOW, DEAR GRELLE...
WHEN THERE'S A DOOR, MAKE SURE YOU USE IT.
PARDON THE INTERRUPTION, LADIES AND GENTS! ^_^
HUSH, OTHELLO! THINGS LIKE ENTRANCES ARE ALL ABOUT BEING COOL!

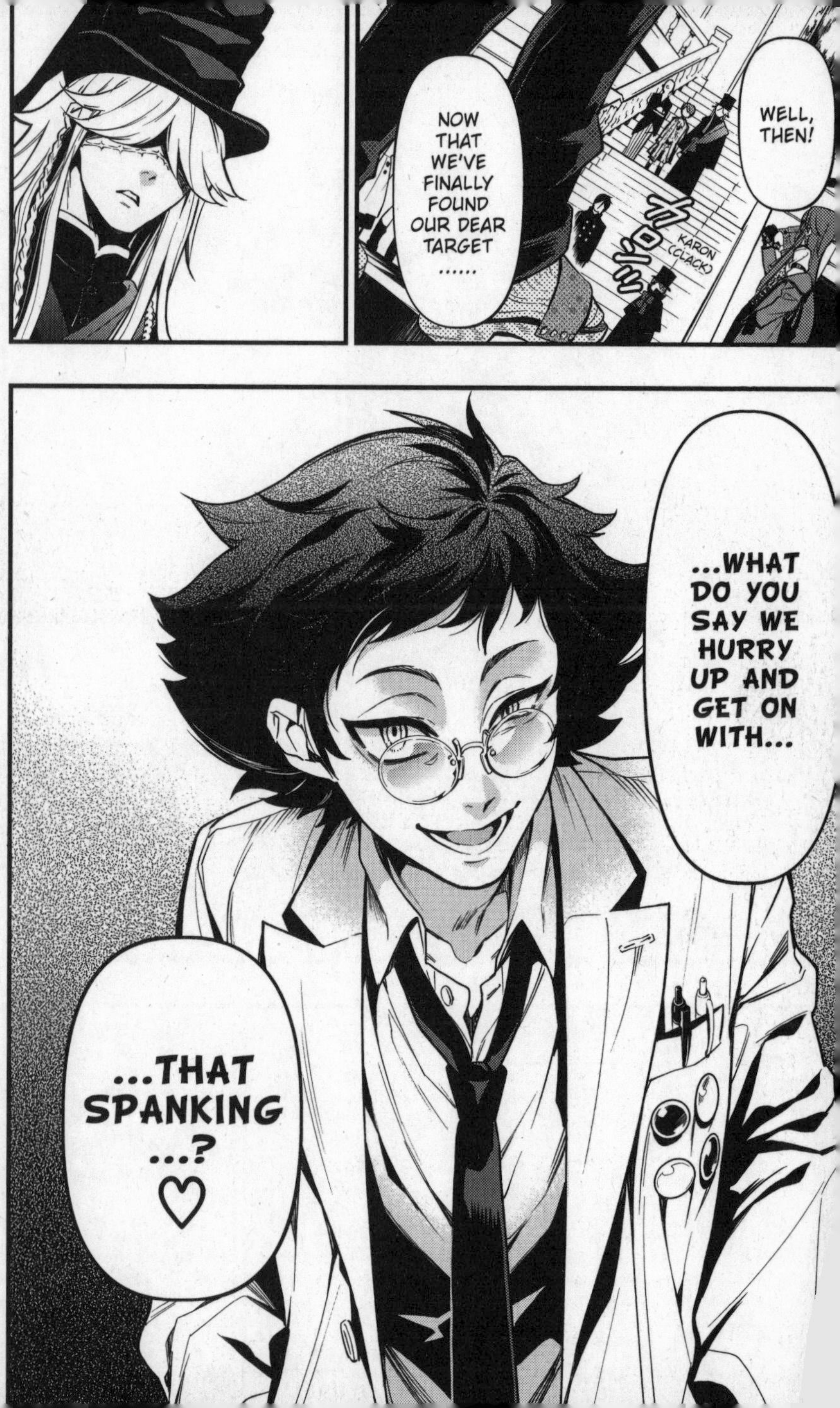
WELL, THEN!
NOW THAT WE'VE FINALLY FOUND OUR DEAR TARGET......
KARON (CLACK)
...WHAT DO YOU SAY WE HURRY UP AND GET ON WITH...
...THAT SPANKING ...? ♡

Black Butler

Chapter 142

At noon : The Butler, Chastised

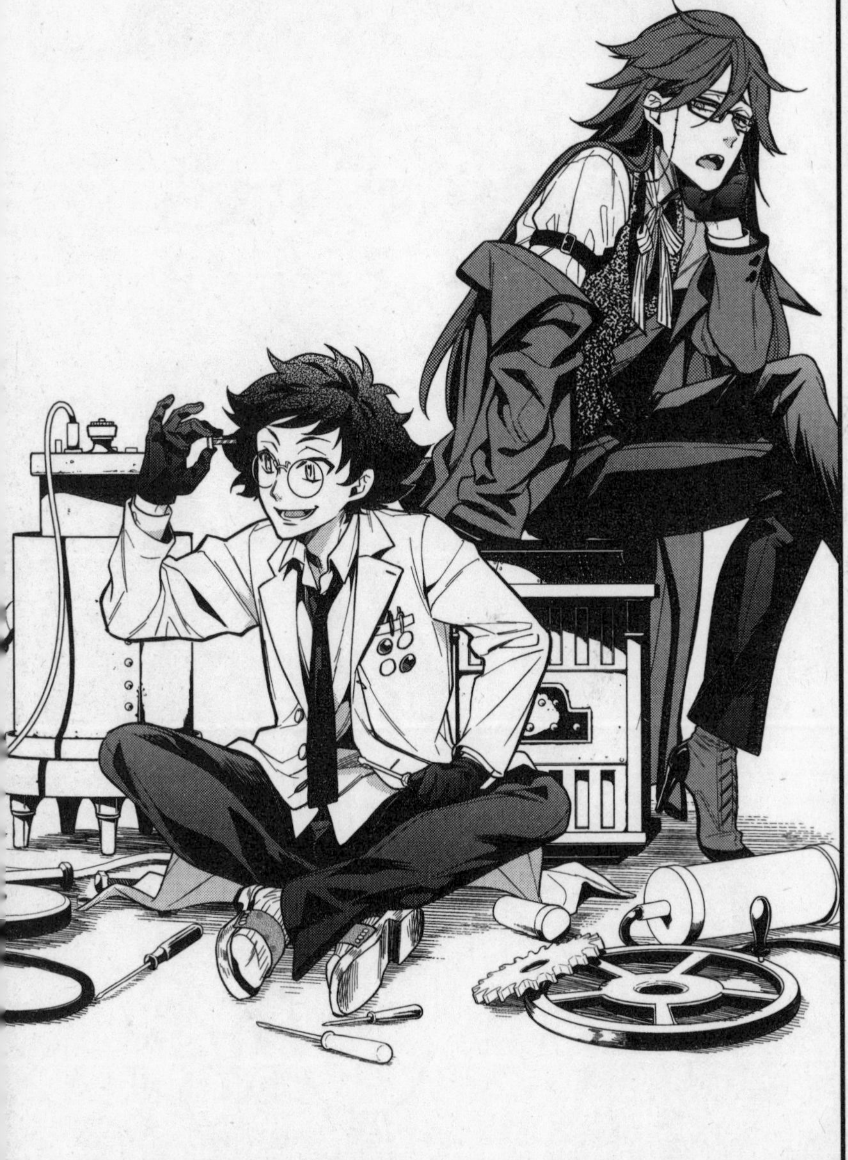

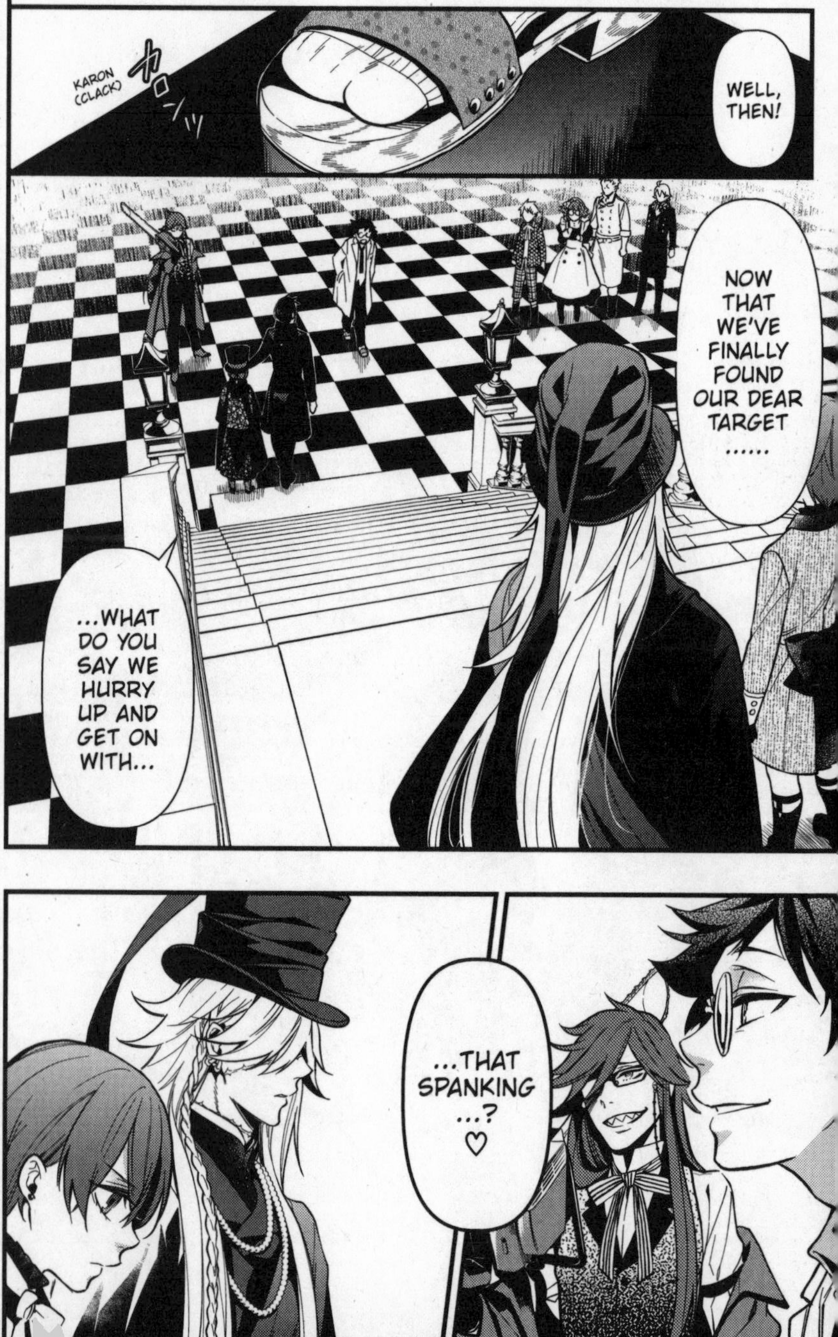
WELL, THEN!
KARON (CLACK)
NOW THAT WE'VE FINALLY FOUND OUR DEAR TARGET ......
...WHAT DO YOU SAY WE HURRY UP AND GET ON WITH...
...THAT SPANKING ...? ♡

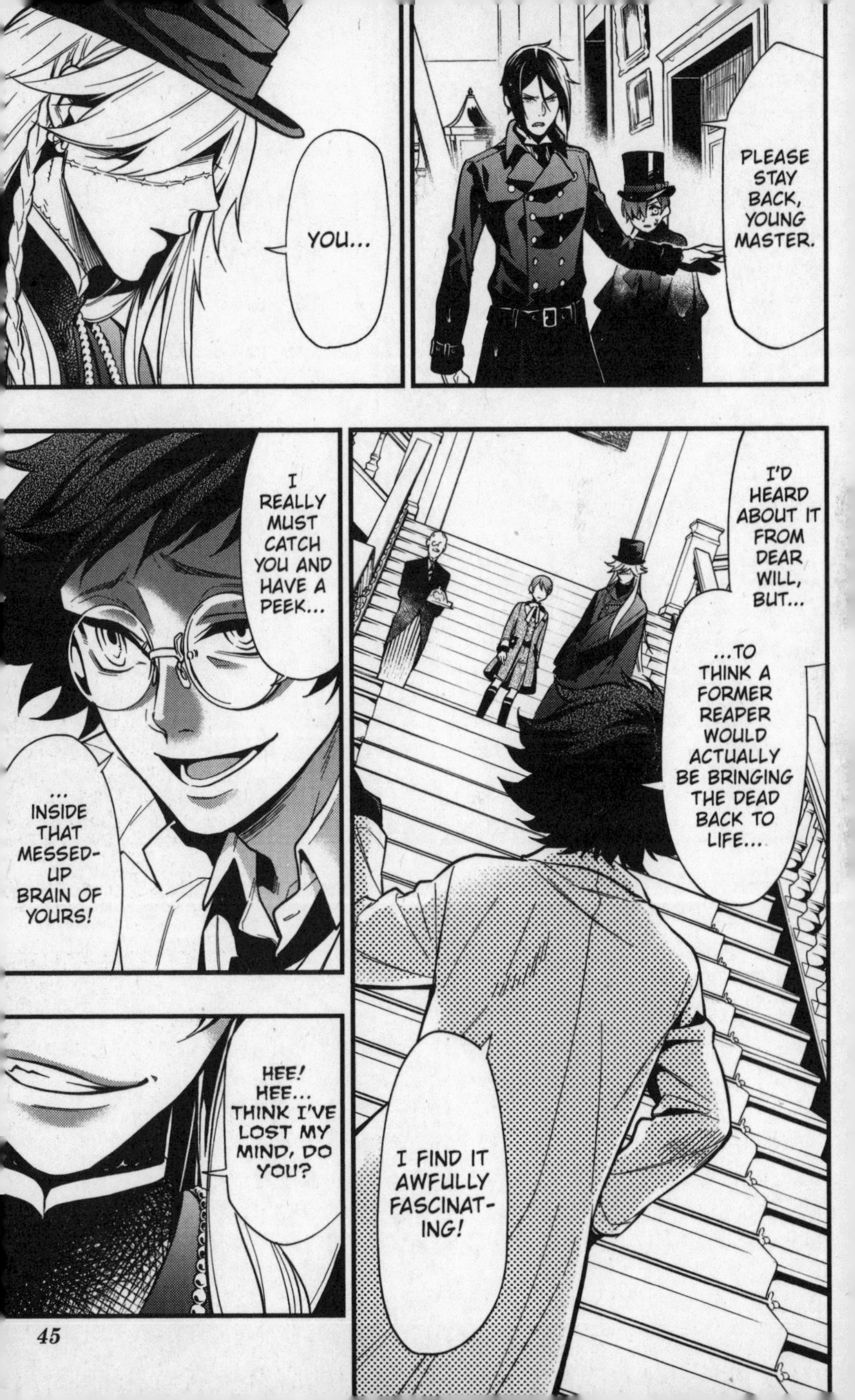
PLEASE STAY BACK, YOUNG MASTER.
YOU...
I'D HEARD ABOUT IT FROM DEAR WILL, BUT...
...TO THINK A FORMER REAPER WOULD ACTUALLY BE BRINGING THE DEAD BACK TO LIFE...
I FIND IT AWFULLY FASCINAT-ING!
I REALLY MUST CATCH YOU AND HAVE A PEEK...
...INSIDE THAT MESSED-UP BRAIN OF YOURS!
HEE! HEE... THINK I'VE LOST MY MIND, DO YOU?

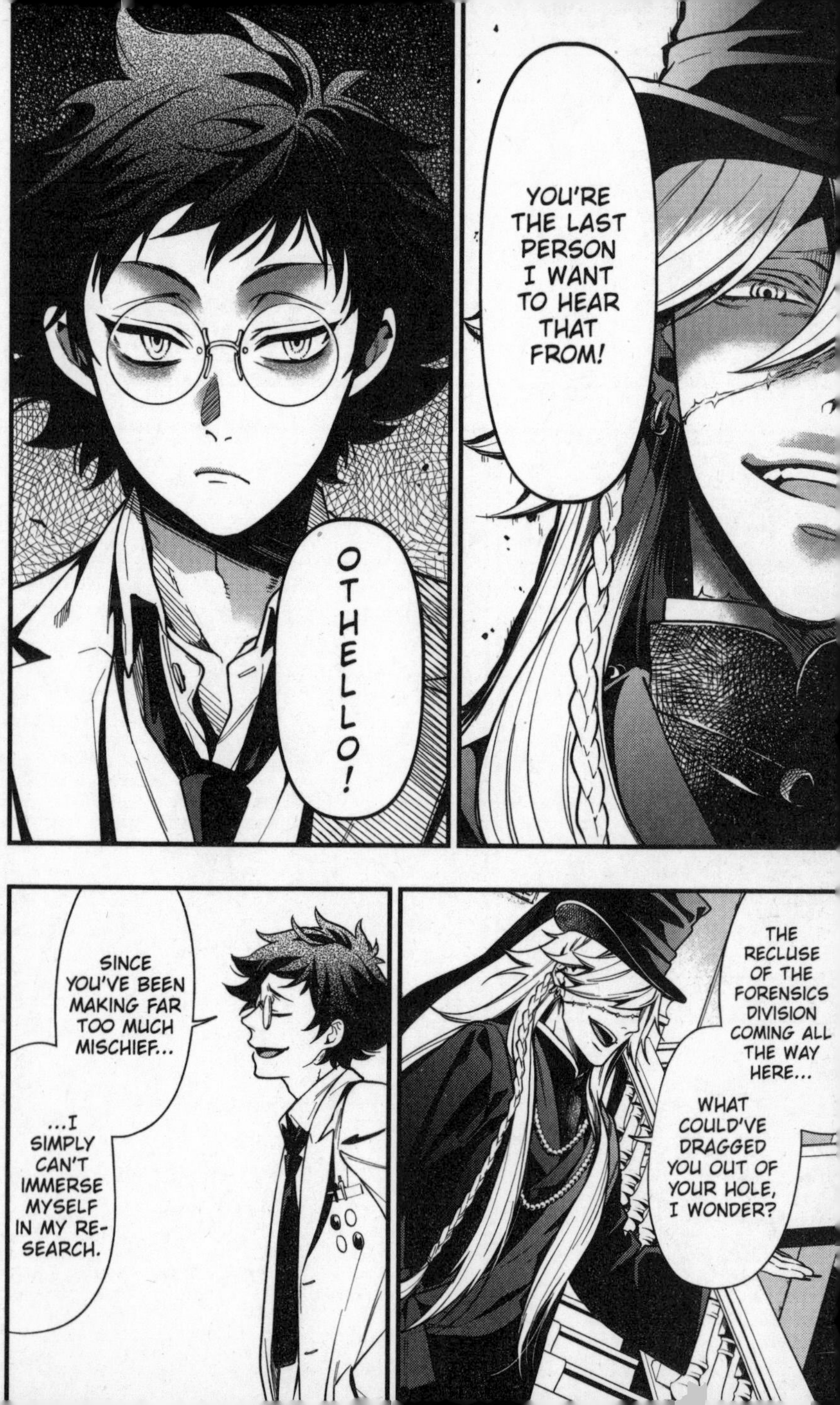
YOU'RE THE LAST PERSON I WANT TO HEAR THAT FROM!
OTHELLO!
THE RECLUSE OF THE FORENSICS DIVISION COMING ALL THE WAY HERE...
WHAT COULD'VE DRAGGED YOU OUT OF YOUR HOLE, I WONDER?
SINCE YOU'VE BEEN MAKING FAR TOO MUCH MISCHIEF...
...I SIMPLY CAN'T IMMERSE MYSELF IN MY RE-SEARCH.

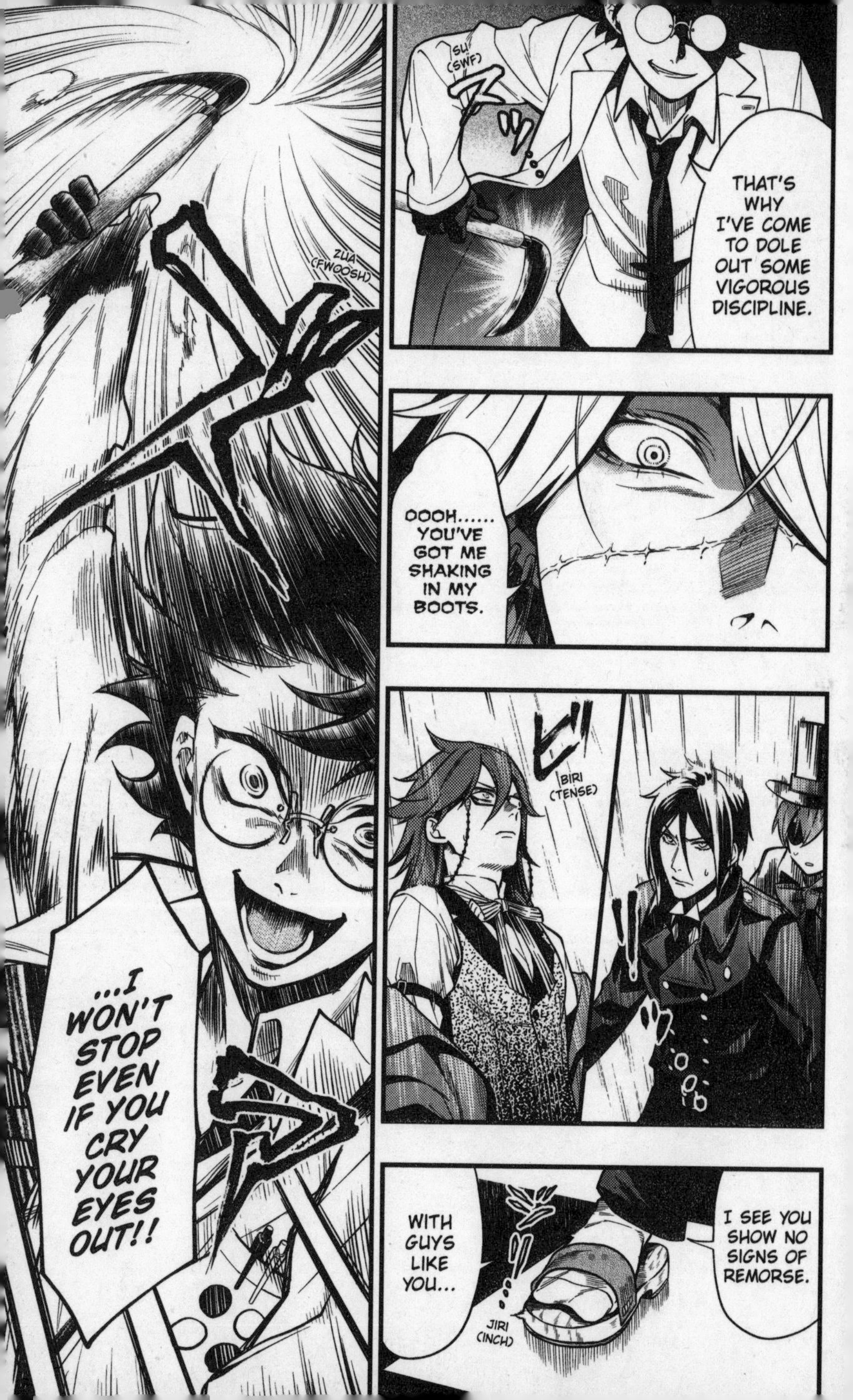
SU (SWF)
THAT'S WHY I'VE COME TO DOLE OUT SOME VIGOROUS DISCIPLINE.
OOOH...... YOU'VE GOT ME SHAKING IN MY BOOTS.
BIRI (TENSE)
I SEE YOU SHOW NO SIGNS OF REMORSE.
JIRI (INCH)
WITH GUYS LIKE YOU...
ZUA (FWOOSH)
...I WON'T STOP EVEN IF YOU CRY YOUR EYES OUT!!

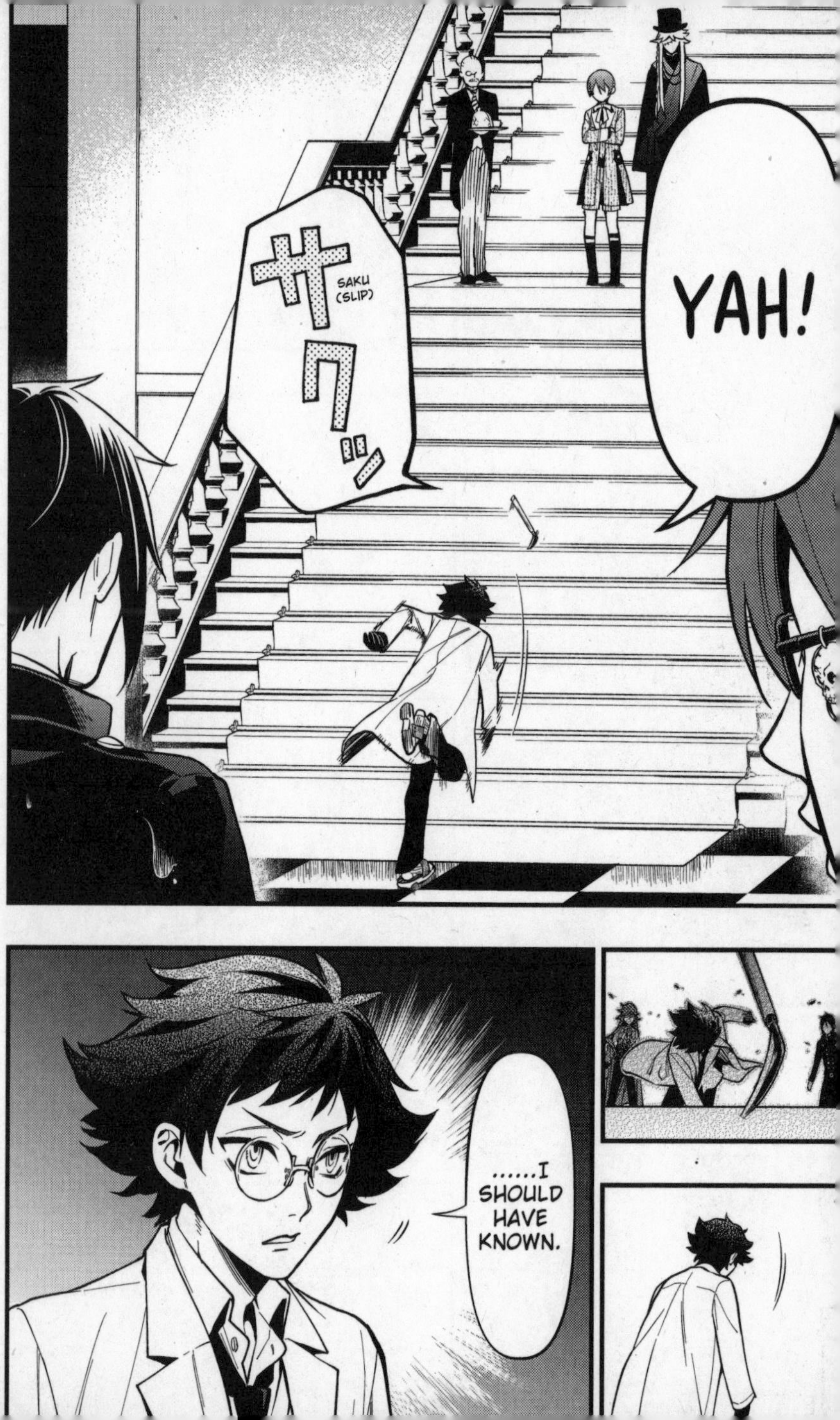
YAH!
サク
SAKU (SLIP)
......I SHOULD HAVE KNOWN.

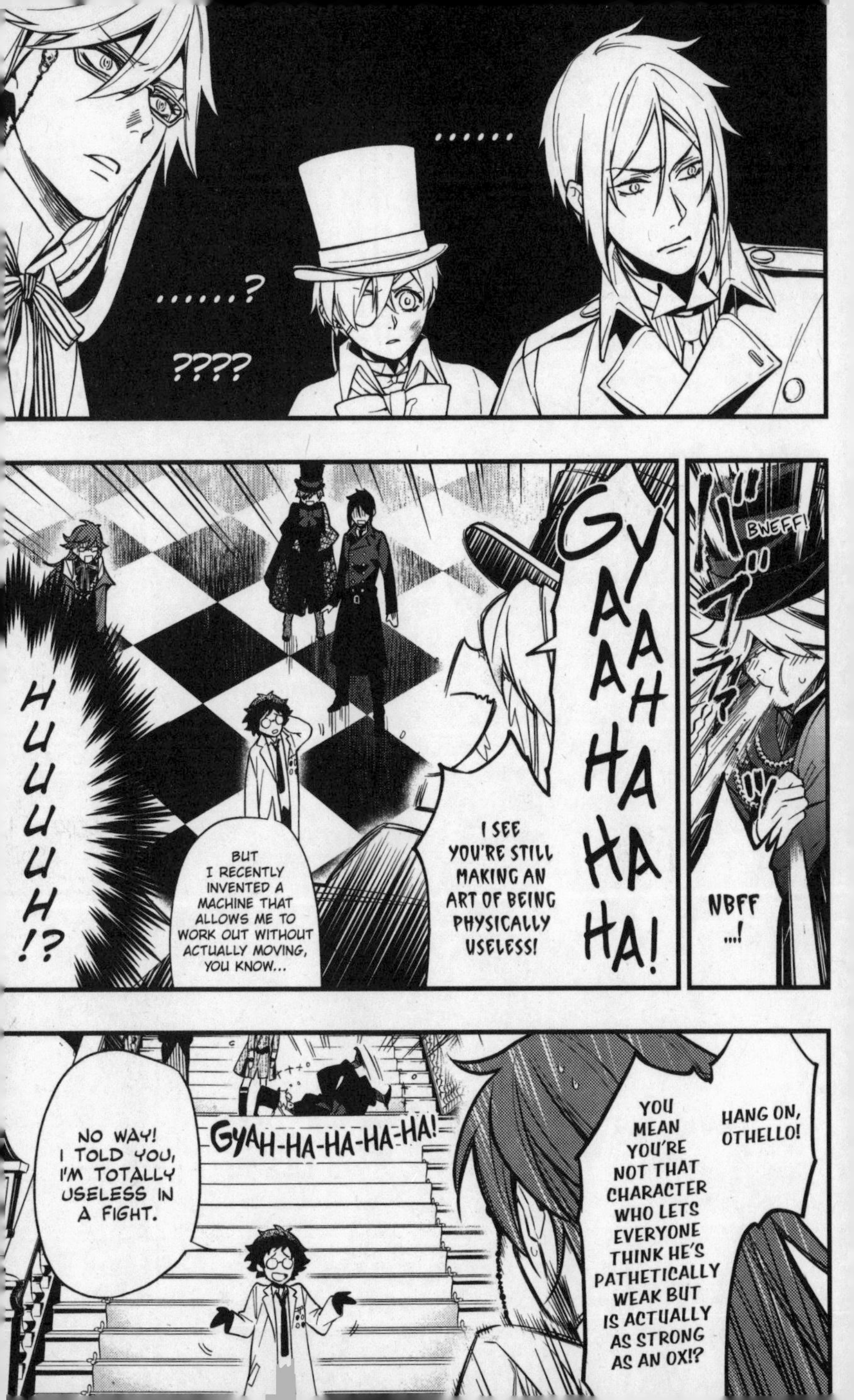
......
......?
????
BWEFF!
NBFF ...!
GYAAAHHAHAHAHA!
I SEE YOU'RE STILL MAKING AN ART OF BEING PHYSICALLY USELESS!
BUT I RECENTLY INVENTED A MACHINE THAT ALLOWS ME TO WORK OUT WITHOUT ACTUALLY MOVING, YOU KNOW...
HUUUUH!?
HANG ON, OTHELLO!
YOU MEAN YOU'RE NOT THAT CHARACTER WHO LETS EVERYONE THINK HE'S PATHETICALLY WEAK BUT IS ACTUALLY AS STRONG AS AN OX!?
GYAH-HA-HA-HA-HA!
NO WAY! I TOLD YOU, I'M TOTALLY USELESS IN A FIGHT.

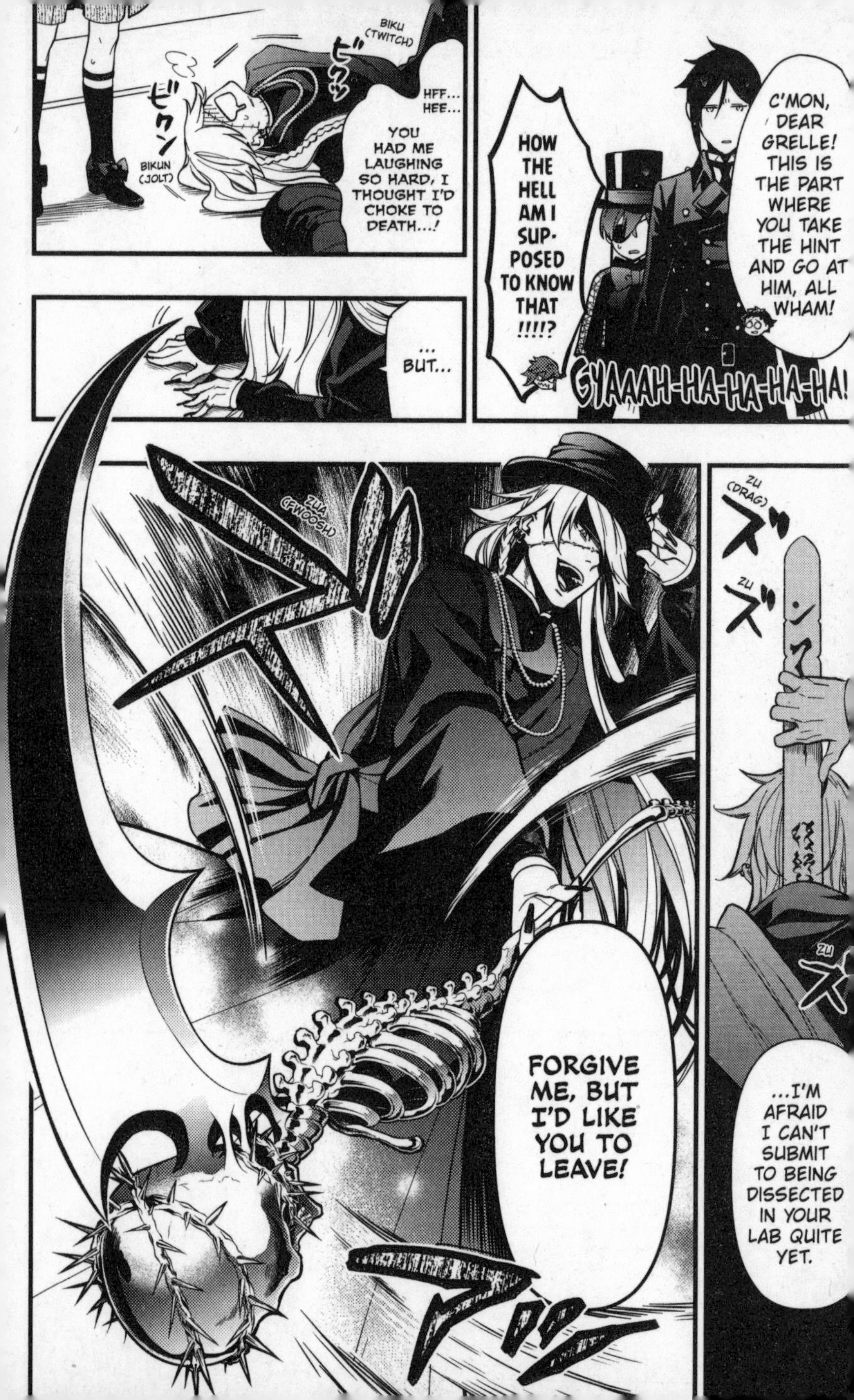
C'MON, DEAR GRELLE! THIS IS THE PART WHERE YOU TAKE THE HINT AND GO AT HIM, ALL WHAM!
HOW THE HELL AM I SUPPOSED TO KNOW THAT!!!!?
GYAAAH-HA-HA-HA-HA!
ビクッ
BIKU (TWITCH)
ビクン
BIKUN (JOLT)
HFF... HEE...
YOU HAD ME LAUGHING SO HARD, I THOUGHT I'D CHOKE TO DEATH...!
...BUT...
ズッ
ZU (DRAG)
ズ
ZU
ズ
ZU
...I'M AFRAID I CAN'T SUBMIT TO BEING DISSECTED IN YOUR LAB QUITE YET.
ZUA (FWOOSH)
FORGIVE ME, BUT I'D LIKE YOU TO LEAVE!

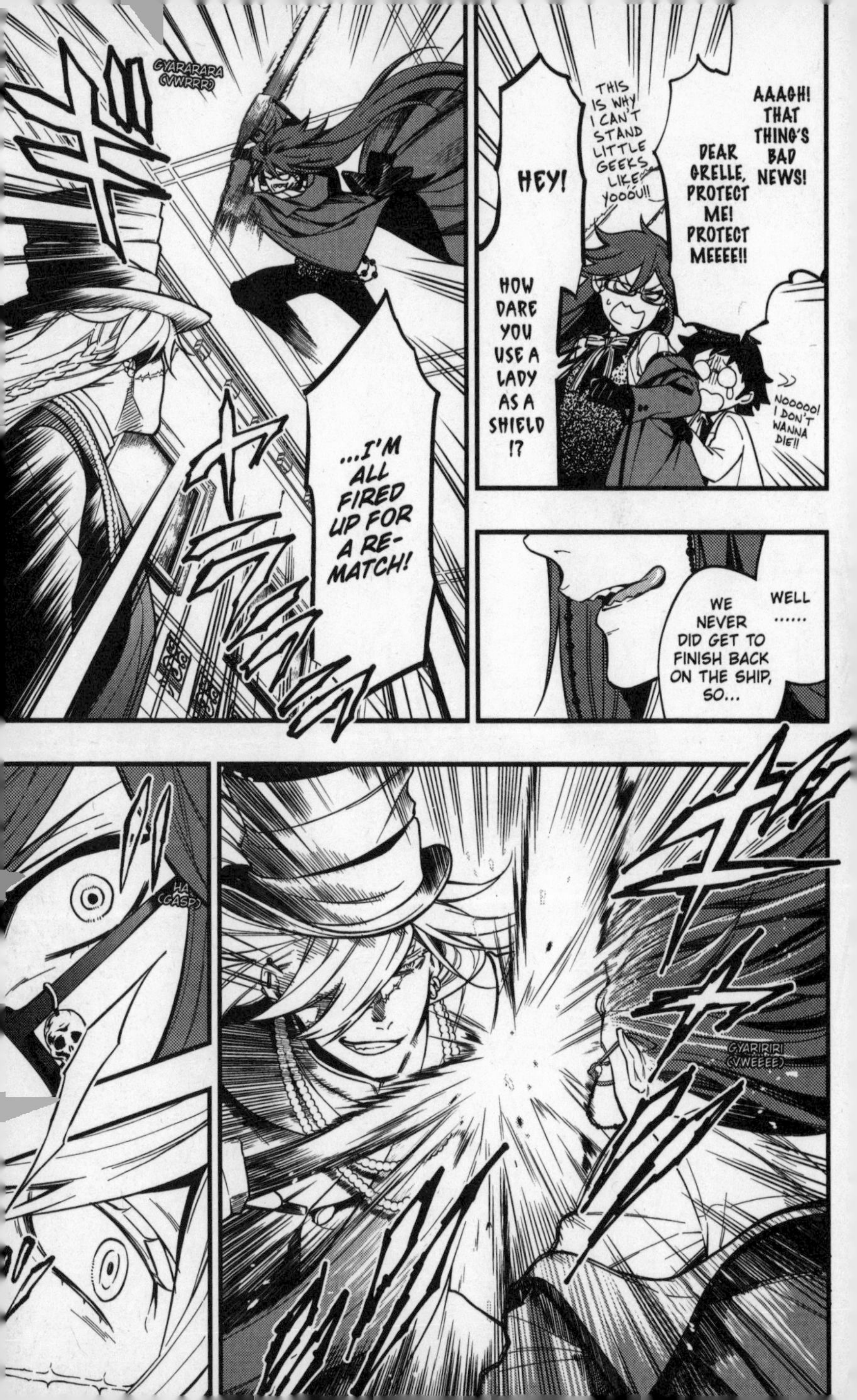
AAAGH! THAT THING'S BAD NEWS!
DEAR GRELLE, PROTECT ME! PROTECT MEEEE!!
THIS IS WHY I CAN'T STAND LITTLE GEEKS LIKE YOOOU!!
HEY!
NOOOOO! I DON'T WANNA DIE!!
HOW DARE YOU USE A LADY AS A SHIELD !?
WELL ......
WE NEVER DID GET TO FINISH BACK ON THE SHIP, SO...
GYARARARA (VWRRR)
...I'M ALL FIRED UP FOR A RE-MATCH!
GYARIRIRI (VWEEEE)
HA (GASP)

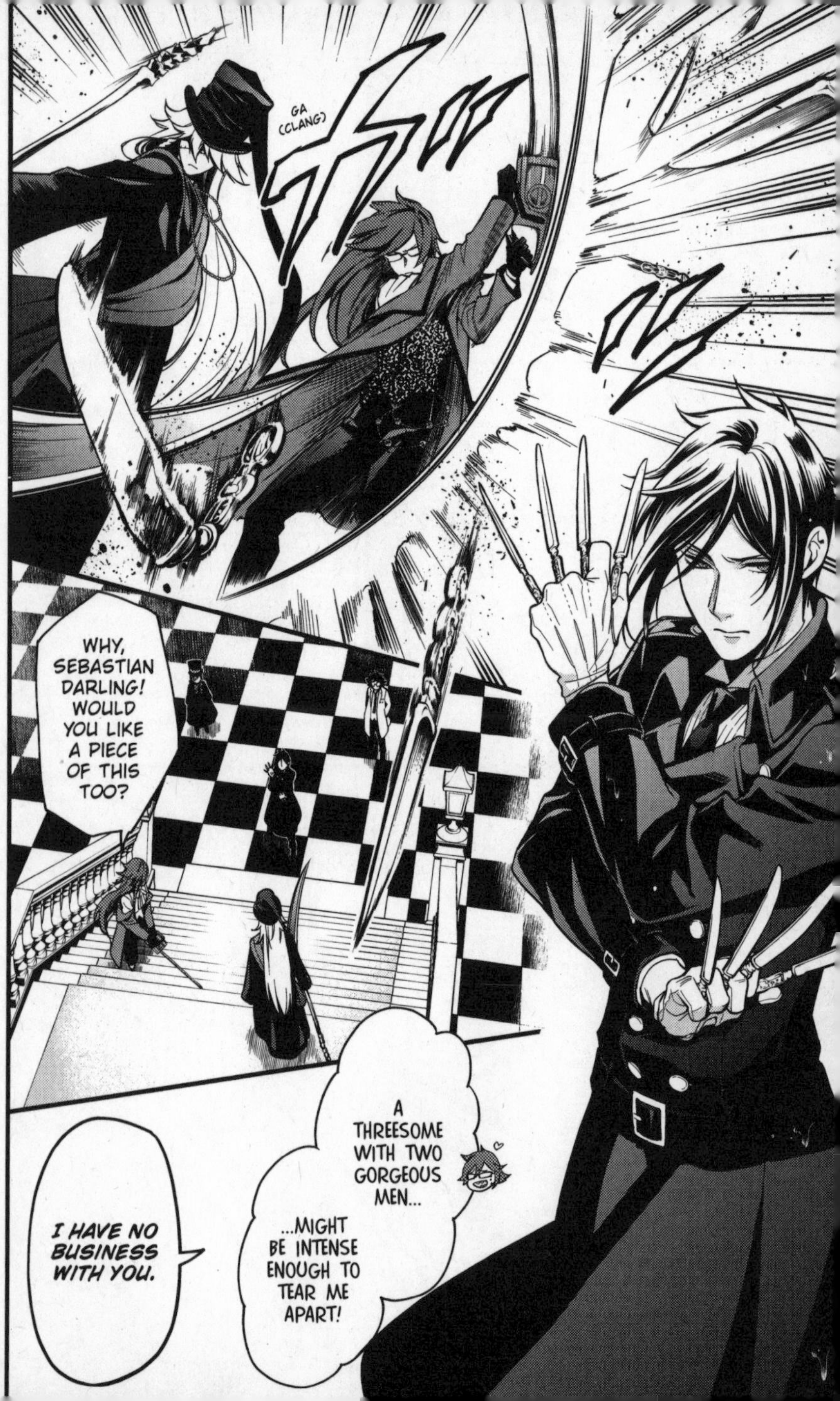
GA (CLANG)
WHY, SEBASTIAN DARLING! WOULD YOU LIKE A PIECE OF THIS TOO?
A THREESOME WITH TWO GORGEOUS MEN...
...MIGHT BE INTENSE ENOUGH TO TEAR ME APART!
I HAVE NO BUSINESS WITH YOU.

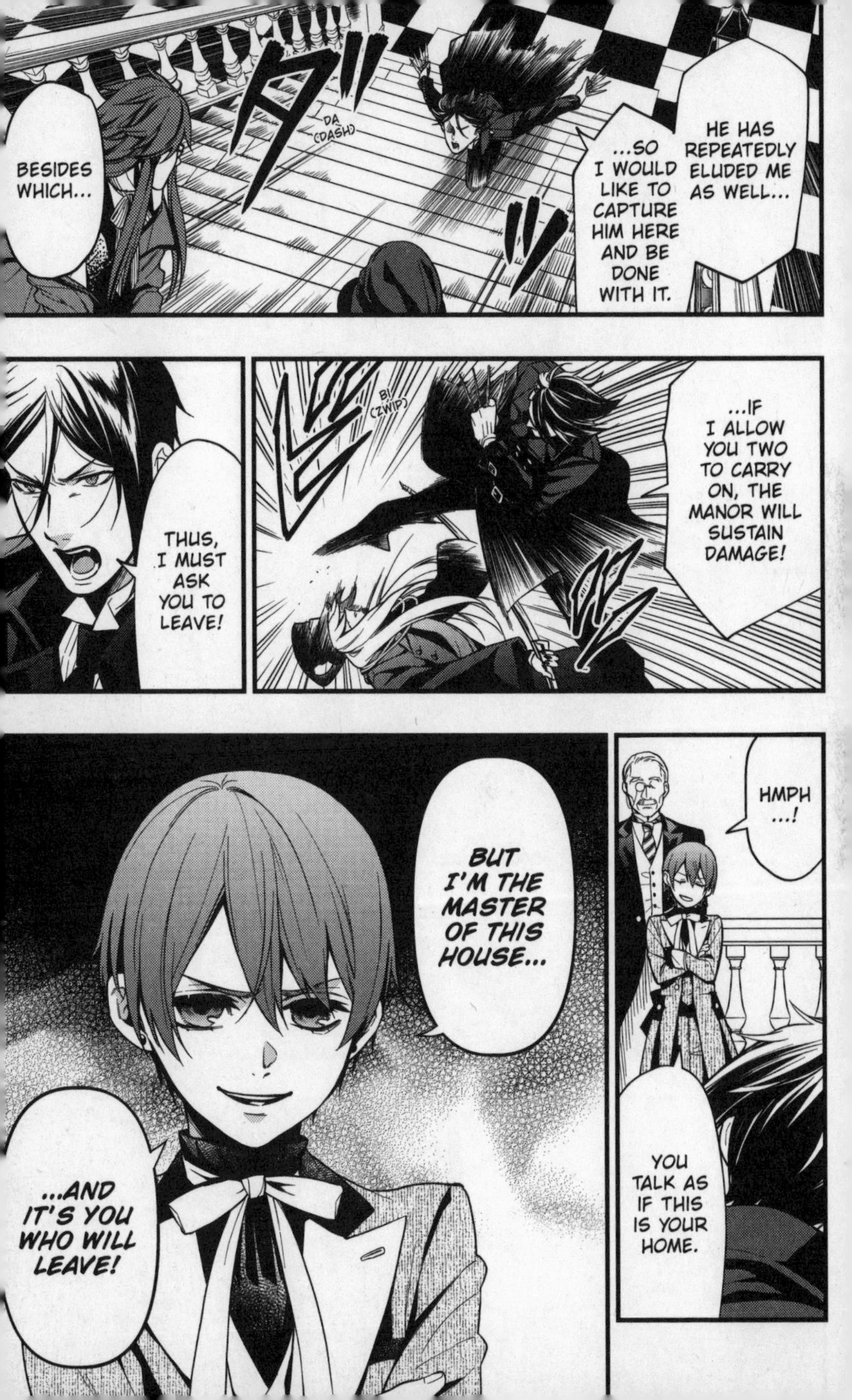
HE HAS REPEATEDLY ELUDED ME AS WELL...
...SO I WOULD LIKE TO CAPTURE HIM HERE AND BE DONE WITH IT.
DA (DASH)
BESIDES WHICH...
...IF I ALLOW YOU TWO TO CARRY ON, THE MANOR WILL SUSTAIN DAMAGE!
BI (ZWIP)
THUS, I MUST ASK YOU TO LEAVE!
HMPH...!
YOU TALK AS IF THIS IS YOUR HOME.
BUT I'M THE MASTER OF THIS HOUSE...
...AND IT'S YOU WHO WILL LEAVE!

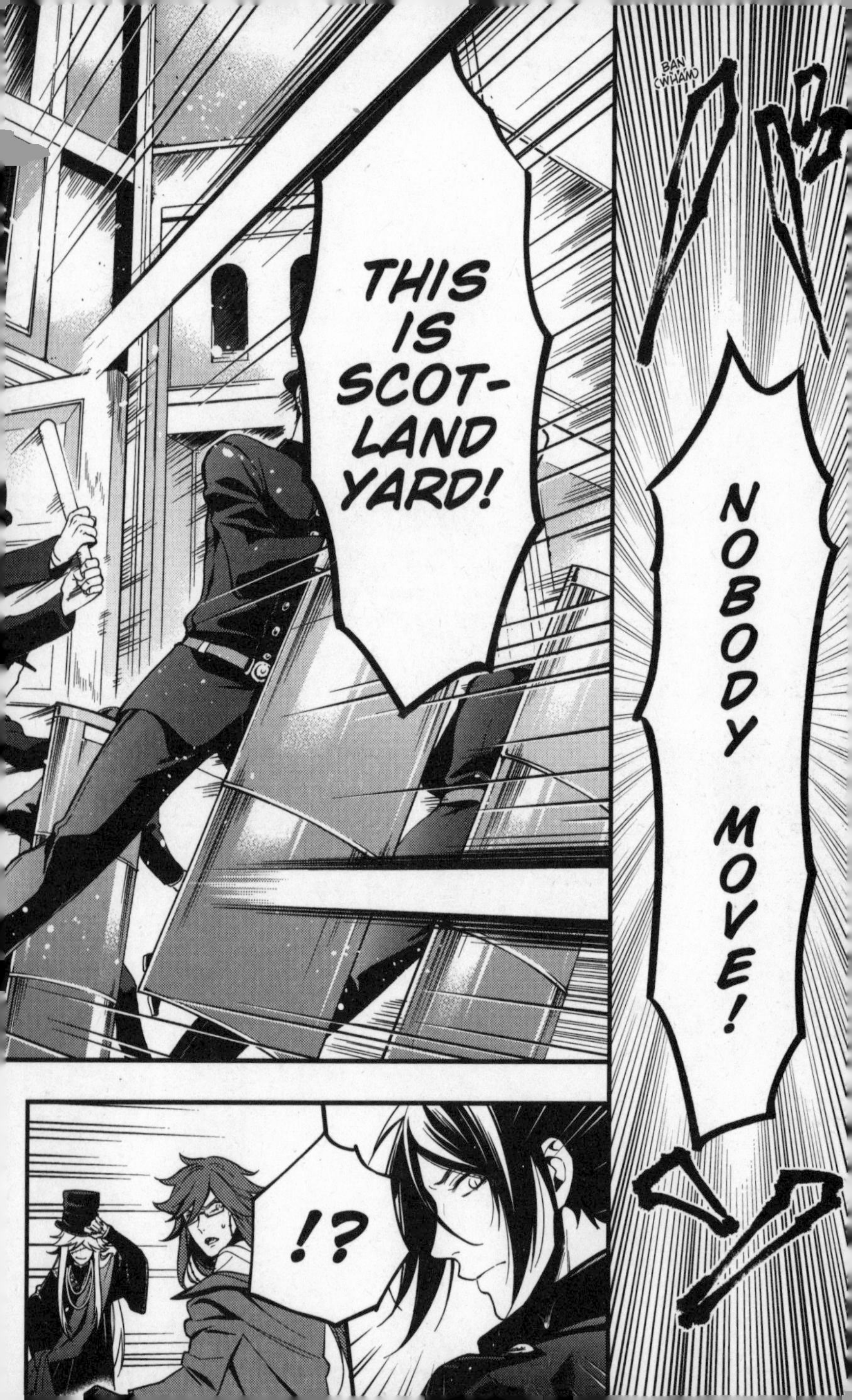
BAN (WHAM)
NOBODY MOVE!
THIS IS SCOT-LAND YARD!
!?

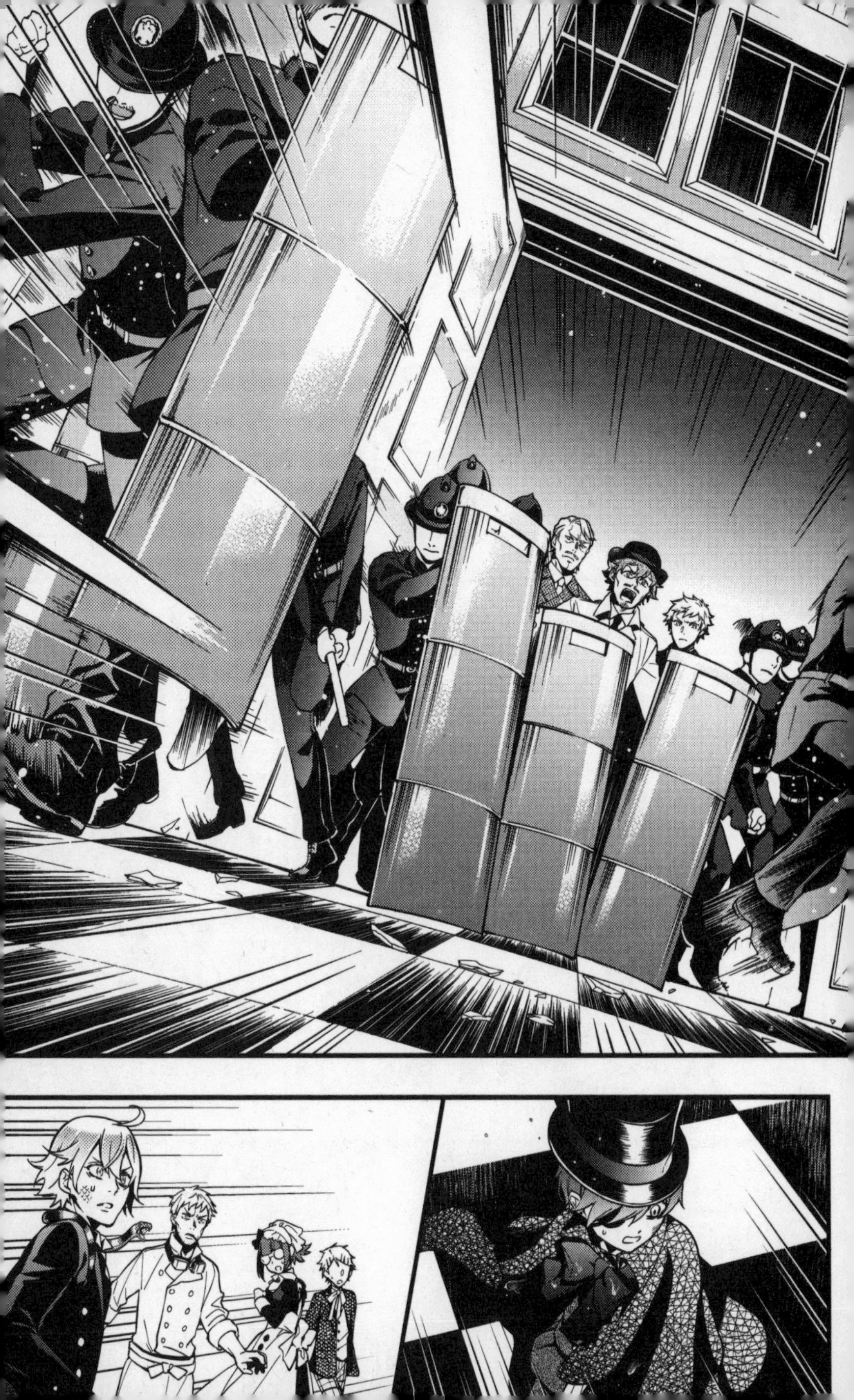

THE MARQUESS OF MIDFORD...!?

CHIEF INSPECTOR ABBERLINE!

WE RECEIVED AN ANONYMOUS REPORT ALLEGING THAT BLAVAT SKY, MASTERMIND OF THE SPHERE MUSIC HALL SERIAL MURDERS...

...AND HIS CONSPIRATORS ARE HIDING OUT IN THE PHANTOMHIVE MANOR!

EARL PHANTOMHIVE...

IF YOU WOULD PLEASE EXPLAIN YOURS—

EX-CUSE ME!?

EVERYONE, PUT YOUR WEAPONS DOWN!

DEAR GRELLE, JUST DO AS THEY SAY NOW.

......!?

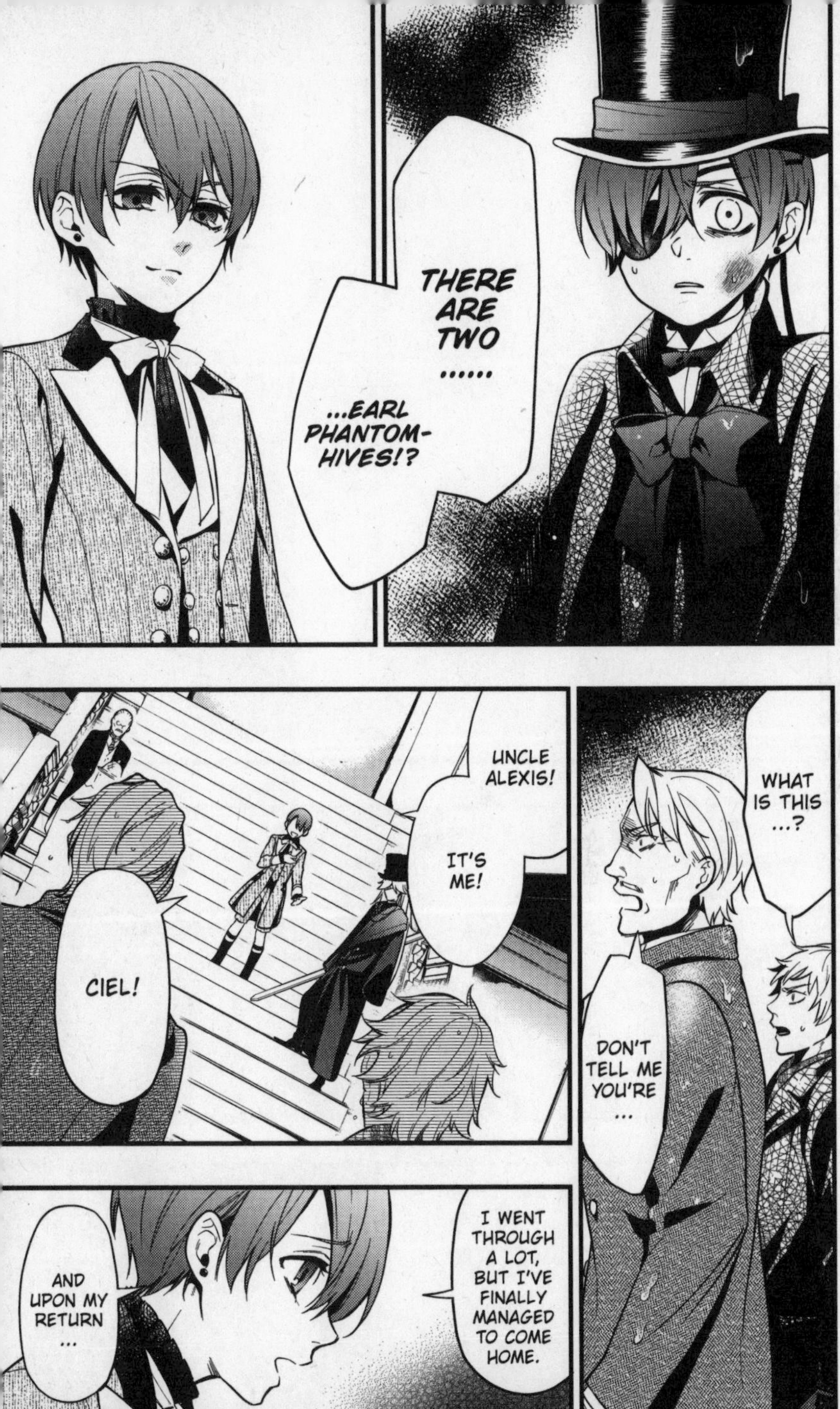
THERE ARE TWO ......
...EARL PHANTOM-HIVES!?
WHAT IS THIS ...?
DON'T TELL ME YOU'RE ...
UNCLE ALEXIS!
IT'S ME!
CIEL!
I WENT THROUGH A LOT, BUT I'VE FINALLY MANAGED TO COME HOME.
AND UPON MY RETURN ...

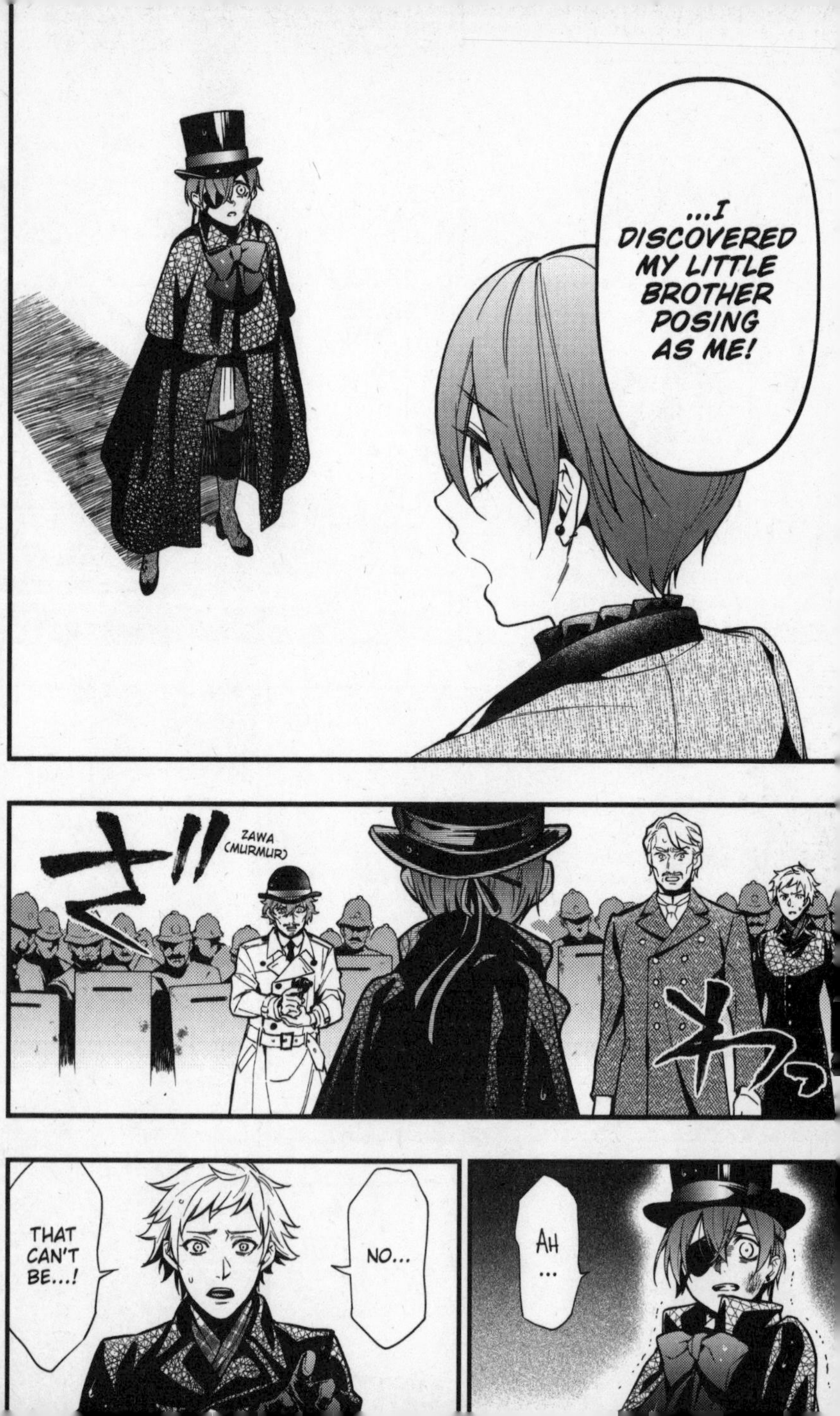

...I DISCOVERED MY LITTLE BROTHER POSING AS ME!
ZAWA (MURMUR)
AH ...
NO...
THAT CAN'T BE...!

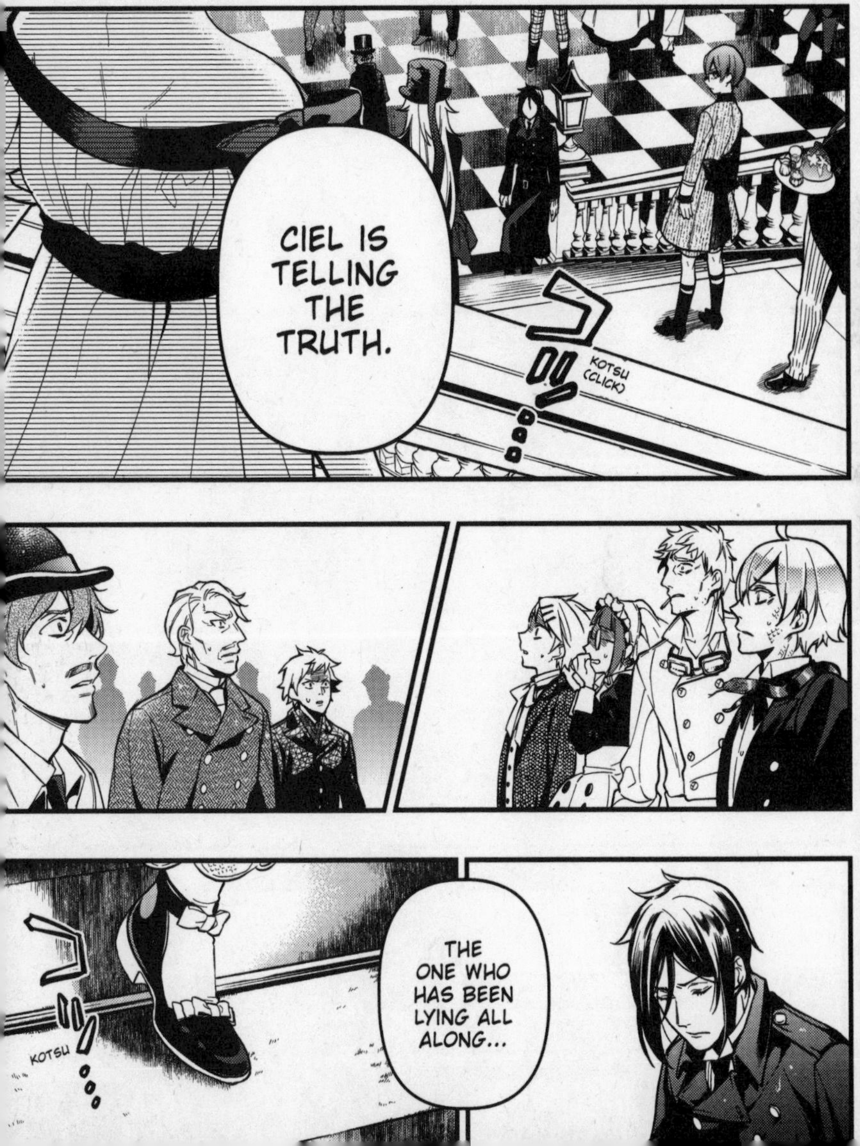
CIEL IS TELLING THE TRUTH.
KOTSU (CLICK)
THE ONE WHO HAS BEEN LYING ALL ALONG...
KOTSU

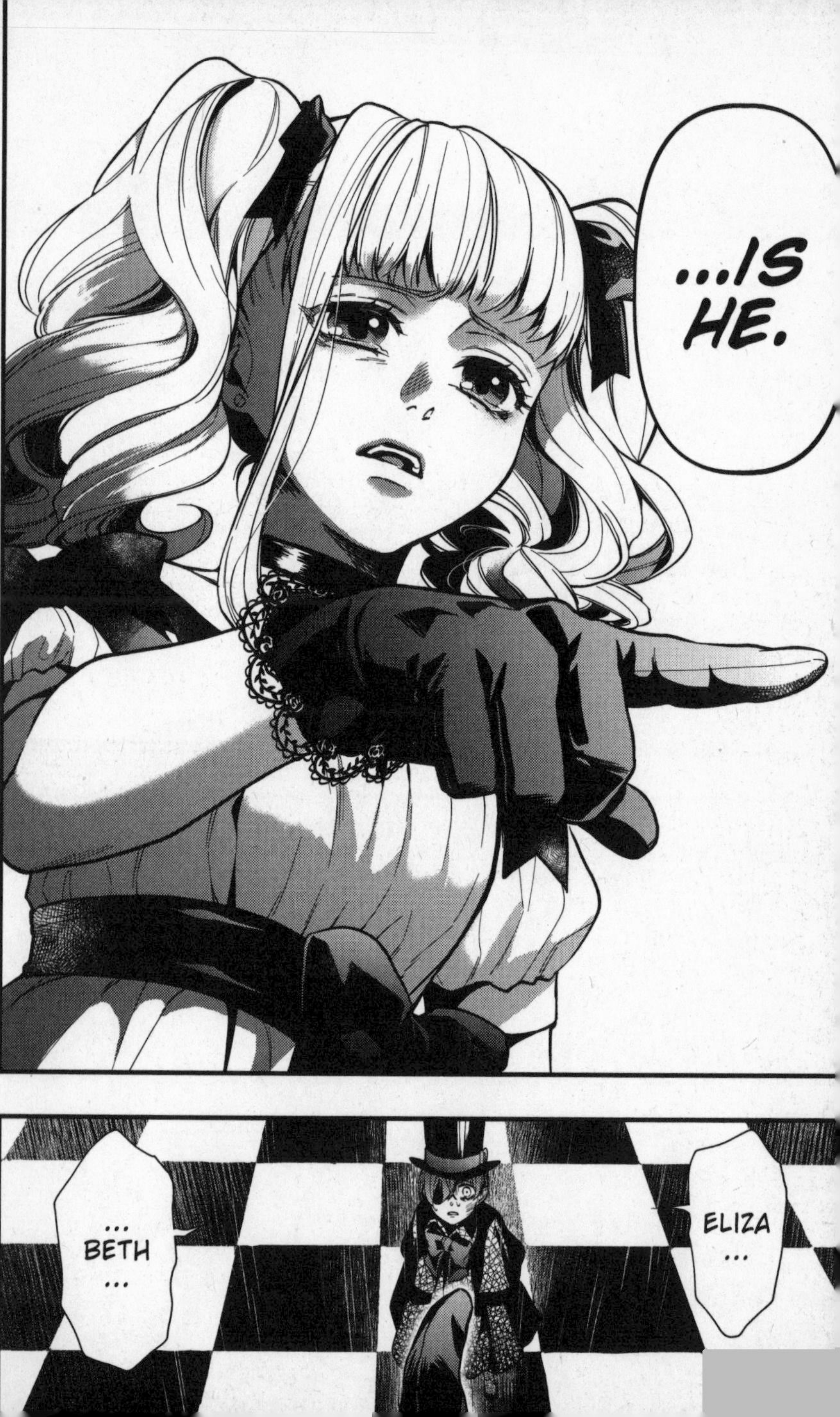
...IS HE.
ELIZA ...
... BETH ...

Black Butler

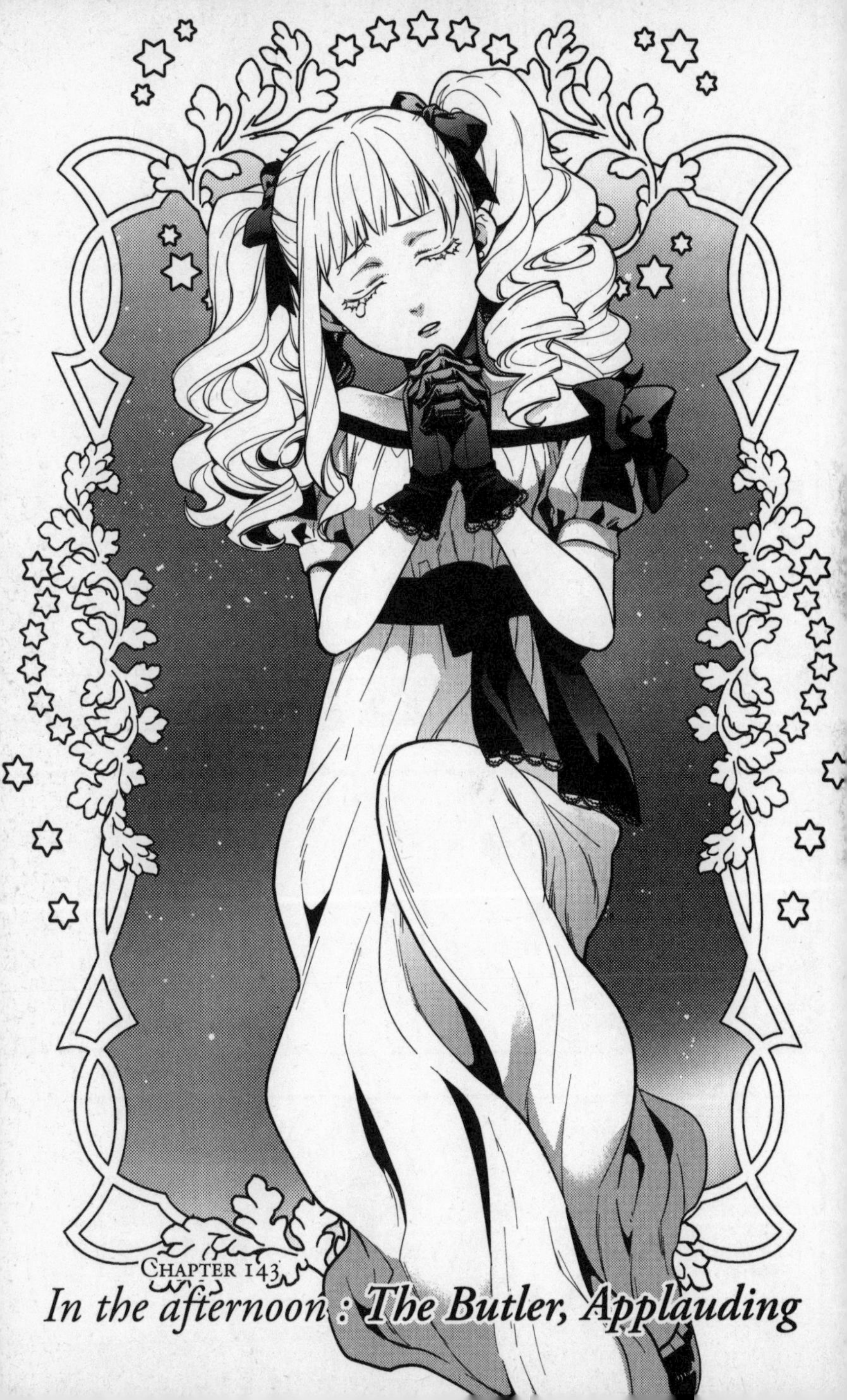

CHAPTER 143

In the afternoon : The Butler, Applauding

THE ONE WHO HAS BEEN LYING ALL ALONG...

...IS HE.

ELIZA... BETH...

I SEE. THE REASON FOR LADY ELIZABETH'S REFUSAL TO RETURN HOME......

IT WAS BECAUSE SHE HAD REUNITED WITH HER BETROTHED.

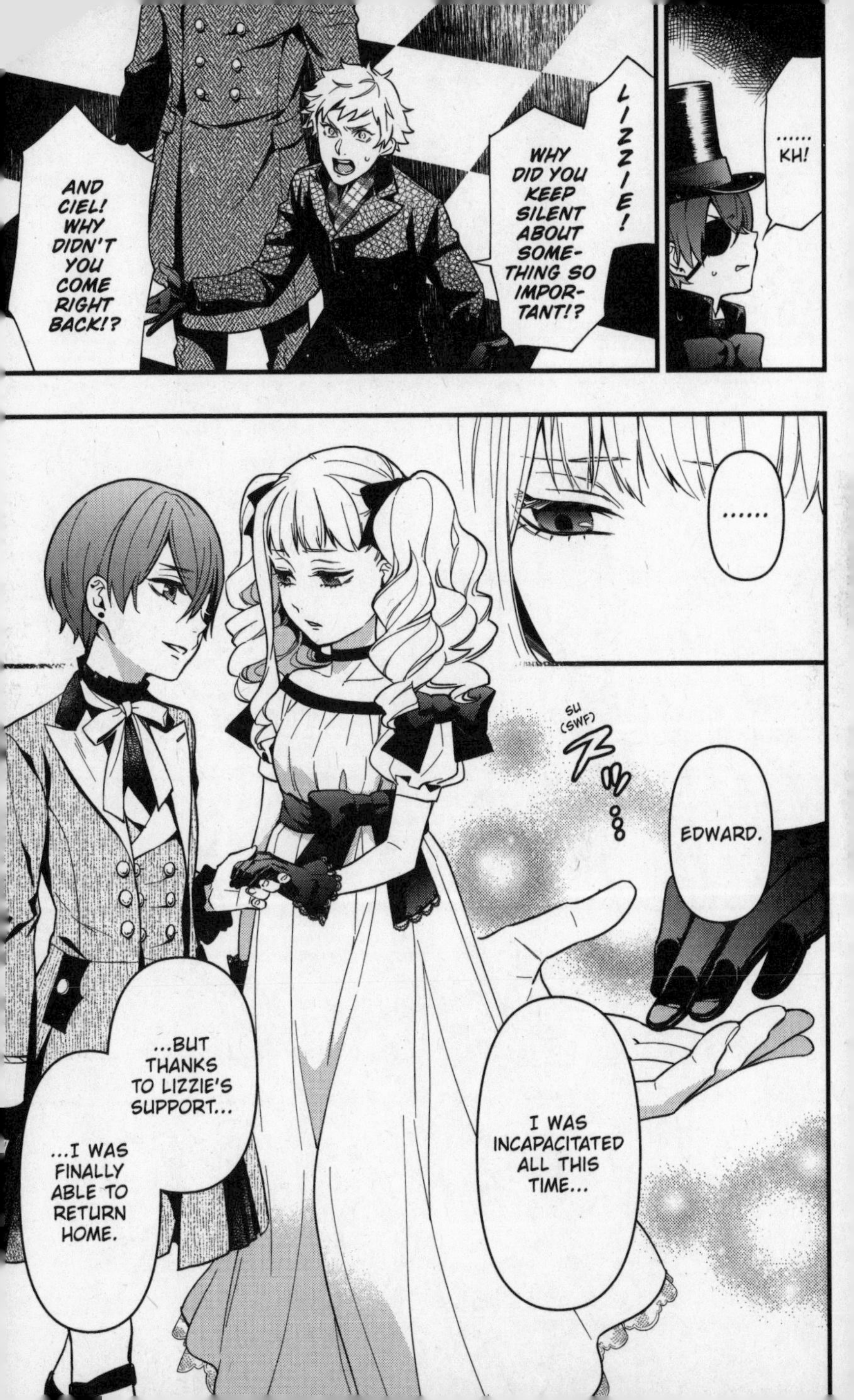
......KH!
LIZZIE!
WHY DID YOU KEEP SILENT ABOUT SOMETHING SO IMPORTANT!?
AND CIEL! WHY DIDN'T YOU COME RIGHT BACK!?
......
SU (SWF)
EDWARD.
I WAS INCAPACITATED ALL THIS TIME...
...BUT THANKS TO LIZZIE'S SUPPORT...
...I WAS FINALLY ABLE TO RETURN HOME.

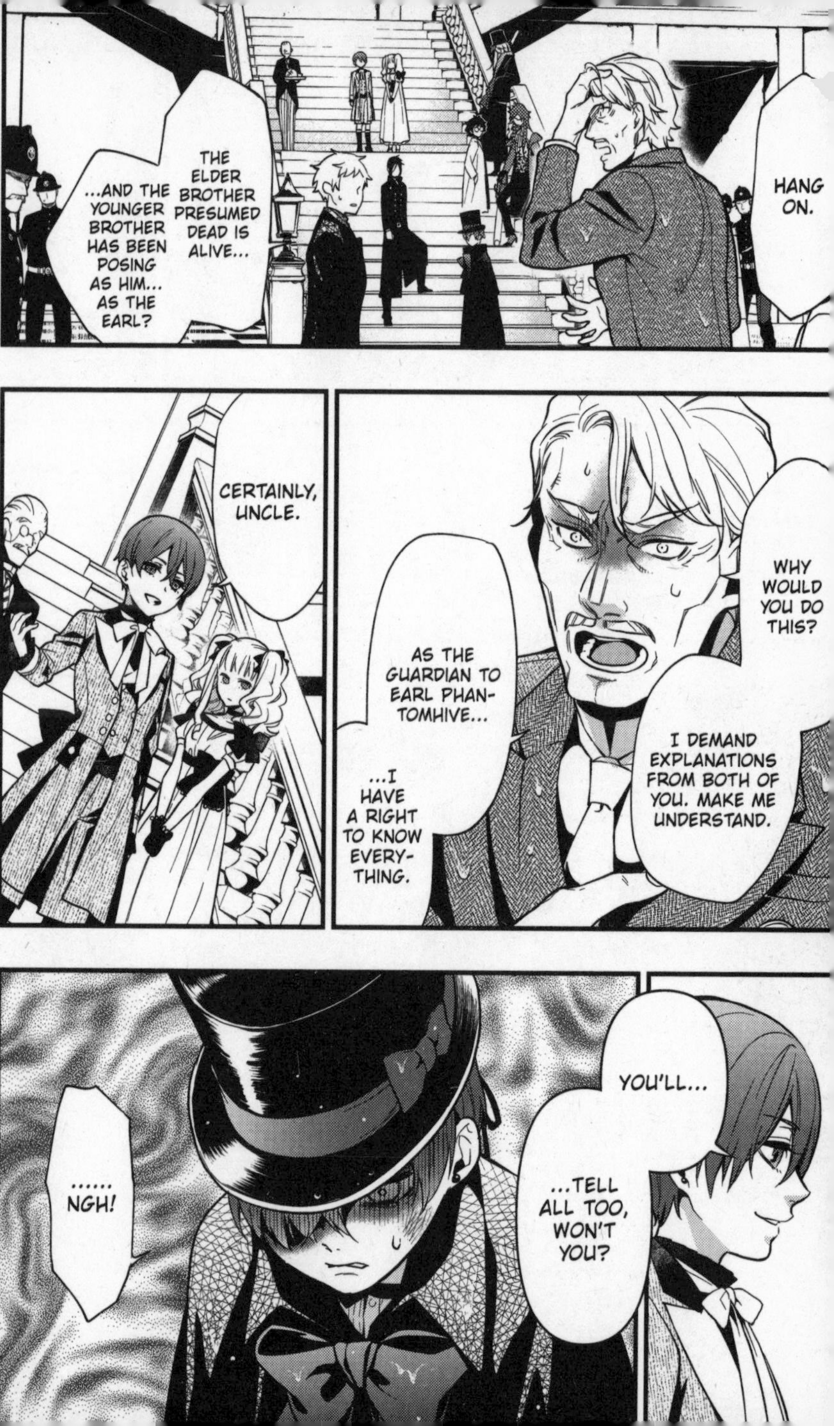
HANG ON.
THE ELDER BROTHER PRESUMED DEAD IS ALIVE...
...AND THE YOUNGER BROTHER HAS BEEN POSING AS HIM... AS THE EARL?
WHY WOULD YOU DO THIS?
I DEMAND EXPLANATIONS FROM BOTH OF YOU. MAKE ME UNDERSTAND.
AS THE GUARDIAN TO EARL PHANTOMHIVE...
...I HAVE A RIGHT TO KNOW EVERYTHING.
CERTAINLY, UNCLE.
YOU'LL...
...TELL ALL TOO, WON'T YOU?
...... NGH!

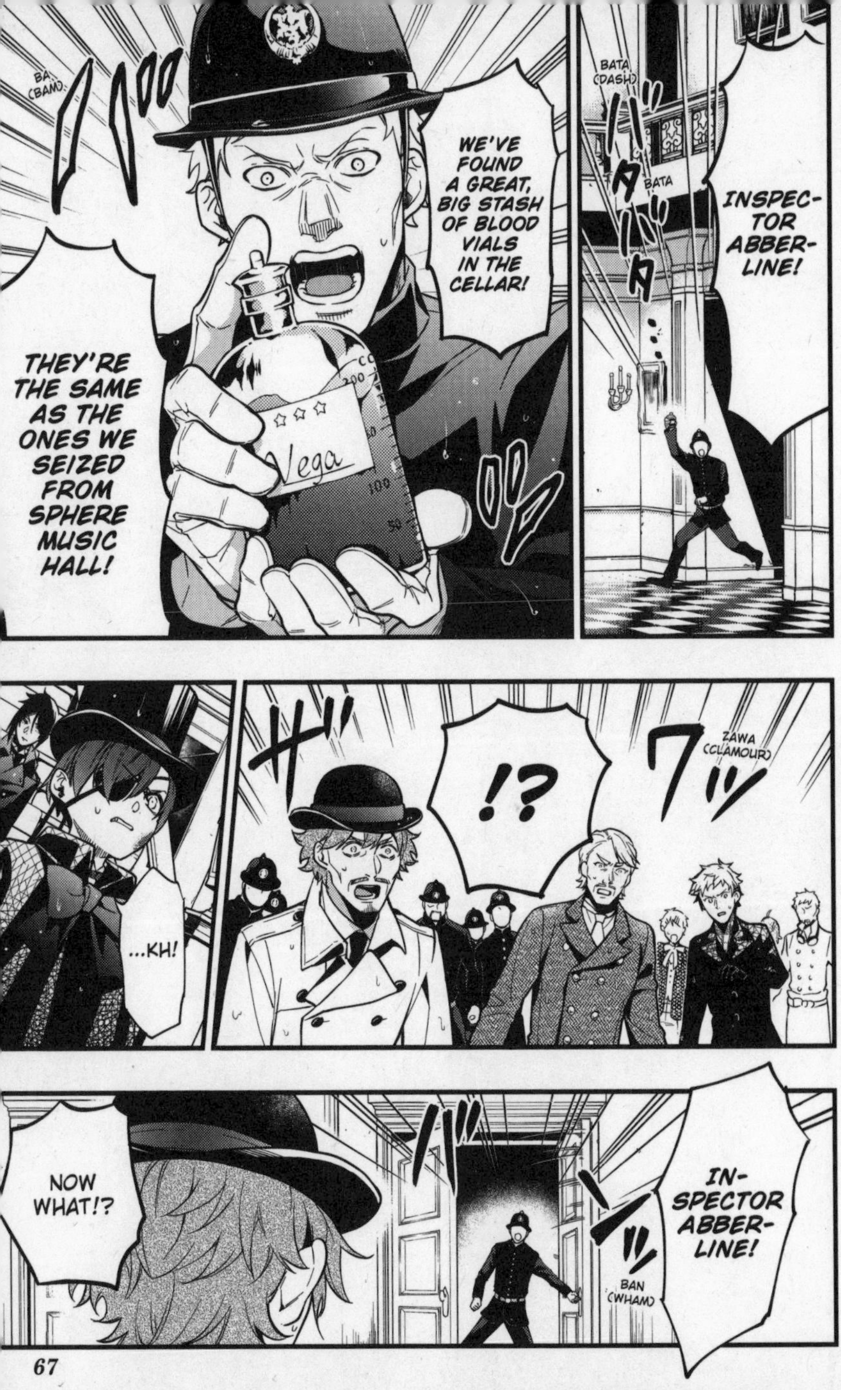
BATA (DASH)
BATA
INSPECTOR ABBERLINE!
BA (BAM)
WE'VE FOUND A GREAT, BIG STASH OF BLOOD VIALS IN THE CELLAR!
THEY'RE THE SAME AS THE ONES WE SEIZED FROM SPHERE MUSIC HALL!
Vega
!?
ZAWA (CLAMOUR)
...KH!
INSPECTOR ABBERLINE!
BAN (WHAM)
NOW WHAT!?

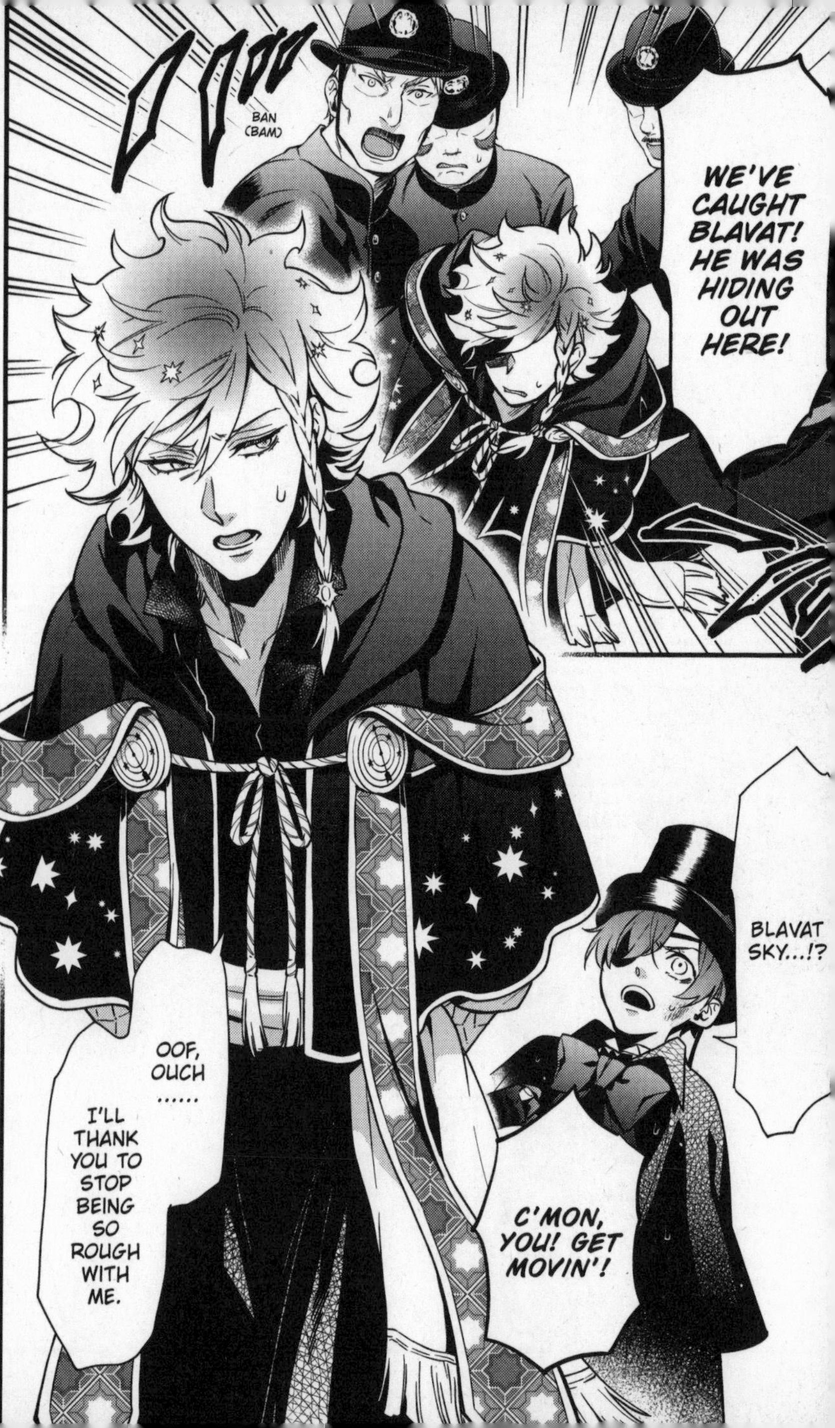
WE'VE CAUGHT BLAVAT! HE WAS HIDING OUT HERE!
BAN (BAM)
BLAVAT SKY...!?
C'MON, YOU! GET MOVIN'!
OOF, OUCH ......
I'LL THANK YOU TO STOP BEING SO ROUGH WITH ME.

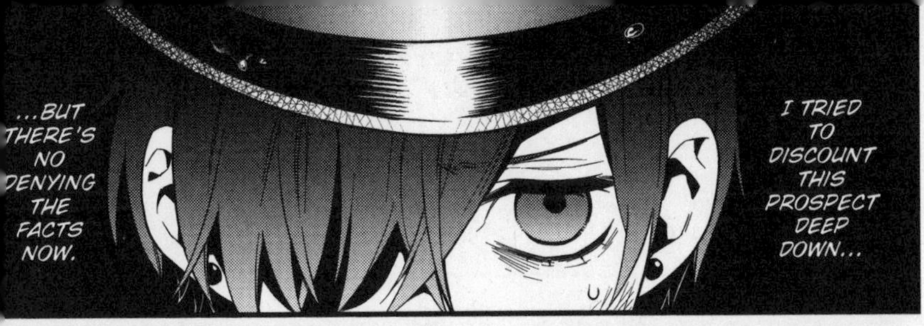
I TRIED TO DISCOUNT THIS PROSPECT DEEP DOWN...
...BUT THERE'S NO DENYING THE FACTS NOW.

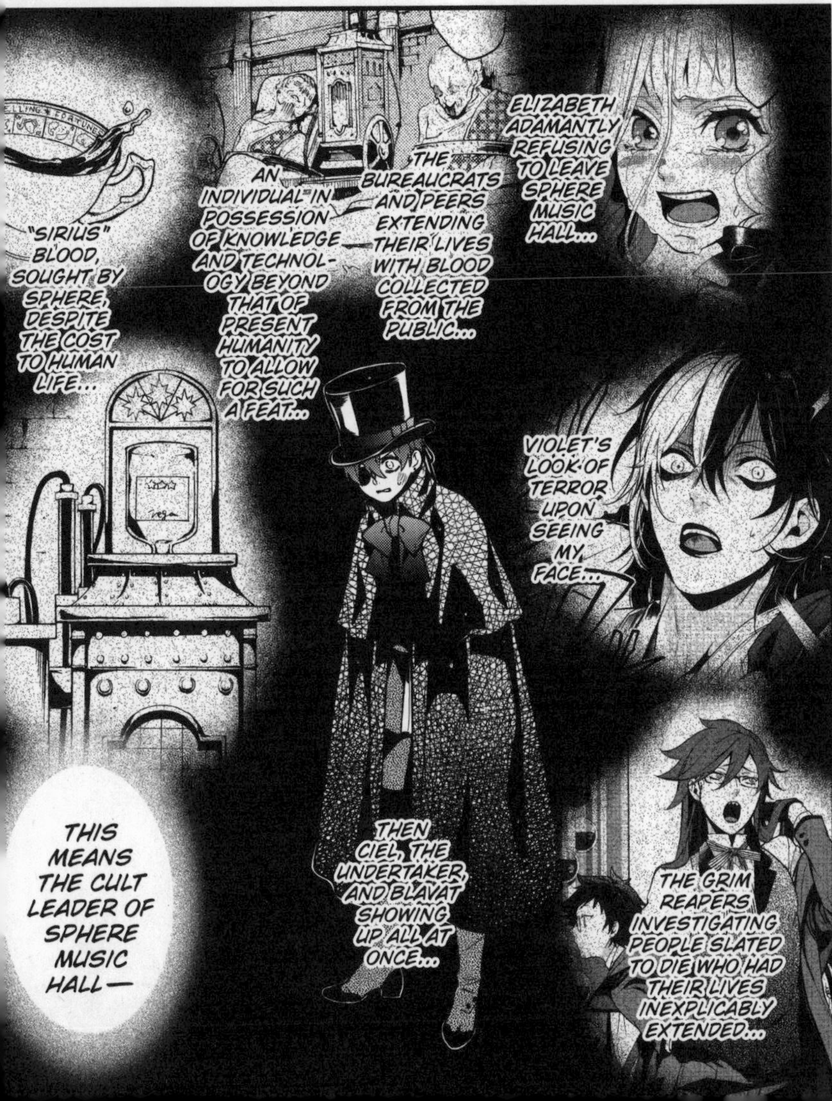
ELIZABETH ADAMANTLY REFUSING TO LEAVE SPHERE MUSIC HALL...
THE BUREAUCRATS AND PEERS EXTENDING THEIR LIVES WITH BLOOD COLLECTED FROM THE PUBLIC...
AN INDIVIDUAL IN POSSESSION OF KNOWLEDGE AND TECHNOLOGY BEYOND THAT OF PRESENT HUMANITY TO ALLOW FOR SUCH A FEAT...
"SIRIUS" BLOOD, SOUGHT BY SPHERE, DESPITE THE COST TO HUMAN LIFE...
VIOLET'S LOOK OF TERROR UPON SEEING MY FACE...
THE GRIM REAPERS INVESTIGATING PEOPLE SLATED TO DIE WHO HAD THEIR LIVES INEXPLICABLY EXTENDED...
THEN CIEL, THE UNDERTAKER, AND BLAVAT SHOWING UP ALL AT ONCE...
THIS MEANS THE CULT LEADER OF SPHERE MUSIC HALL—

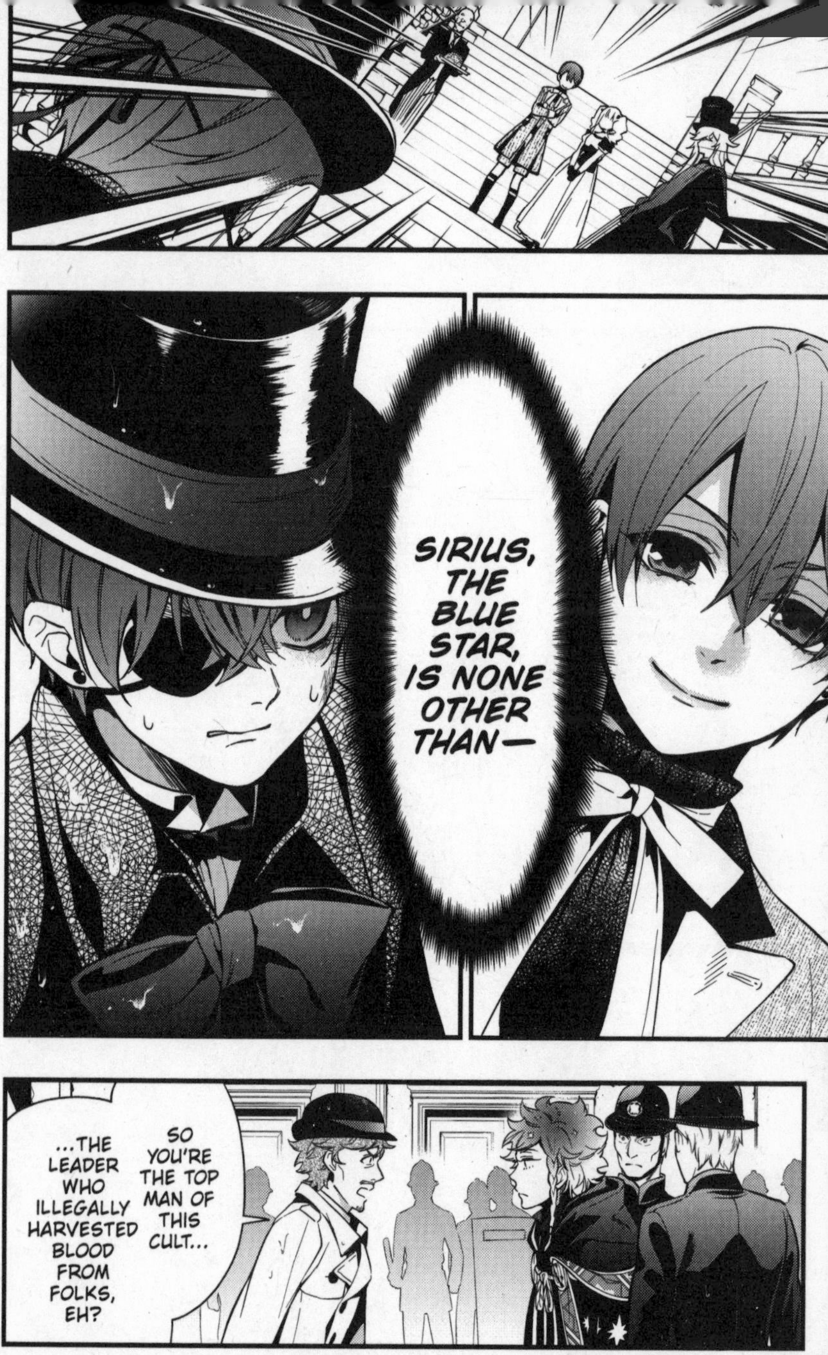
SIRIUS, THE BLUE STAR, IS NONE OTHER THAN—
SO YOU'RE THE TOP MAN OF THIS CULT...
...THE LEADER WHO ILLEGALLY HARVESTED BLOOD FROM FOLKS, EH?

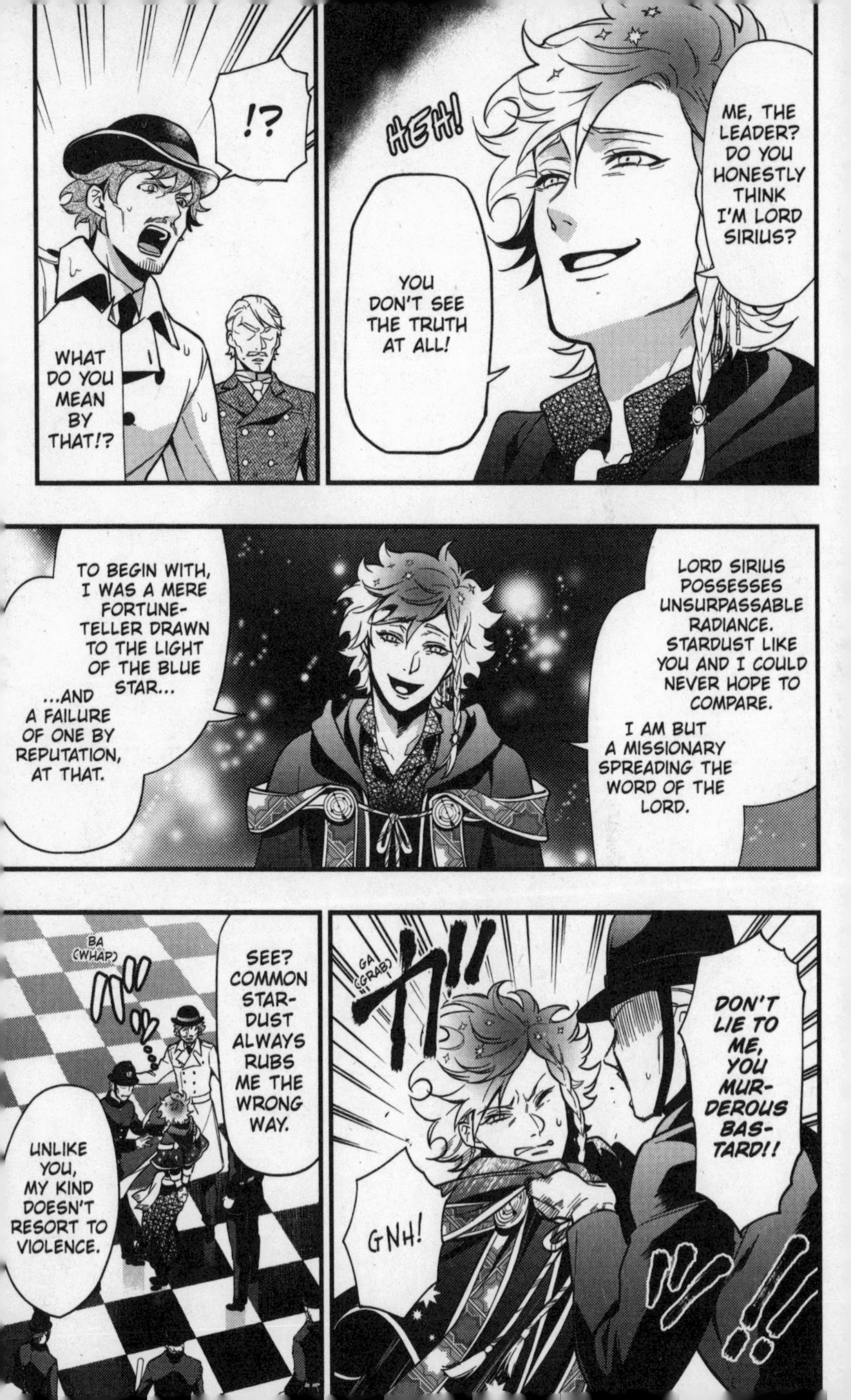
HEH!
ME, THE LEADER? DO YOU HONESTLY THINK I'M LORD SIRIUS?
YOU DON'T SEE THE TRUTH AT ALL!
!?
WHAT DO YOU MEAN BY THAT!?
LORD SIRIUS POSSESSES UNSURPASSABLE RADIANCE. STARDUST LIKE YOU AND I COULD NEVER HOPE TO COMPARE.
I AM BUT A MISSIONARY SPREADING THE WORD OF THE LORD.
TO BEGIN WITH, I WAS A MERE FORTUNE-TELLER DRAWN TO THE LIGHT OF THE BLUE STAR...
...AND A FAILURE OF ONE BY REPUTATION, AT THAT.
GA (GRAB)
DON'T LIE TO ME, YOU MUR-DEROUS BAS-TARD!!
GNH!
BA (WHAP)
SEE? COMMON STAR-DUST ALWAYS RUBS ME THE WRONG WAY.
UNLIKE YOU, MY KIND DOESN'T RESORT TO VIOLENCE.

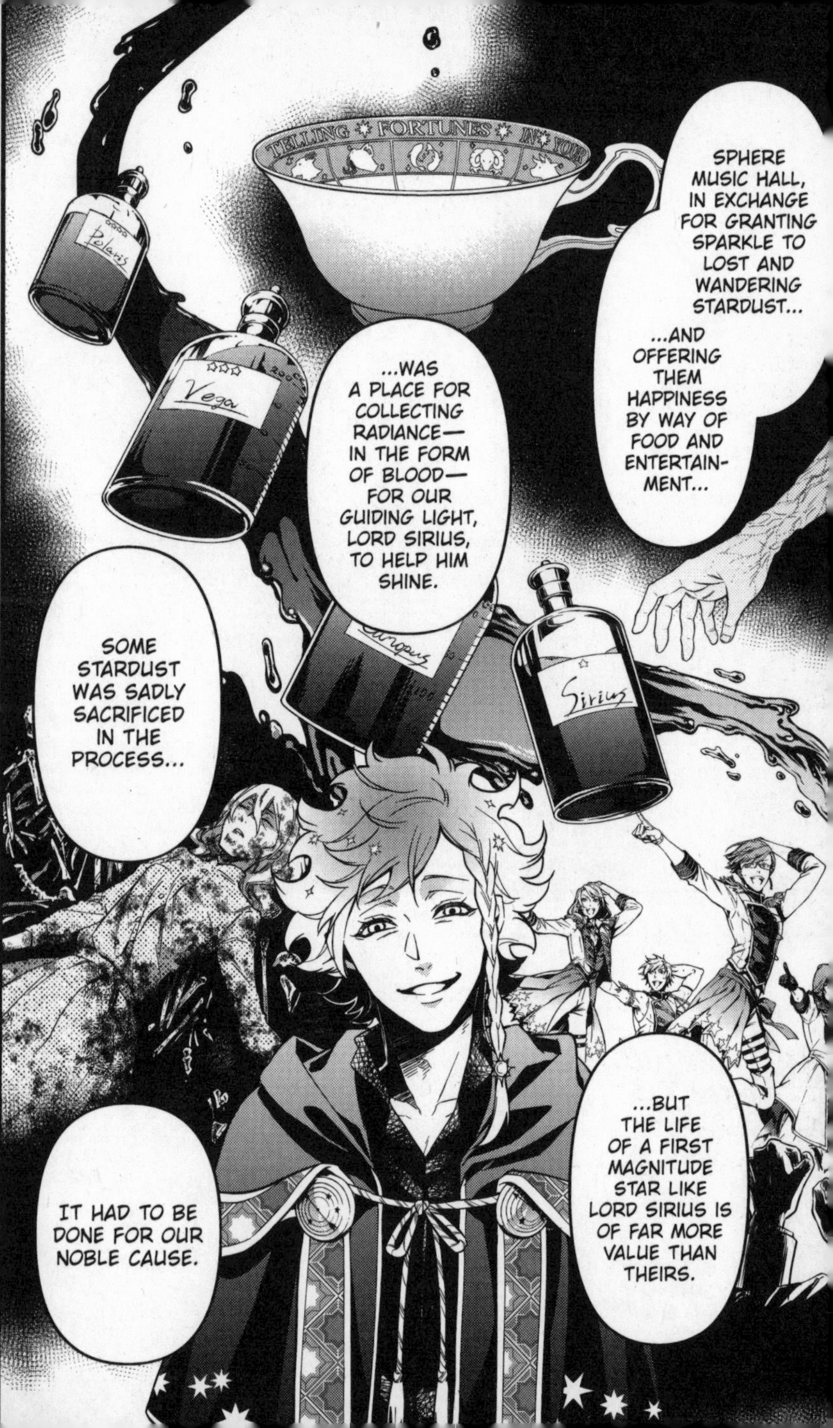
TELLING FORTUNES IN YOUR
Polaris
Vega
Sirius
SPHERE MUSIC HALL, IN EXCHANGE FOR GRANTING SPARKLE TO LOST AND WANDERING STARDUST...
...AND OFFERING THEM HAPPINESS BY WAY OF FOOD AND ENTERTAIN-MENT...
...WAS A PLACE FOR COLLECTING RADIANCE—IN THE FORM OF BLOOD—FOR OUR GUIDING LIGHT, LORD SIRIUS, TO HELP HIM SHINE.
SOME STARDUST WAS SADLY SACRIFICED IN THE PROCESS...
...BUT THE LIFE OF A FIRST MAGNITUDE STAR LIKE LORD SIRIUS IS OF FAR MORE VALUE THAN THEIRS.
IT HAD TO BE DONE FOR OUR NOBLE CAUSE.

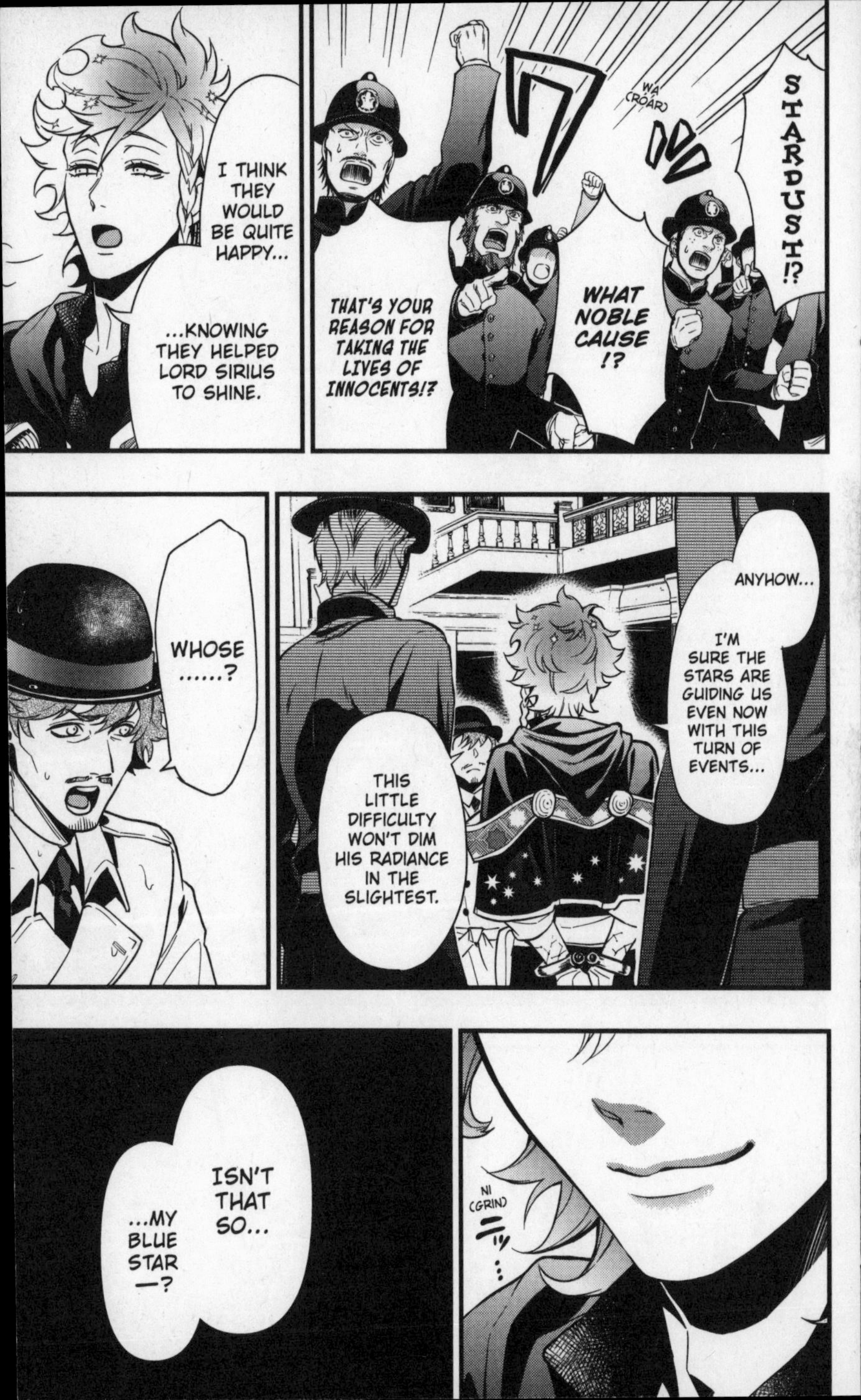
STARDUST!?
WA (ROAR)
WHAT NOBLE CAUSE !?
THAT'S YOUR REASON FOR TAKING THE LIVES OF INNOCENTS!?
I THINK THEY WOULD BE QUITE HAPPY...
...KNOWING THEY HELPED LORD SIRIUS TO SHINE.
ANYHOW...
I'M SURE THE STARS ARE GUIDING US EVEN NOW WITH THIS TURN OF EVENTS...
THIS LITTLE DIFFICULTY WON'T DIM HIS RADIANCE IN THE SLIGHTEST.
WHOSE ......?
NI (GRIN)
ISN'T THAT SO...
...MY BLUE STAR —?

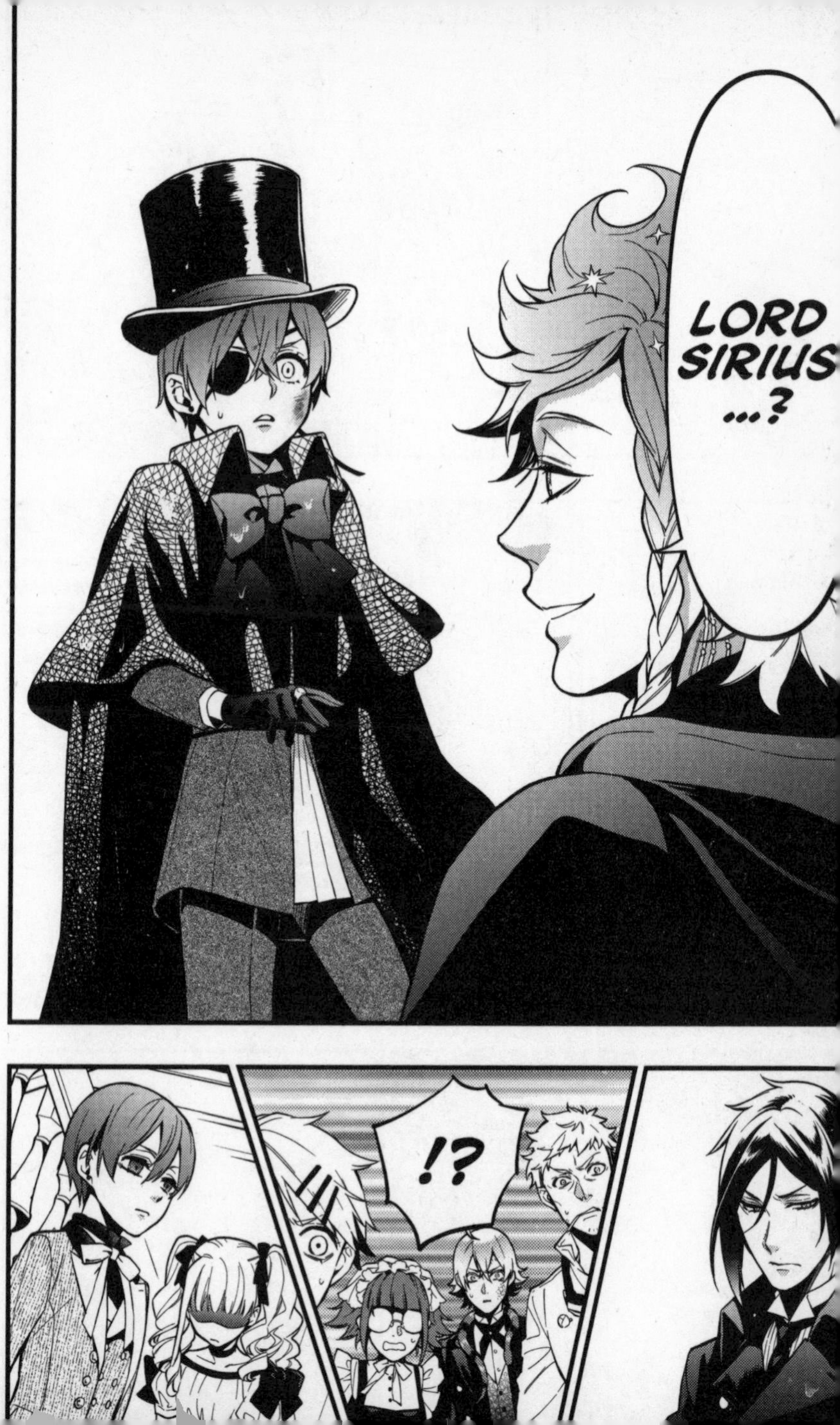
LORD SIRIUS ...?
!?

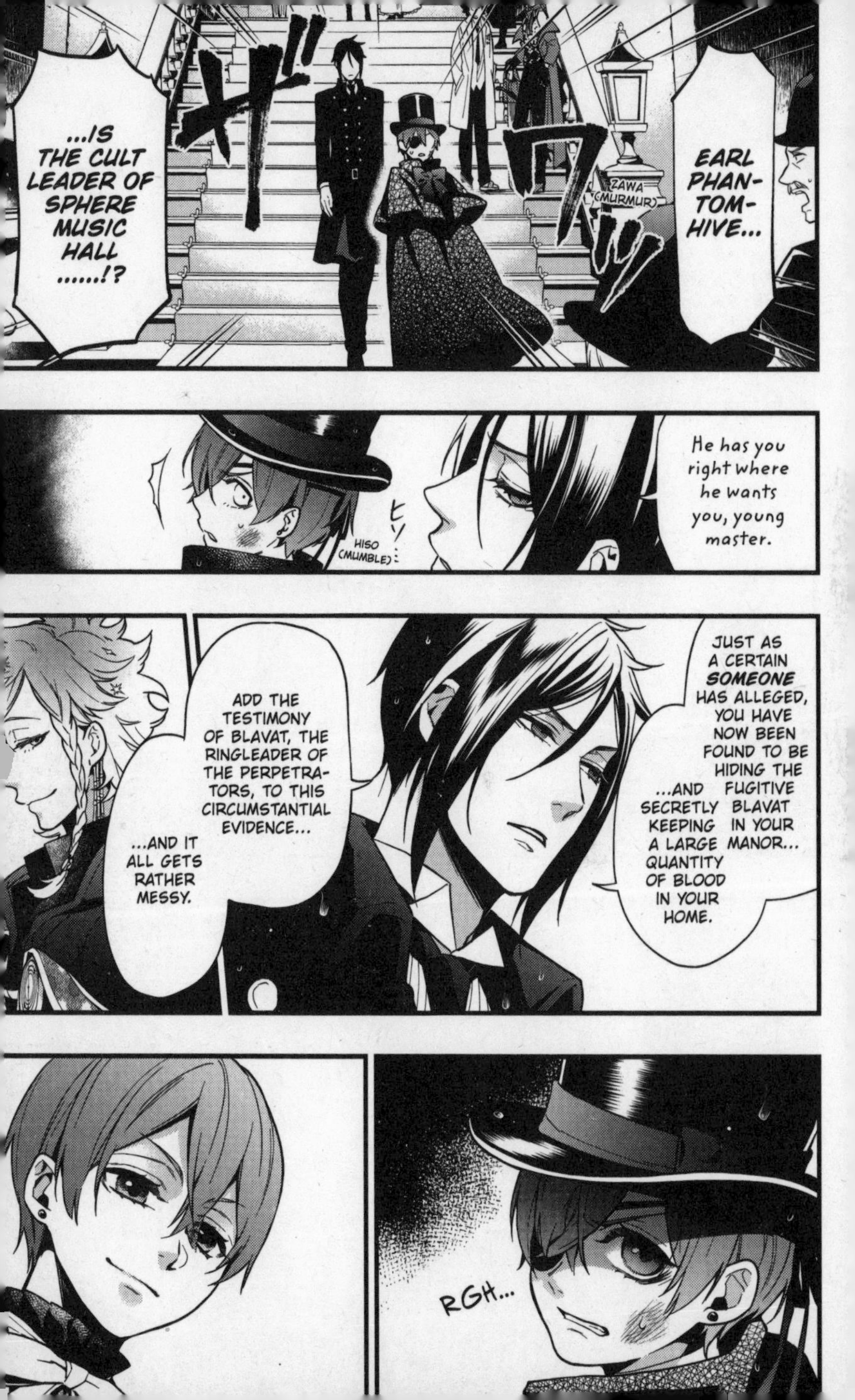
EARL PHANTOMHIVE...
ZAWA (MURMUR)
...IS THE CULT LEADER OF SPHERE MUSIC HALL ......!?
He has you right where he wants you, young master.
HISO (MUMBLE)
JUST AS A CERTAIN ***SOMEONE*** HAS ALLEGED, YOU HAVE NOW BEEN FOUND TO BE HIDING THE FUGITIVE BLAVAT IN YOUR MANOR...
...AND SECRETLY KEEPING A LARGE QUANTITY OF BLOOD IN YOUR HOME.
ADD THE TESTIMONY OF BLAVAT, THE RINGLEADER OF THE PERPETRATORS, TO THIS CIRCUMSTANTIAL EVIDENCE...
...AND IT ALL GETS RATHER MESSY.
RGH...

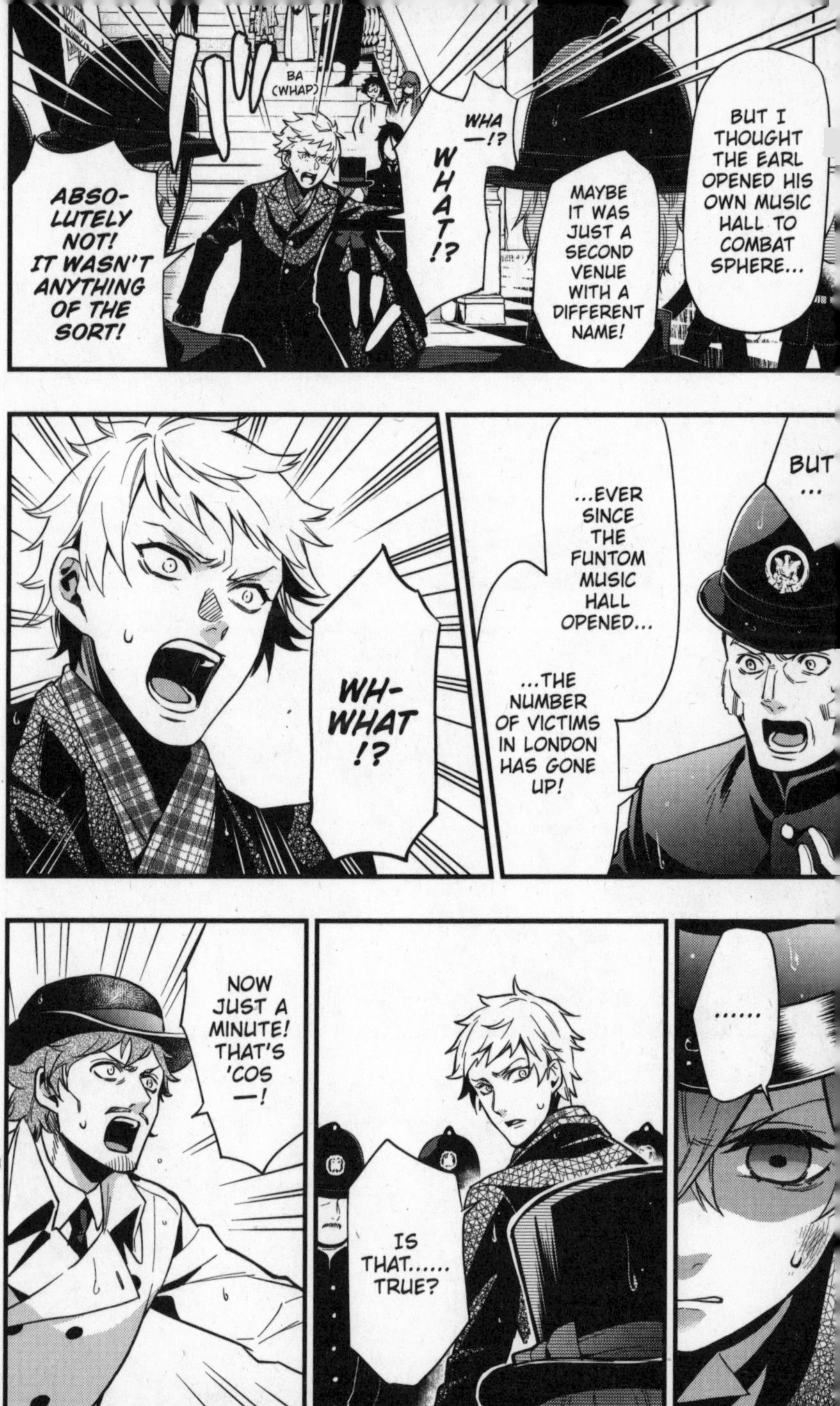
BUT I THOUGHT THE EARL OPENED HIS OWN MUSIC HALL TO COMBAT SPHERE...
MAYBE IT WAS JUST A SECOND VENUE WITH A DIFFERENT NAME!
WHA—!?
WHAT!?
BA (WHAP)
ABSOLUTELY NOT! IT WASN'T ANYTHING OF THE SORT!
BUT...
...EVER SINCE THE FUNTOM MUSIC HALL OPENED...
...THE NUMBER OF VICTIMS IN LONDON HAS GONE UP!
WH-WHAT!?
......
IS THAT...... TRUE?
NOW JUST A MINUTE! THAT'S 'COS—!

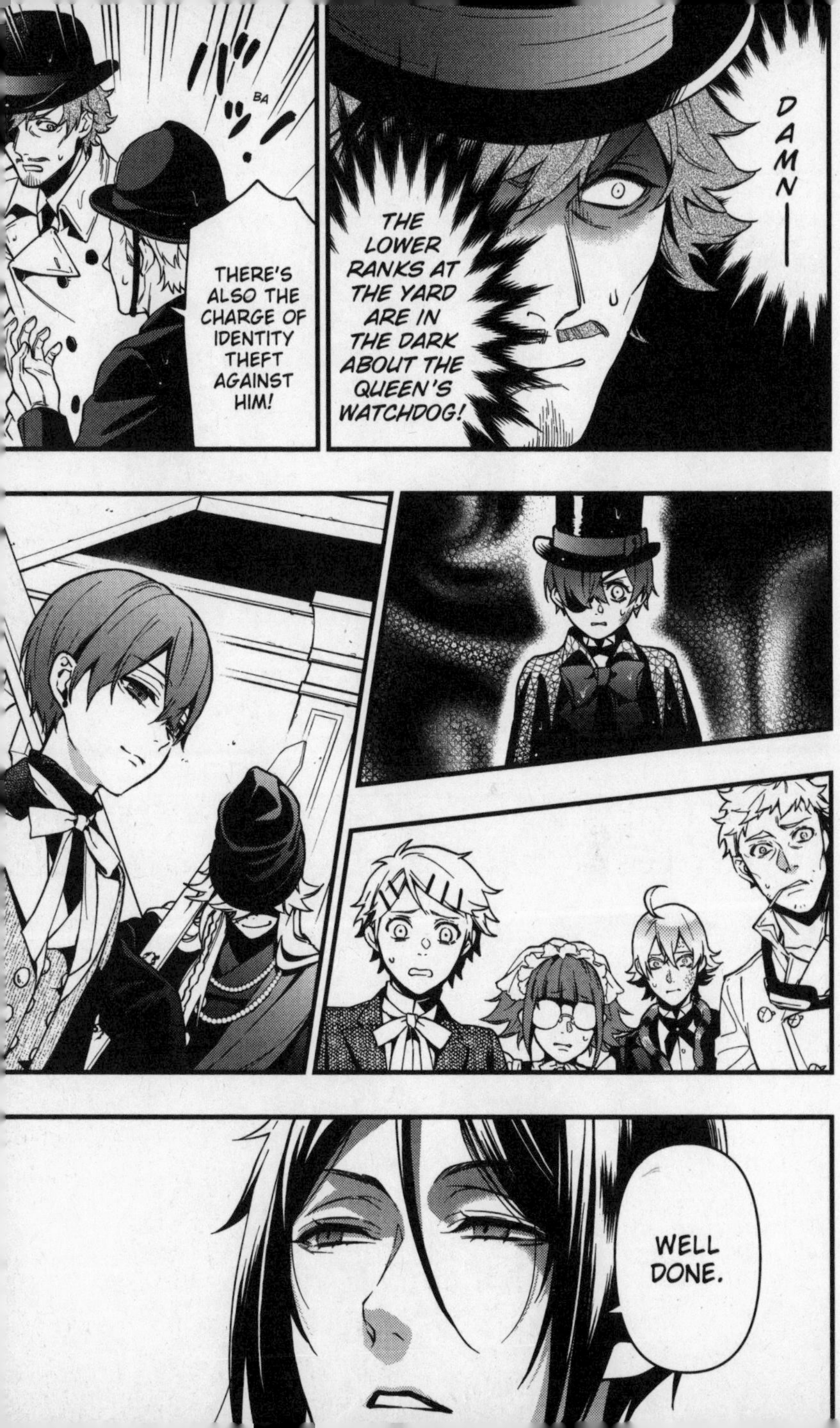
DAMN—
THE LOWER RANKS AT THE YARD ARE IN THE DARK ABOUT THE QUEEN'S WATCHDOG!
BA
THERE'S ALSO THE CHARGE OF IDENTITY THEFT AGAINST HIM!
WELL DONE.

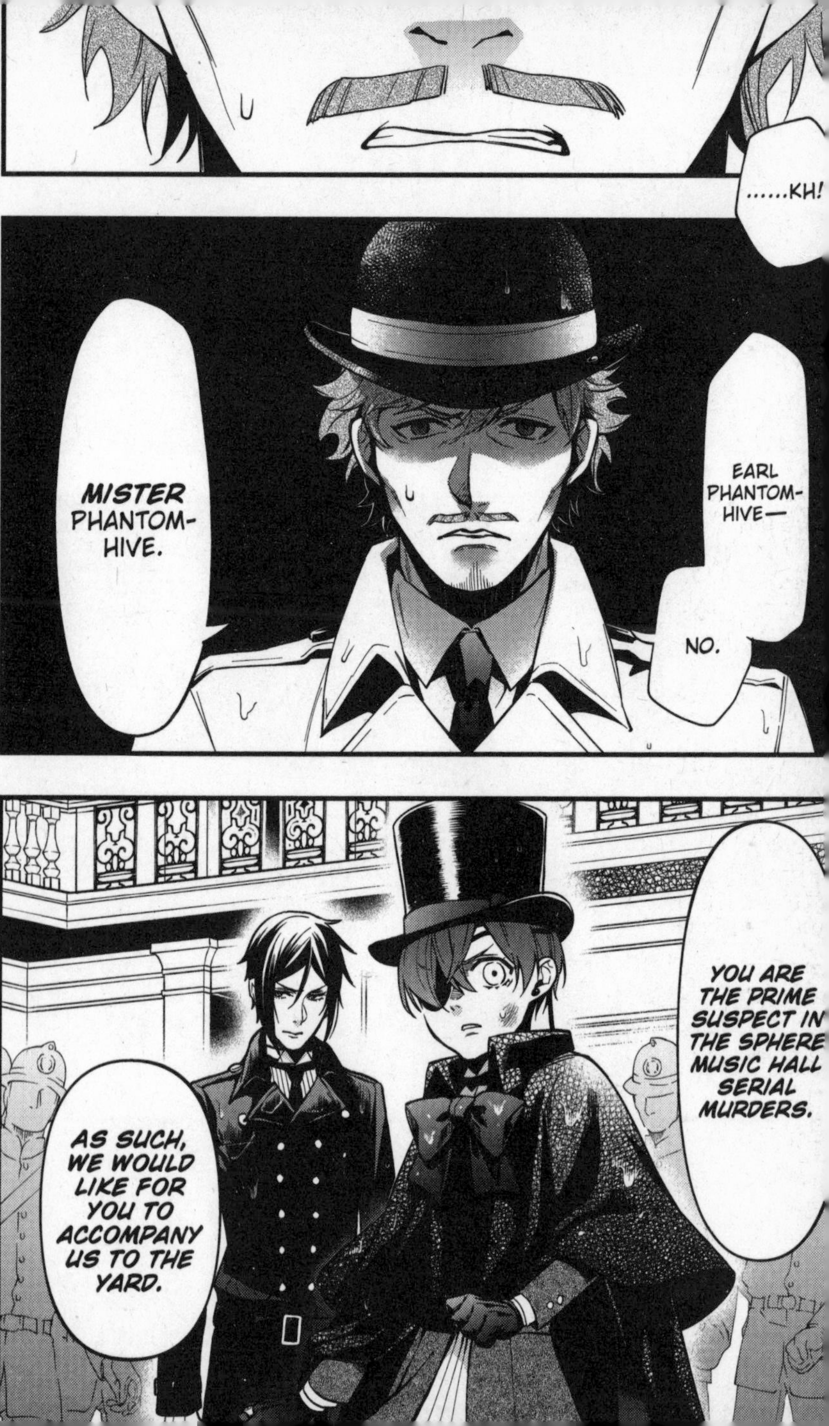

......KH!
EARL PHANTOM-HIVE—
NO.
MISTER PHANTOM-HIVE.
YOU ARE THE PRIME SUSPECT IN THE SPHERE MUSIC HALL SERIAL MURDERS.
AS SUCH, WE WOULD LIKE FOR YOU TO ACCOMPANY US TO THE YARD.

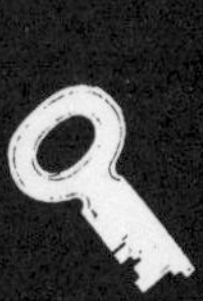

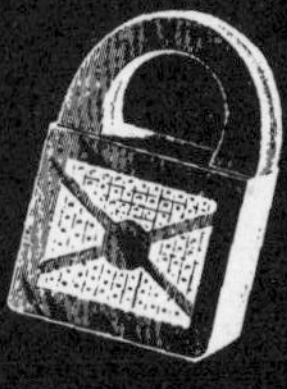

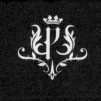

Black Butler

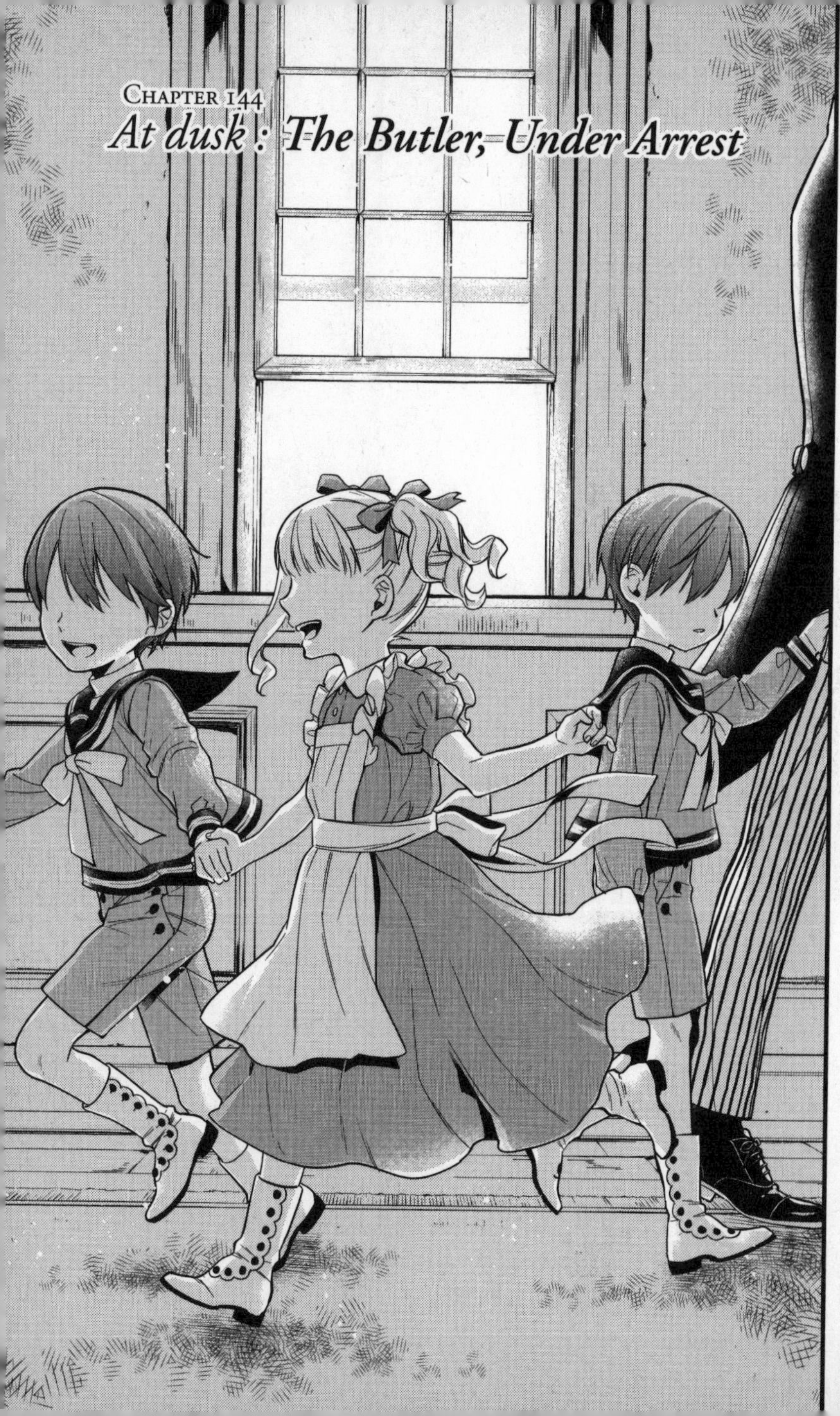
Chapter 144
At dusk : The Butler, Under Arrest

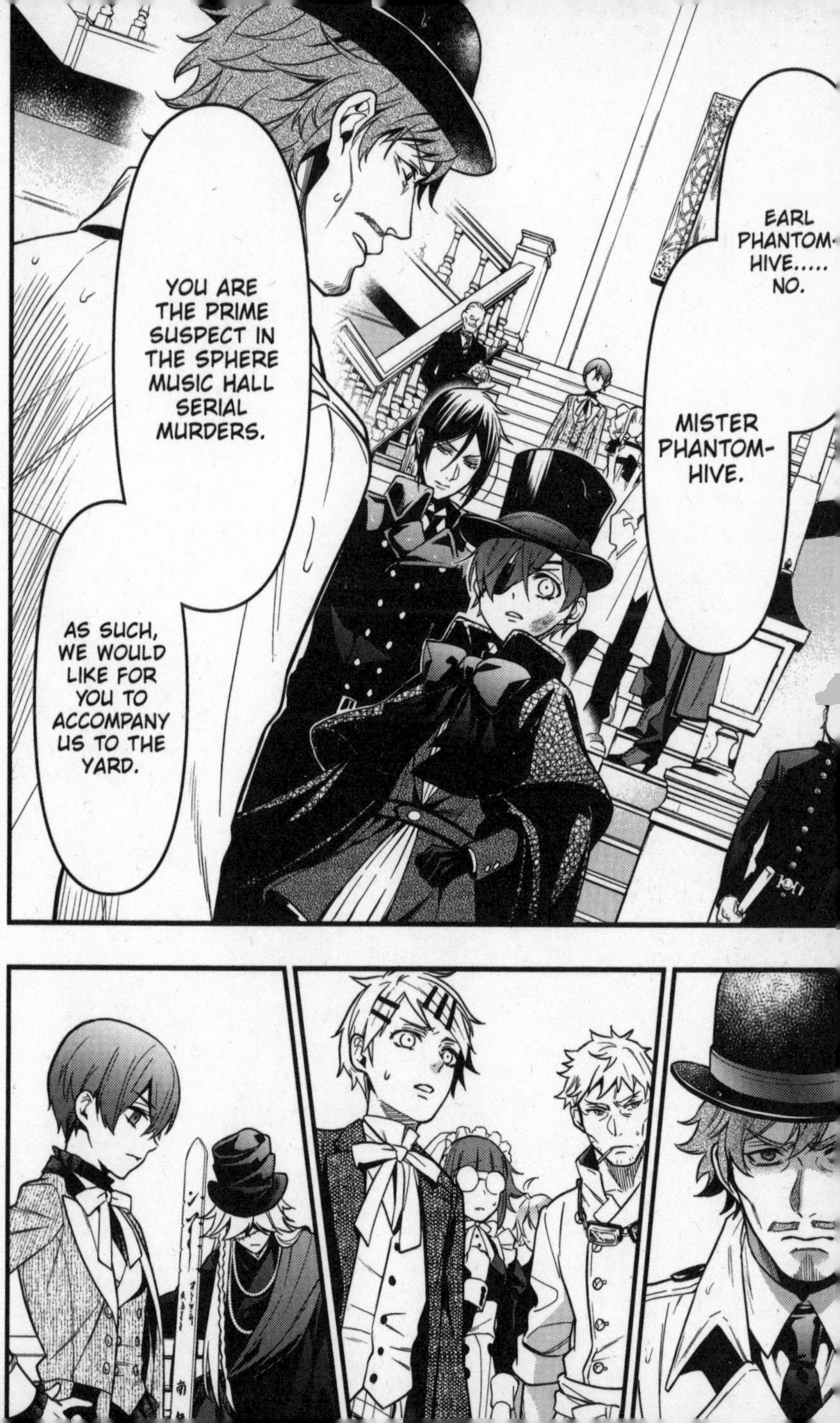
EARL PHANTOM-HIVE..... NO.
MISTER PHANTOM-HIVE.
YOU ARE THE PRIME SUSPECT IN THE SPHERE MUSIC HALL SERIAL MURDERS.
AS SUCH, WE WOULD LIKE FOR YOU TO ACCOMPANY US TO THE YARD.

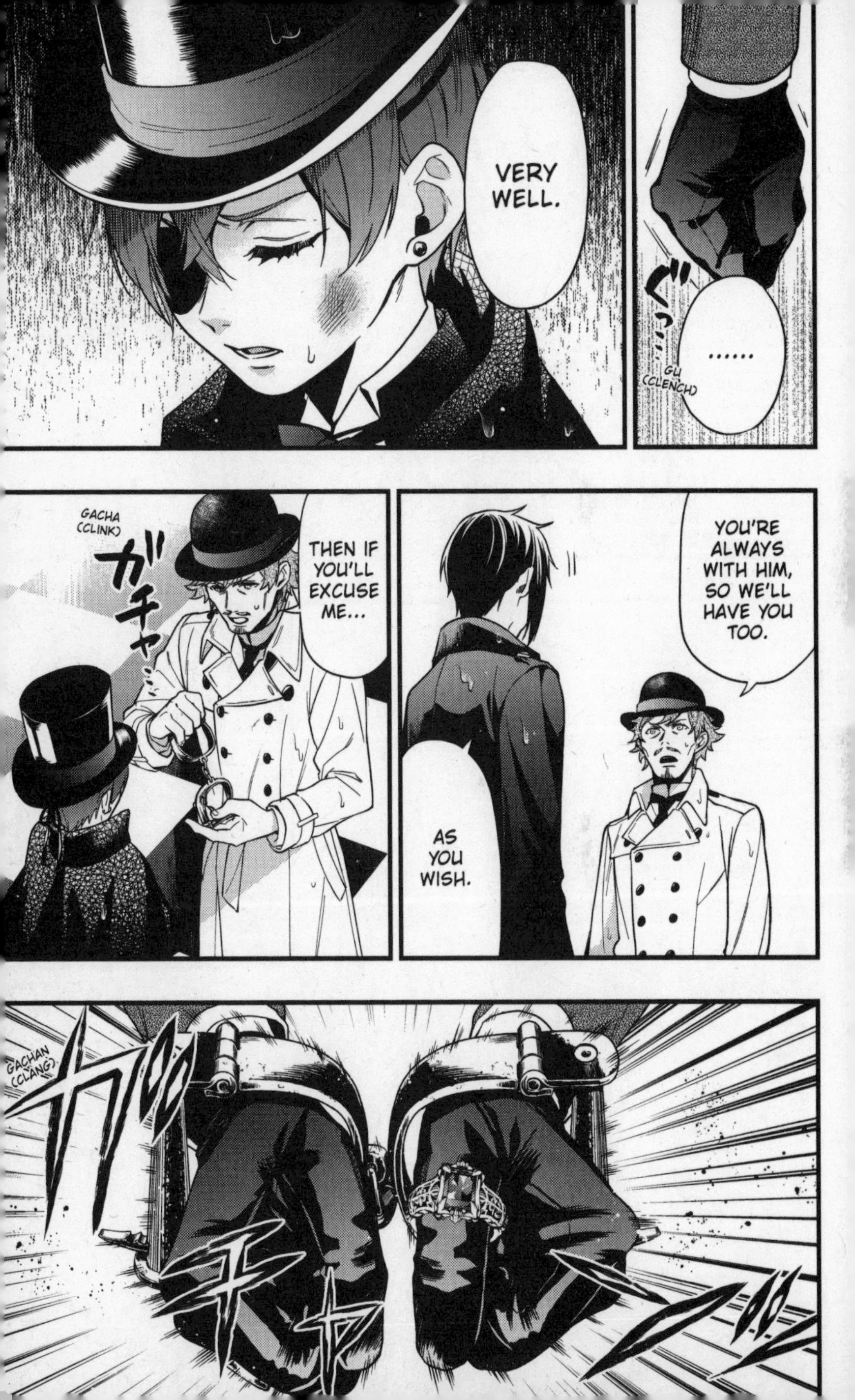

GU (CLENCH)
......
VERY WELL.
YOU'RE ALWAYS WITH HIM, SO WE'LL HAVE YOU TOO.
AS YOU WISH.
GACHA (CLINK)
ガチャ
THEN IF YOU'LL EXCUSE ME...
GACHAN (CLANG)

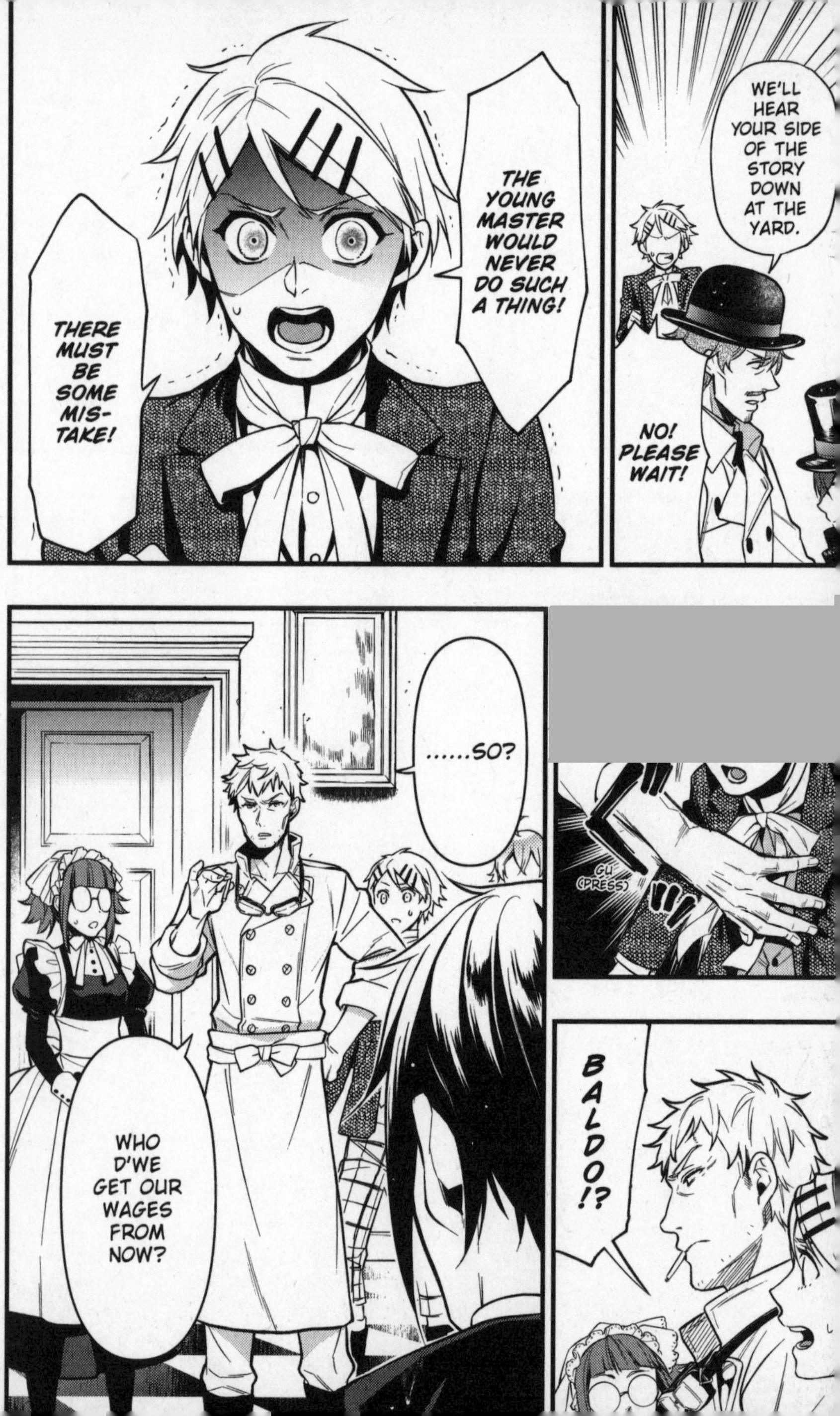
WE'LL HEAR YOUR SIDE OF THE STORY DOWN AT THE YARD.
NO! PLEASE WAIT!
THE YOUNG MASTER WOULD NEVER DO SUCH A THING!
THERE MUST BE SOME MIS-TAKE!
GU (PRESS)
BALDO!?
......SO?
WHO D'WE GET OUR WAGES FROM NOW?

GACHA (CLINK)
ガチャ

AS YOU CAN SEE, I AM AFRAID YOUR PAY WILL HAVE TO WAIT.

....

NOW JUST A MINUTE!

IS THIS REALLY THE TIME TO BE HAGGLING OVER MONEY!?

—SAYS EMILY.

GUI (SHOVE)
ぐいっ

NOW MOVE!

OWWW...... WHY AM I THE ONLY ONE GETTING ROUGH TREATMENT?

COME AND COLLECT IT LATER.

ZAAAA (FWSSH)

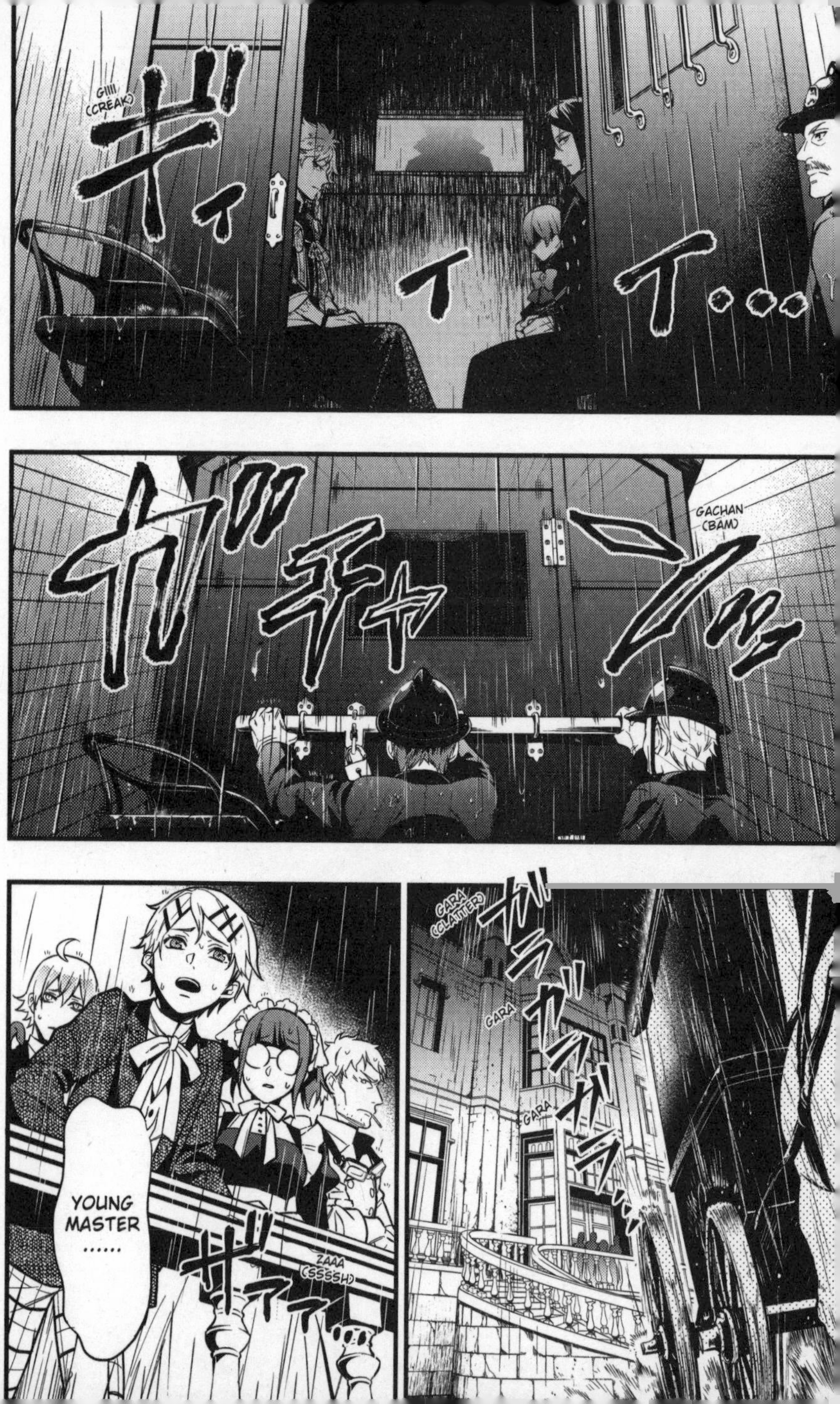
GIIII (CREAK)
GACHAN (BAM)
GARA (CLATTER)
GARA
GARA
YOUNG MASTER ......
ZAAA (SSSSH)

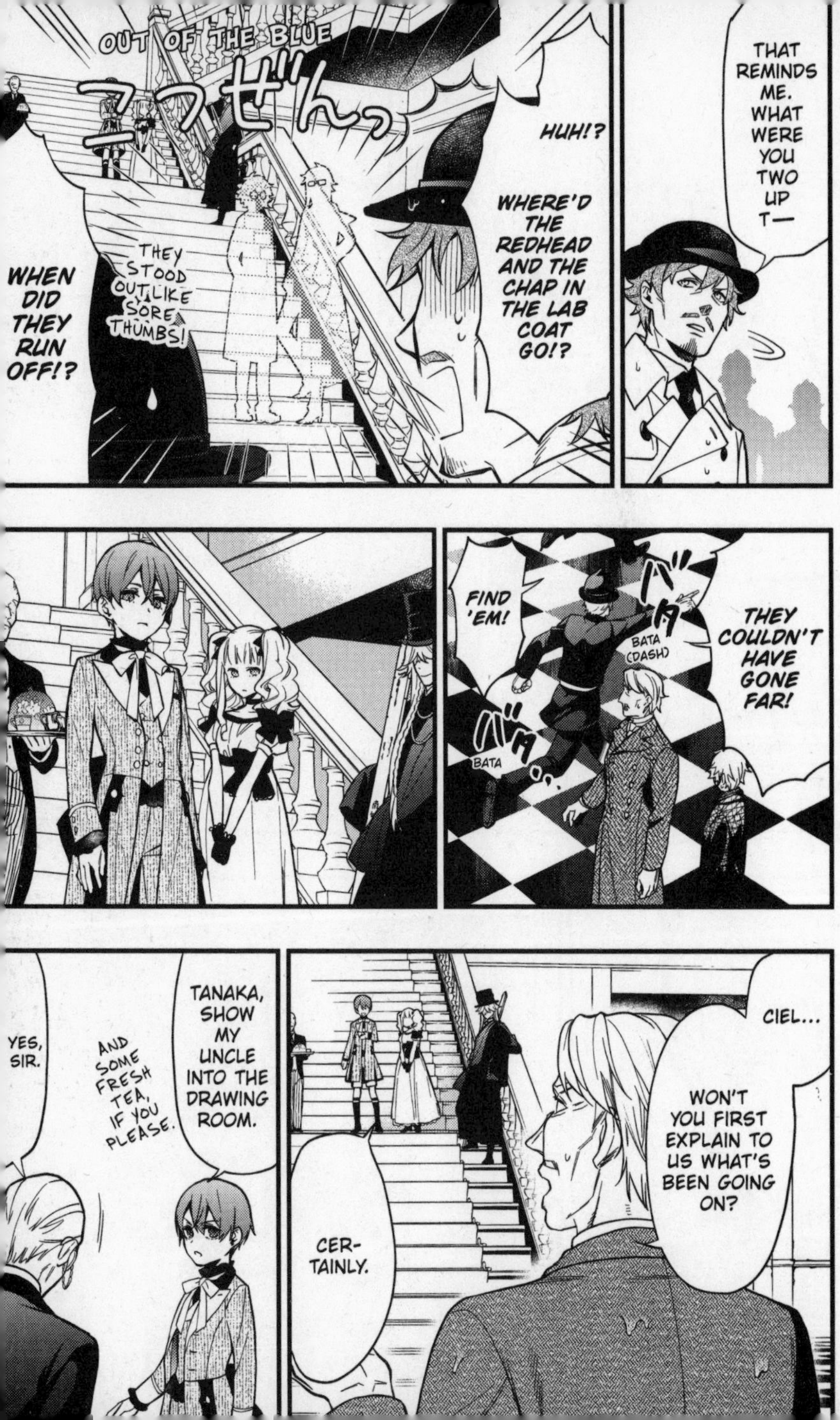
THAT REMINDS ME. WHAT WERE YOU TWO UP T—
HUH!?
WHERE'D THE REDHEAD AND THE CHAP IN THE LAB COAT GO!?
OUT OF THE BLUE
THEY STOOD OUT LIKE SORE THUMBS!
WHEN DID THEY RUN OFF!?
THEY COULDN'T HAVE GONE FAR!
FIND 'EM!
BATA (DASH)
BATA
CIEL...
WON'T YOU FIRST EXPLAIN TO US WHAT'S BEEN GOING ON?
CER-TAINLY.
TANAKA, SHOW MY UNCLE INTO THE DRAWING ROOM.
AND SOME FRESH TEA, IF YOU PLEASE.
YES, SIR.

DO YOU HAVE ANY IDEA HOW WORRIED WE WERE FOR YOU ...!?

AND ELIZA-BETH...

GO HOME.

BUT......

I'M SORRY ... ...FATHER... EDWARD......

...... YES.

I'M SURE AUNT FRANCIS IS SICK WITH WORRY OVER YOU.

LIZZIE...

I'M FINE NOW.

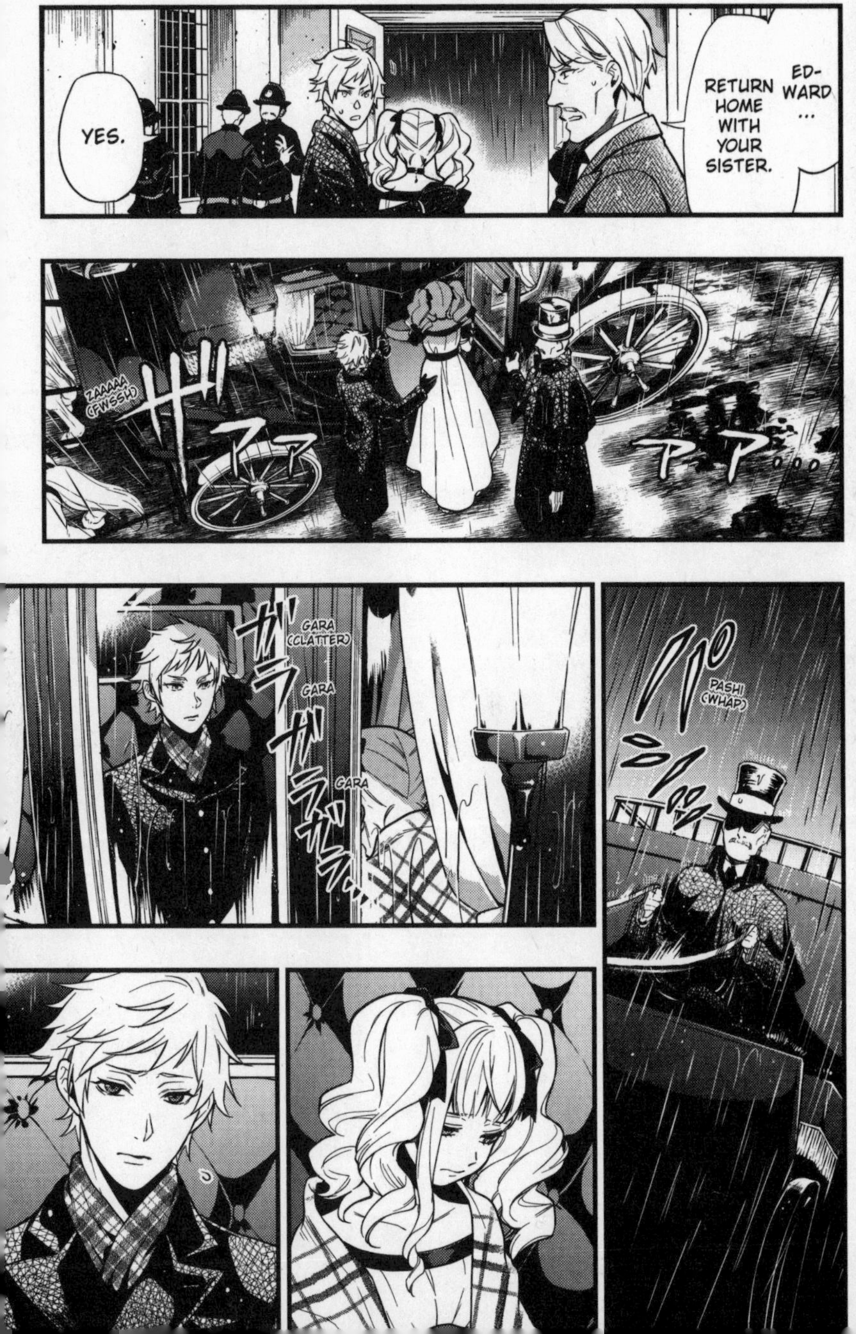
EDWARD...
RETURN HOME WITH YOUR SISTER.
YES.
ZAAAAA (FWSSH)
PASHI (WHAP)
GARA (CLATTER)
GARA
GARA

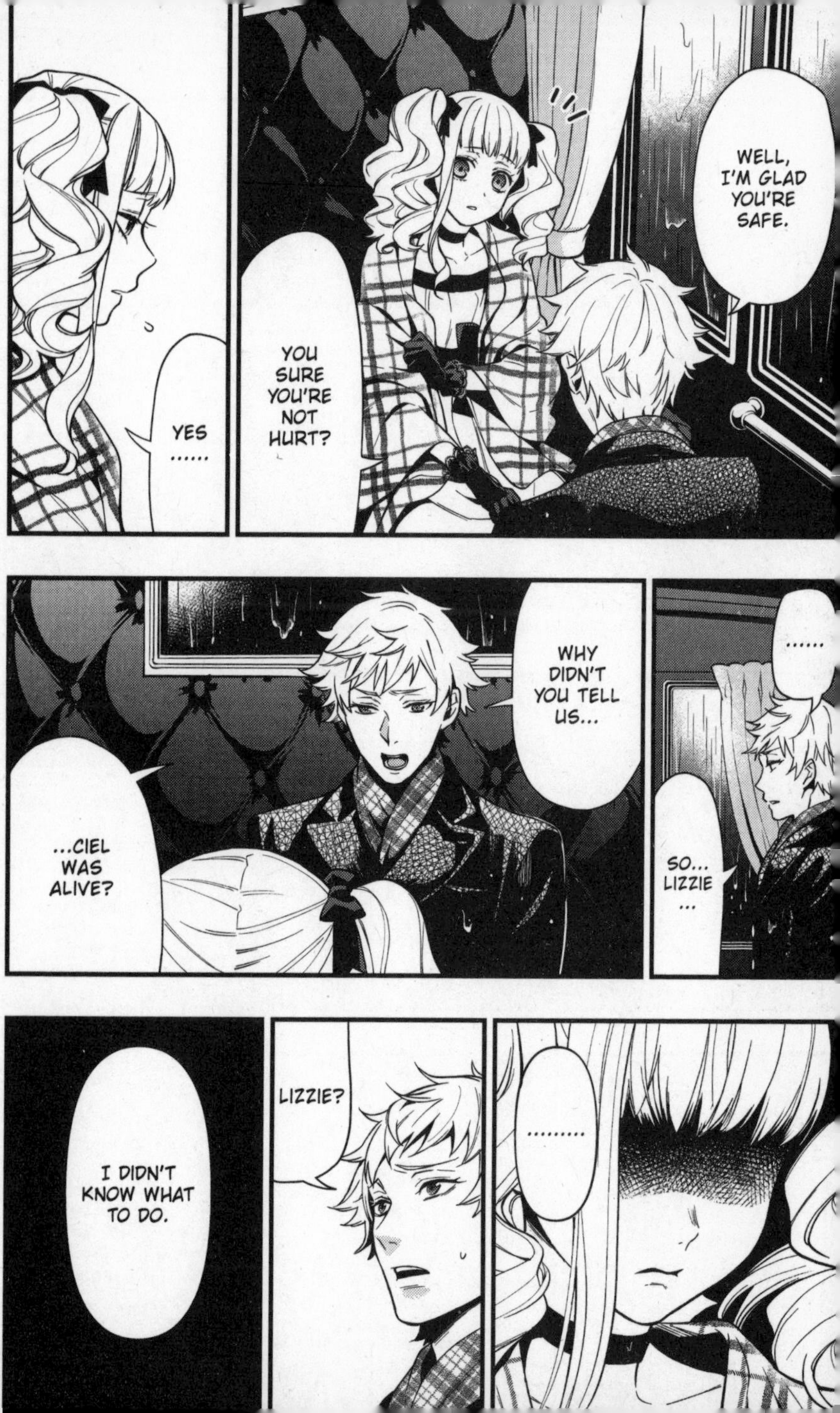
WELL, I'M GLAD YOU'RE SAFE.
YOU SURE YOU'RE NOT HURT?
YES ......
......
SO... LIZZIE ...
WHY DIDN'T YOU TELL US...
...CIEL WAS ALIVE?
....
LIZZIE?
I DIDN'T KNOW WHAT TO DO.

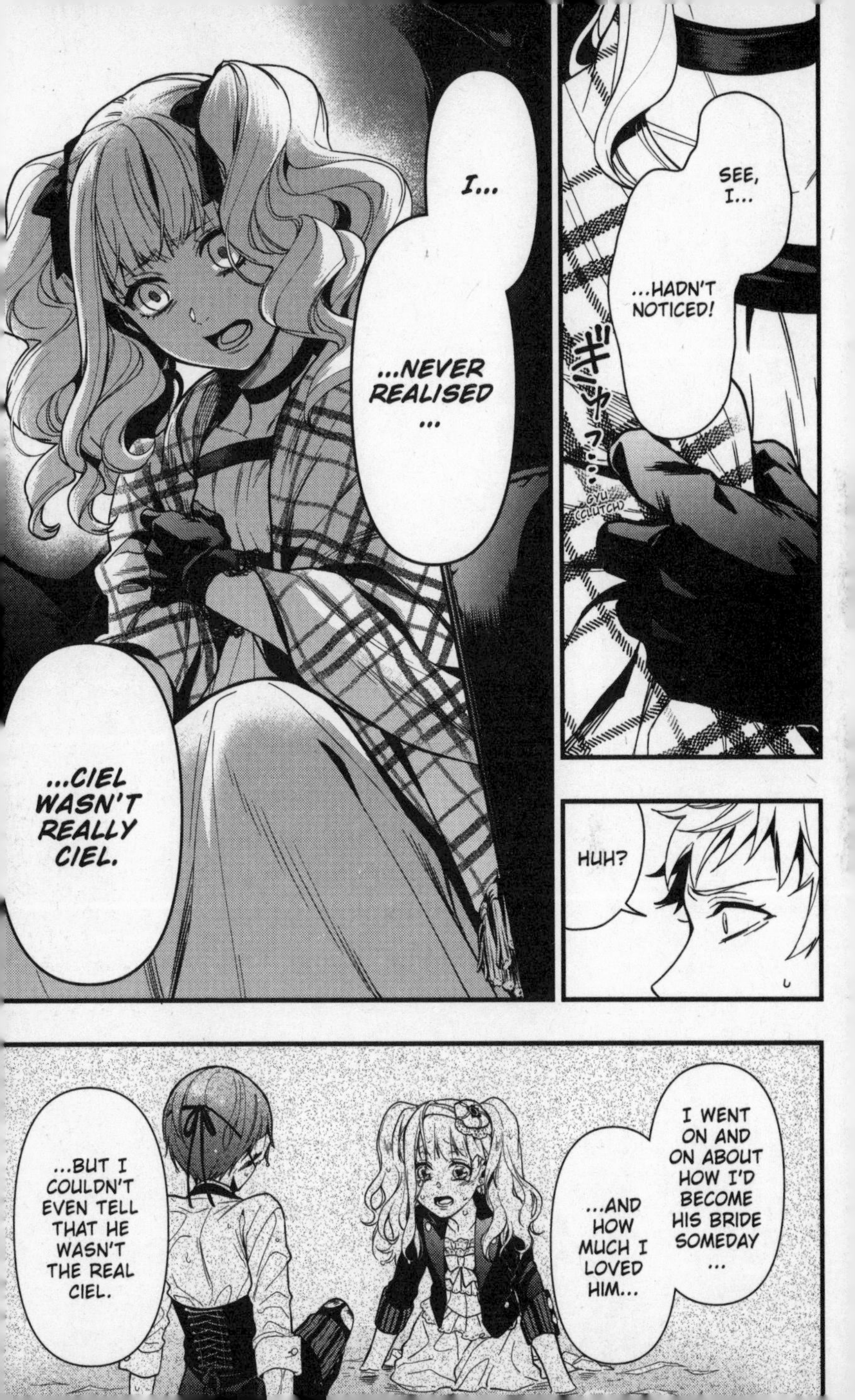

SEE, I...
...HADN'T NOTICED!
ギュッ
GYU (CLUTCH)
HUH?
I...
...NEVER REALISED ...
...CIEL WASN'T REALLY CIEL.
I WENT ON AND ON ABOUT HOW I'D BECOME HIS BRIDE SOMEDAY ...
...AND HOW MUCH I LOVED HIM...
...BUT I COULDN'T EVEN TELL THAT HE WASN'T THE REAL CIEL.

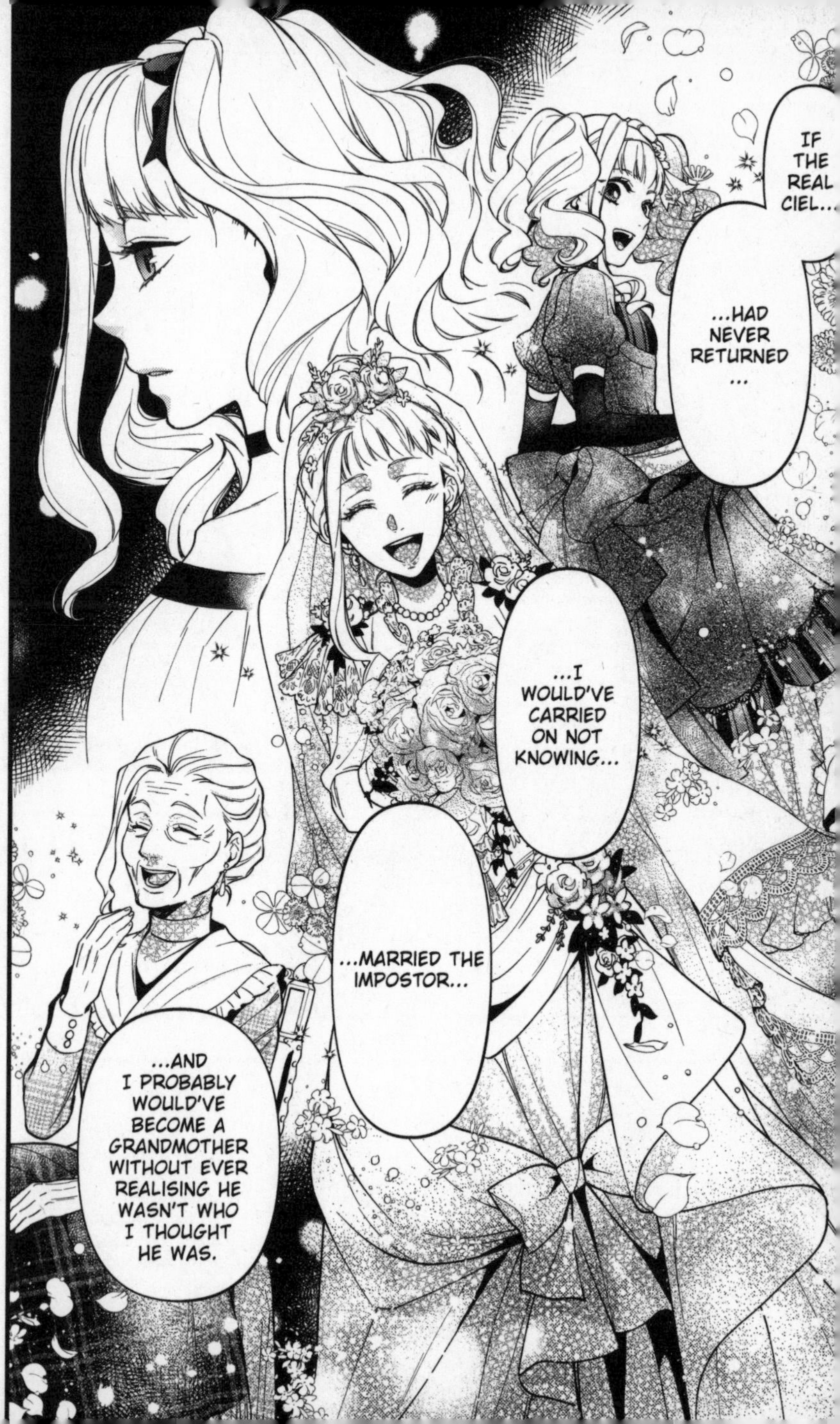
IF THE REAL CIEL...
...HAD NEVER RETURNED ...
...I WOULD'VE CARRIED ON NOT KNOWING...
...MARRIED THE IMPOSTOR...
...AND I PROBABLY WOULD'VE BECOME A GRANDMOTHER WITHOUT EVER REALISING HE WASN'T WHO I THOUGHT HE WAS.

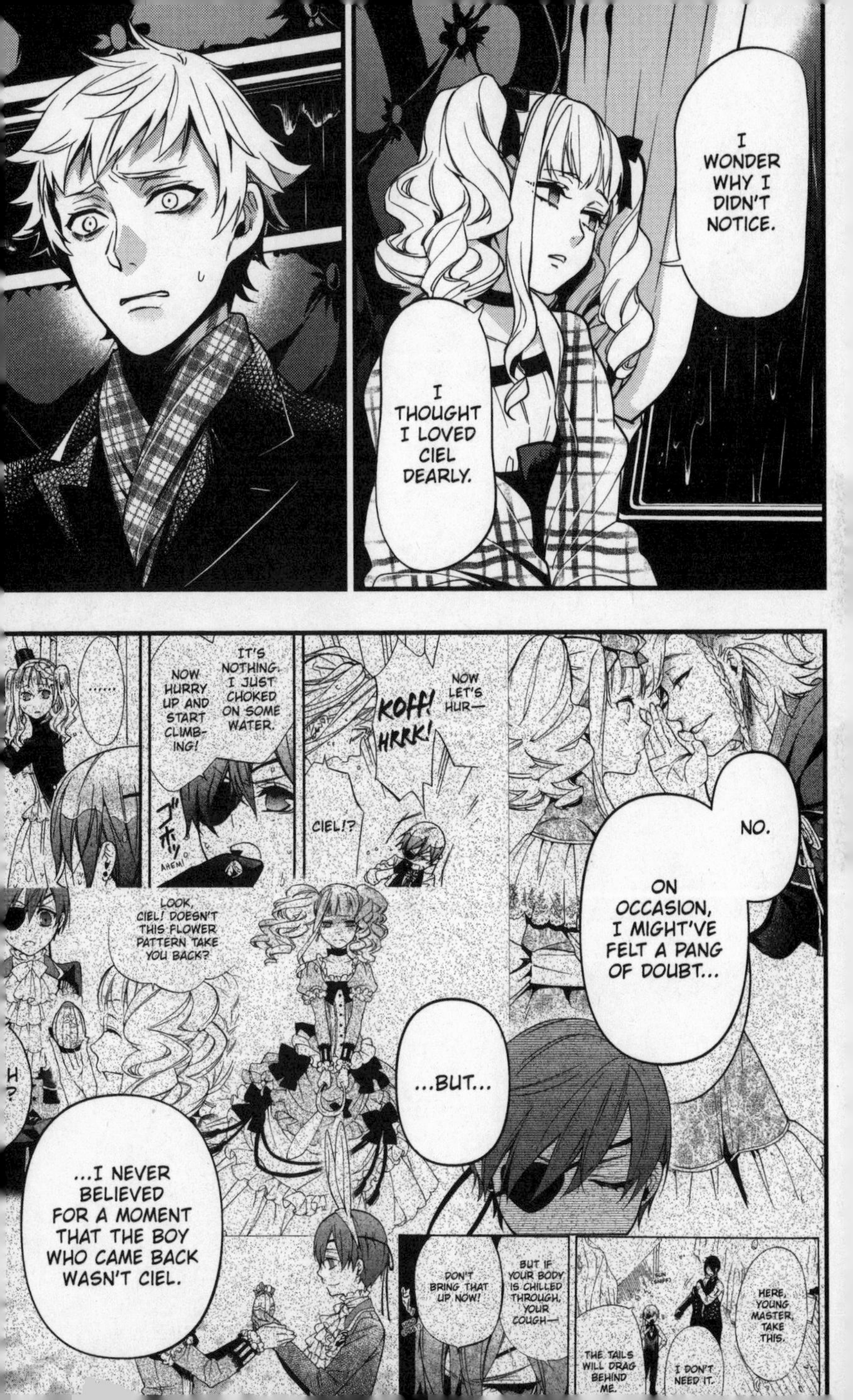

I WONDER WHY I DIDN'T NOTICE.
I THOUGHT I LOVED CIEL DEARLY.
NO.
ON OCCASION, I MIGHT'VE FELT A PANG OF DOUBT...
KOFF! HRRK!
NOW LET'S HUR—
CIEL!?
IT'S NOTHING. I JUST CHOKED ON SOME WATER.
NOW HURRY UP AND START CLIMBING!
ゴホッ
AHEM!
......
LOOK, CIEL! DOESN'T THIS FLOWER PATTERN TAKE YOU BACK?
...BUT...
...I NEVER BELIEVED FOR A MOMENT THAT THE BOY WHO CAME BACK WASN'T CIEL.
HERE, YOUNG MASTER, TAKE THIS.
I DON'T NEED IT.
THE TAILS WILL DRAG BEHIND ME.
BUT IF YOUR BODY IS CHILLED THROUGH, YOUR COUGH—
DON'T BRING THAT UP NOW!

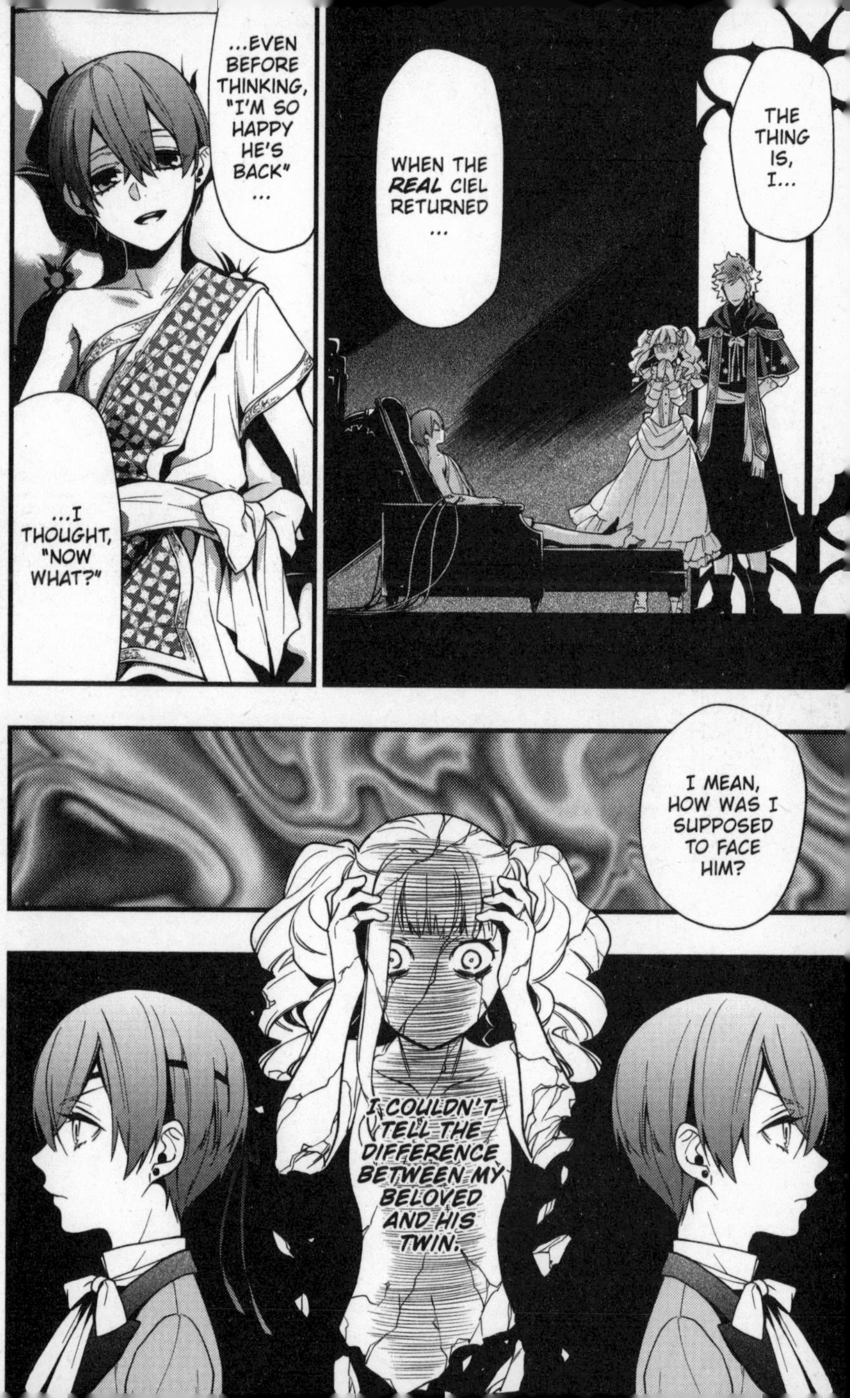
THE THING IS, I...
WHEN THE REAL CIEL RETURNED...
...EVEN BEFORE THINKING, "I'M SO HAPPY HE'S BACK"...
...I THOUGHT, "NOW WHAT?"
I MEAN, HOW WAS I SUPPOSED TO FACE HIM?
I COULDN'T TELL THE DIFFERENCE BETWEEN MY BELOVED AND HIS TWIN.

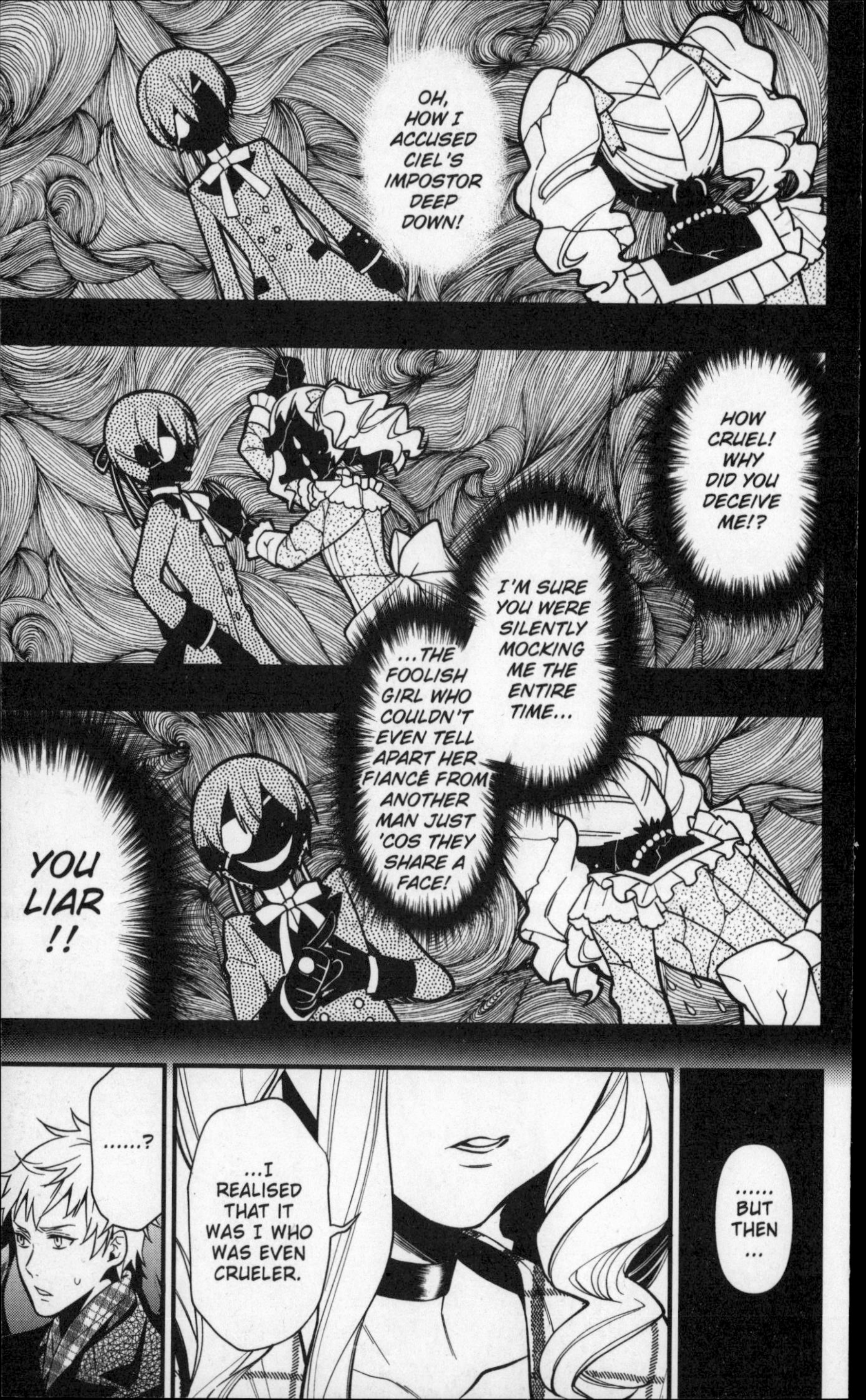
OH, HOW I ACCUSED CIEL'S IMPOSTOR DEEP DOWN!
HOW CRUEL! WHY DID YOU DECEIVE ME!?
I'M SURE YOU WERE SILENTLY MOCKING ME THE ENTIRE TIME...
...THE FOOLISH GIRL WHO COULDN'T EVEN TELL APART HER FIANCÉ FROM ANOTHER MAN JUST 'COS THEY SHARE A FACE!
YOU LIAR!!
......BUT THEN...
...I REALISED THAT IT WAS I WHO WAS EVEN CRUELER.
......?

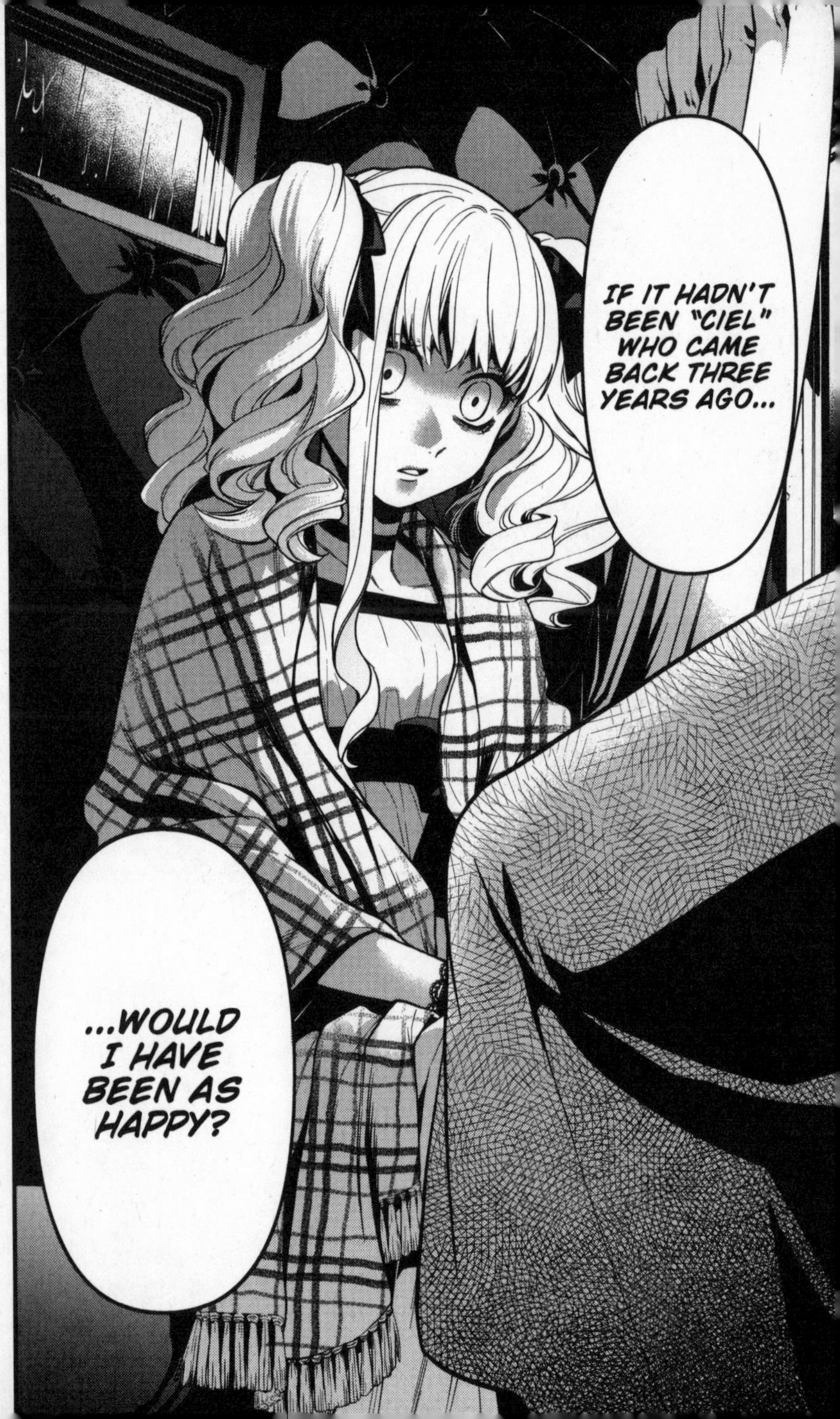
IF IT HADN'T BEEN "CIEL" WHO CAME BACK THREE YEARS AGO...
...WOULD I HAVE BEEN AS HAPPY?

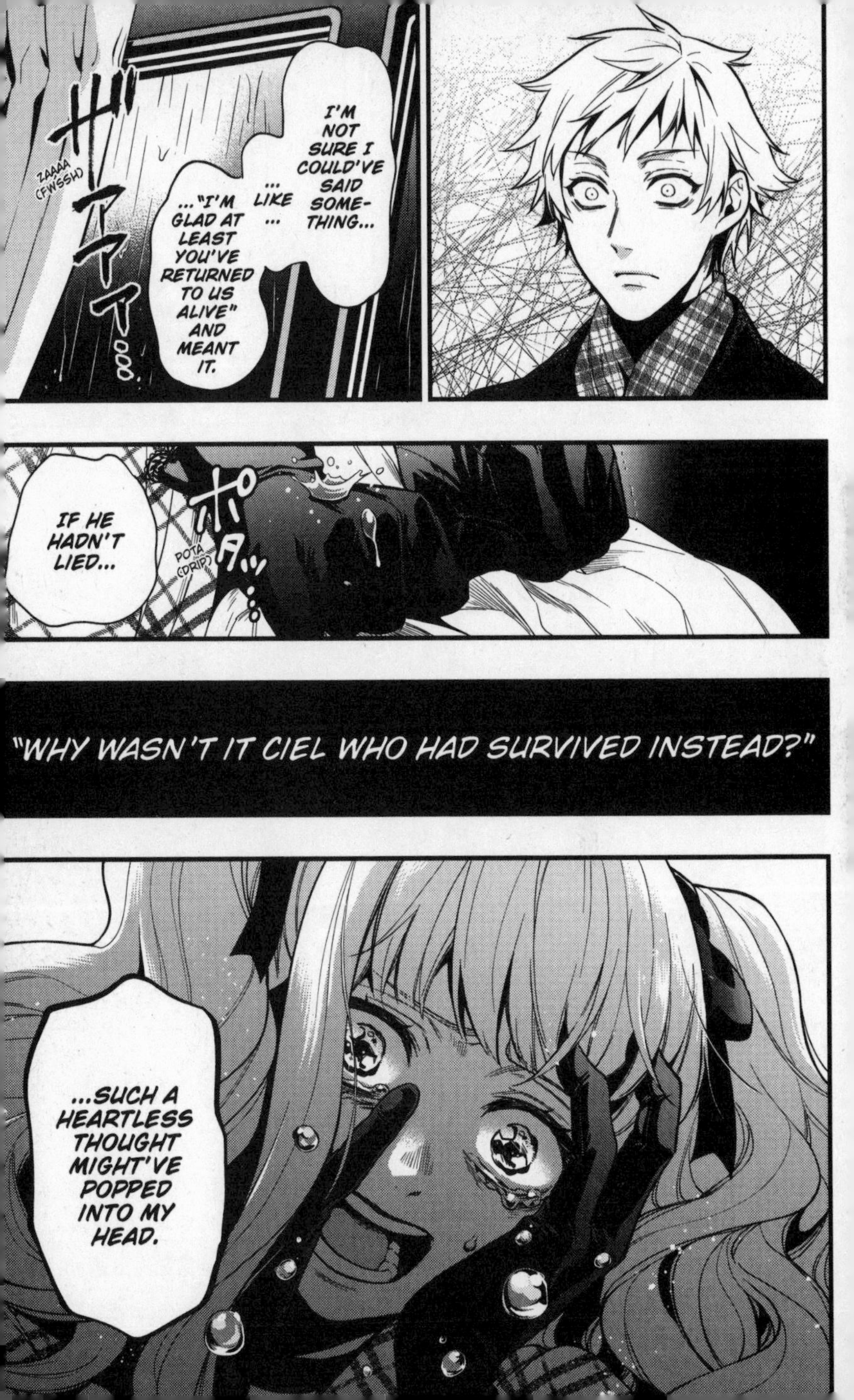
I'M NOT SURE I COULD'VE SAID SOMETHING...
...LIKE...
..."I'M GLAD AT LEAST YOU'VE RETURNED TO US ALIVE" AND MEANT IT.
ZAAAA (FWSSH)
POTA (DRIP)
IF HE HADN'T LIED...
"WHY WASN'T IT CIEL WHO HAD SURVIVED INSTEAD?"
...SUCH A HEARTLESS THOUGHT MIGHT'VE POPPED INTO MY HEAD.

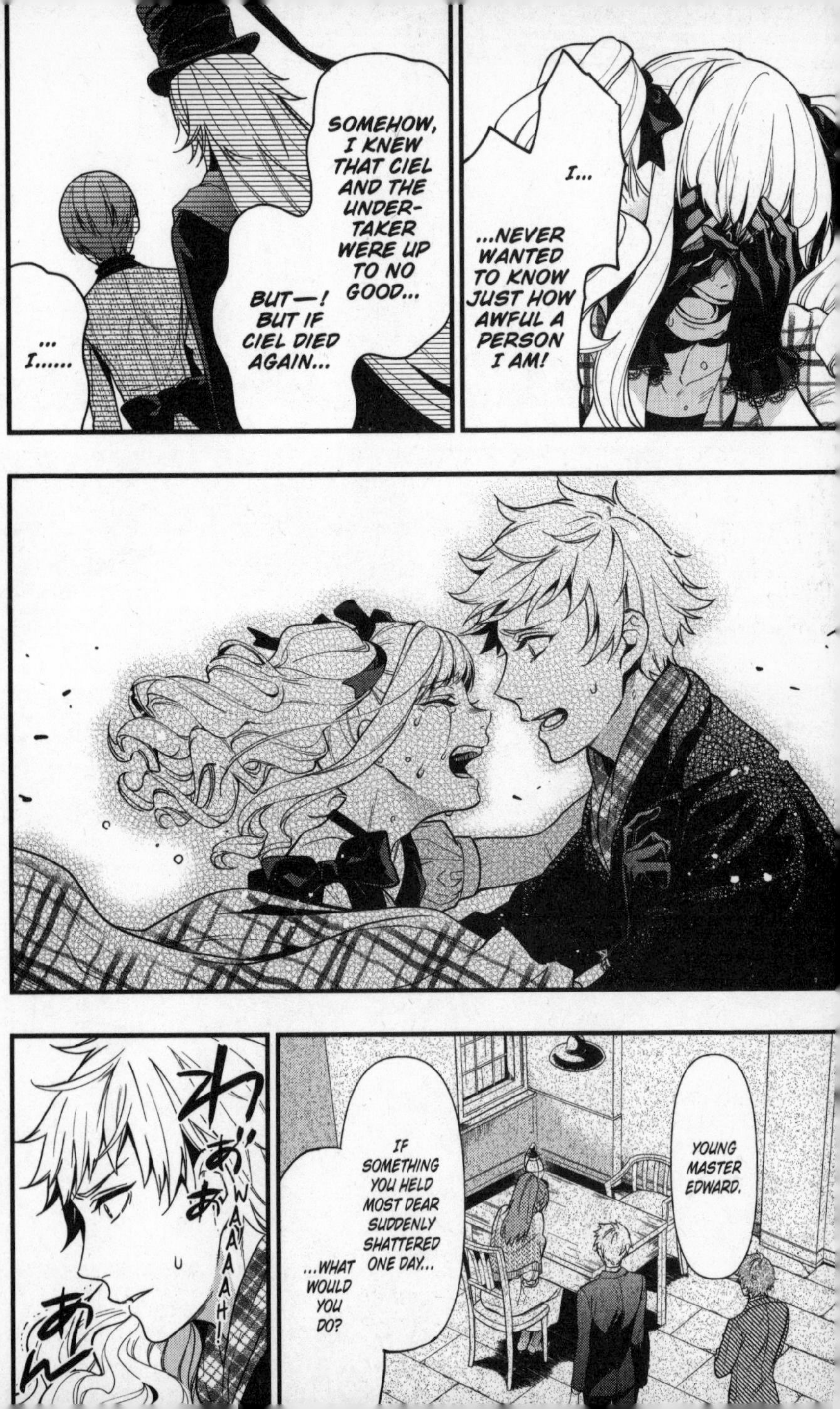
I...
...NEVER WANTED TO KNOW JUST HOW AWFUL A PERSON I AM!
SOMEHOW, I KNEW THAT CIEL AND THE UNDER-TAKER WERE UP TO NO GOOD...
BUT—! BUT IF CIEL DIED AGAIN...
... I......
YOUNG MASTER EDWARD.
IF SOMETHING YOU HELD MOST DEAR SUDDENLY SHATTERED ONE DAY...
...WHAT WOULD YOU DO?
WAAAAAH!

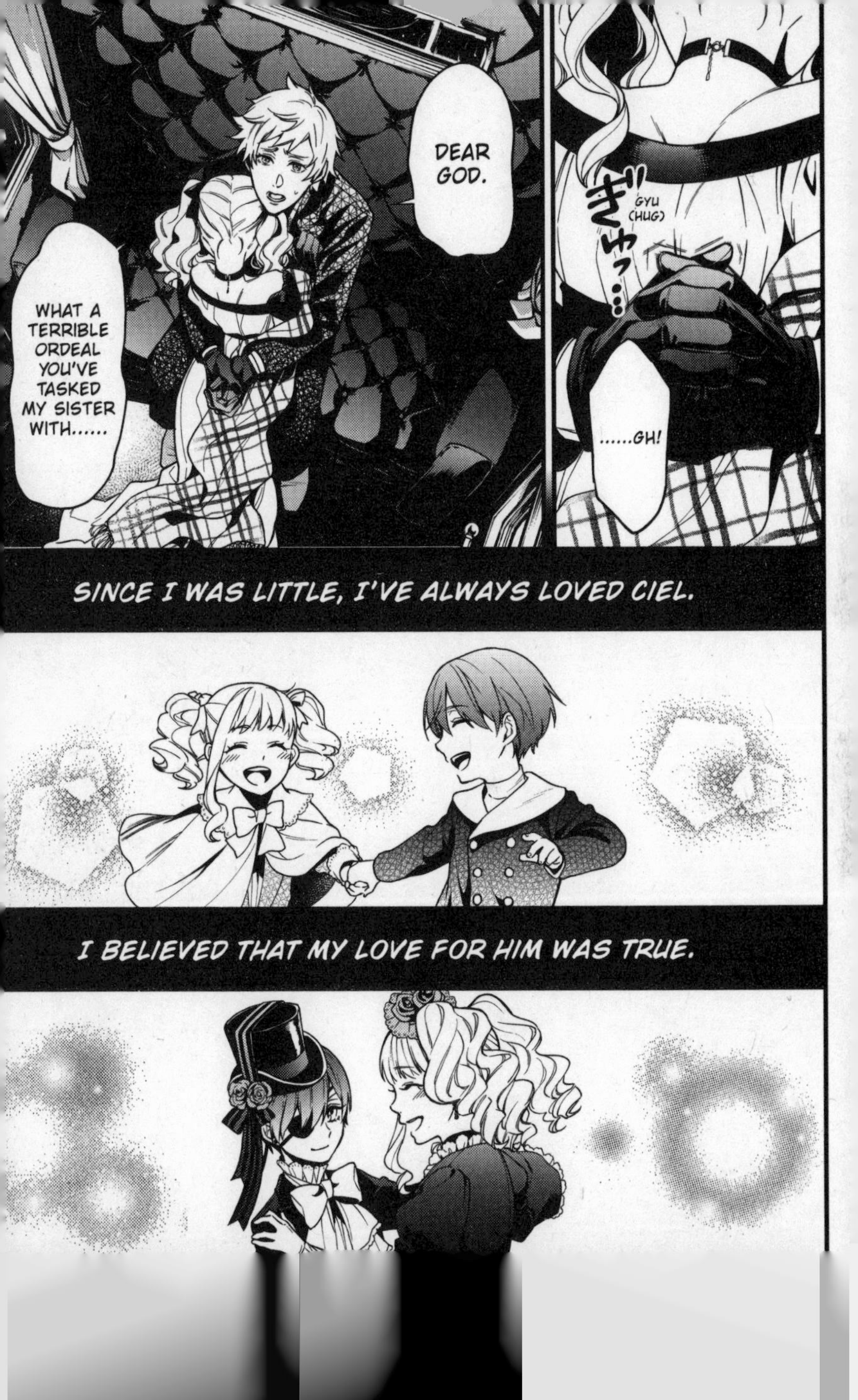
ぎゅっ…
GYU (HUG)
……GH!
DEAR GOD.
WHAT A TERRIBLE ORDEAL YOU'VE TASKED MY SISTER WITH……
SINCE I WAS LITTLE, I'VE ALWAYS LOVED CIEL.
I BELIEVED THAT MY LOVE FOR HIM WAS TRUE.

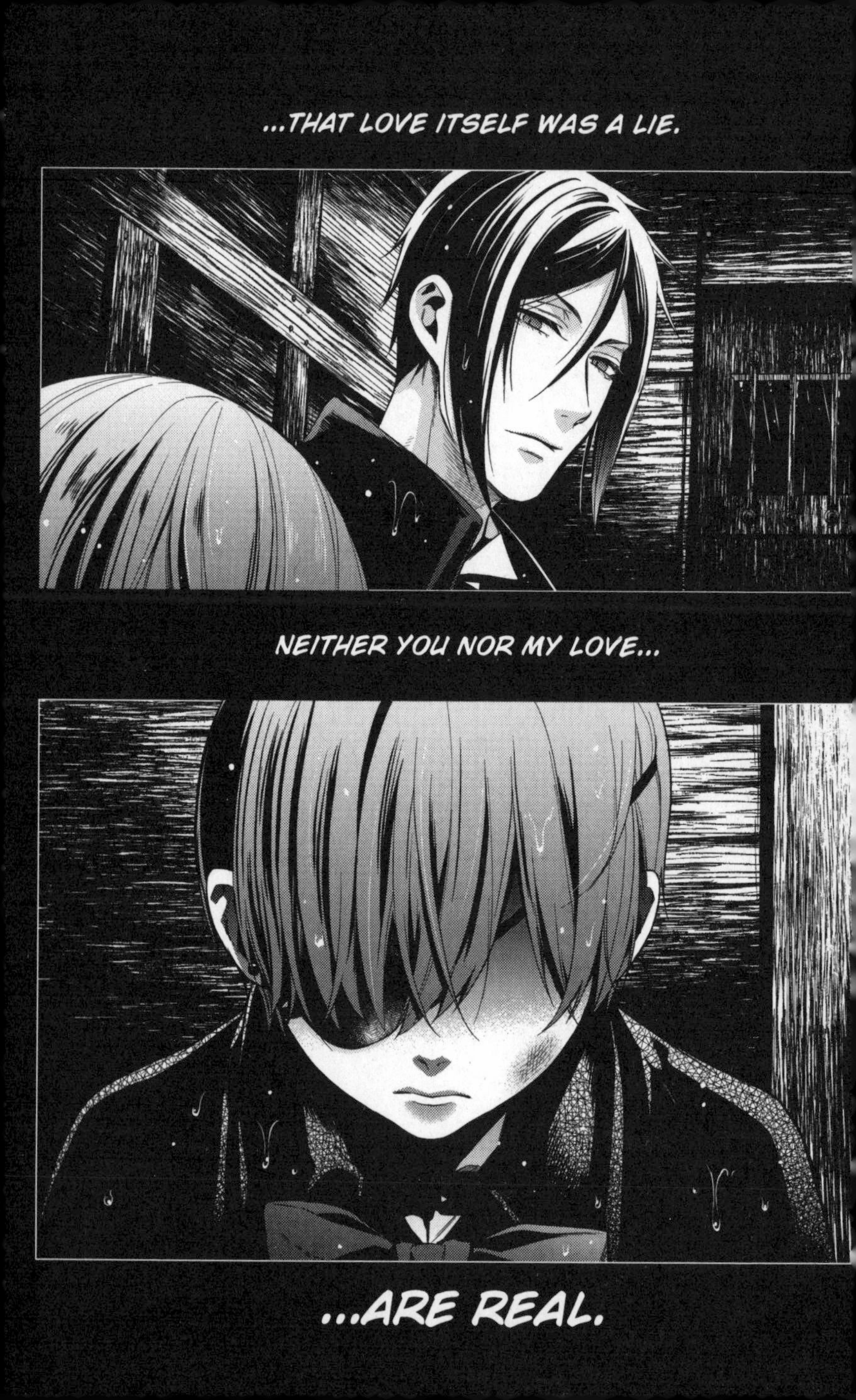
...THAT LOVE ITSELF WAS A LIE.
NEITHER YOU NOR MY LOVE...
...ARE REAL.

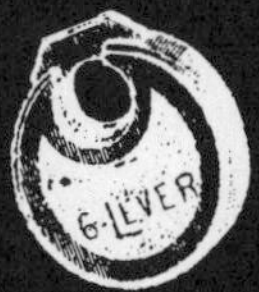
6-LEVER

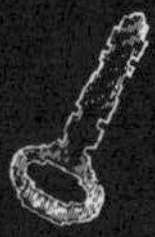

Black Butler

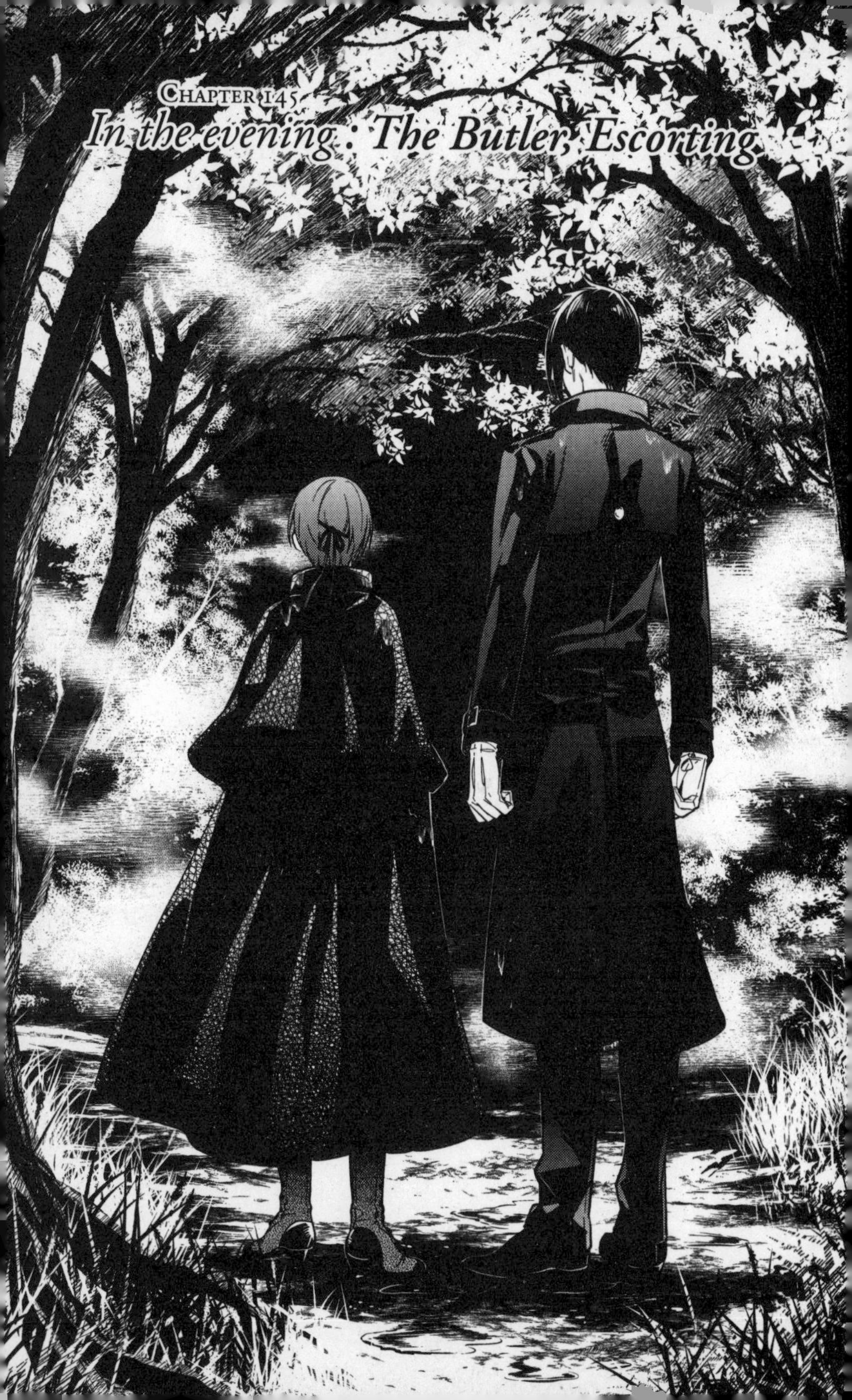
Chapter 145
In the evening : The Butler, Escorting

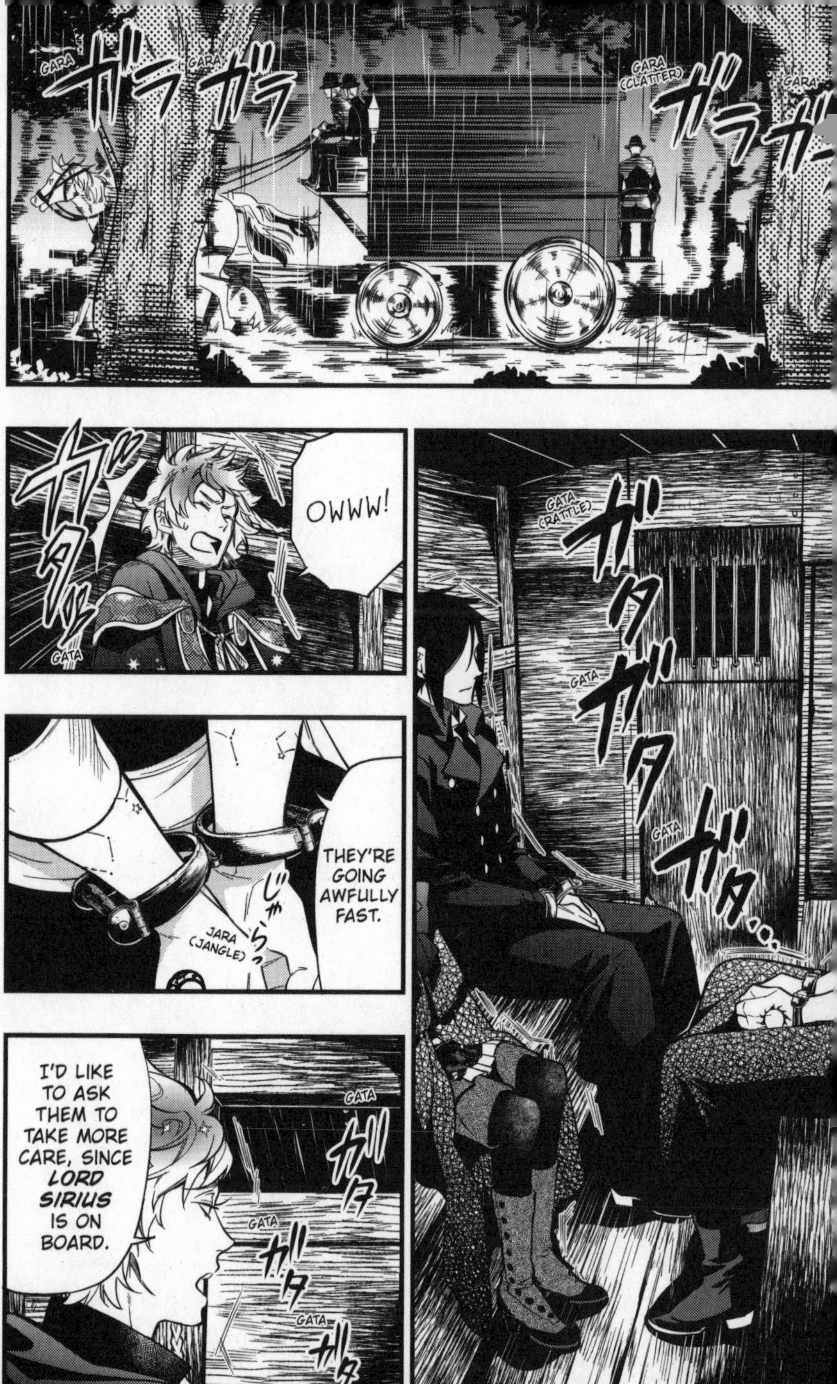
GARA (CLATTER)
GARA
GARA
GARA
GATA (RATTLE)
GATA
GATA
GATA
OWWW!
THEY'RE GOING AWFULLY FAST.
JARA (JANGLE)
I'D LIKE TO ASK THEM TO TAKE MORE CARE, SINCE ***LORD SIRIUS*** IS ON BOARD.
GATA
GATA
GATA

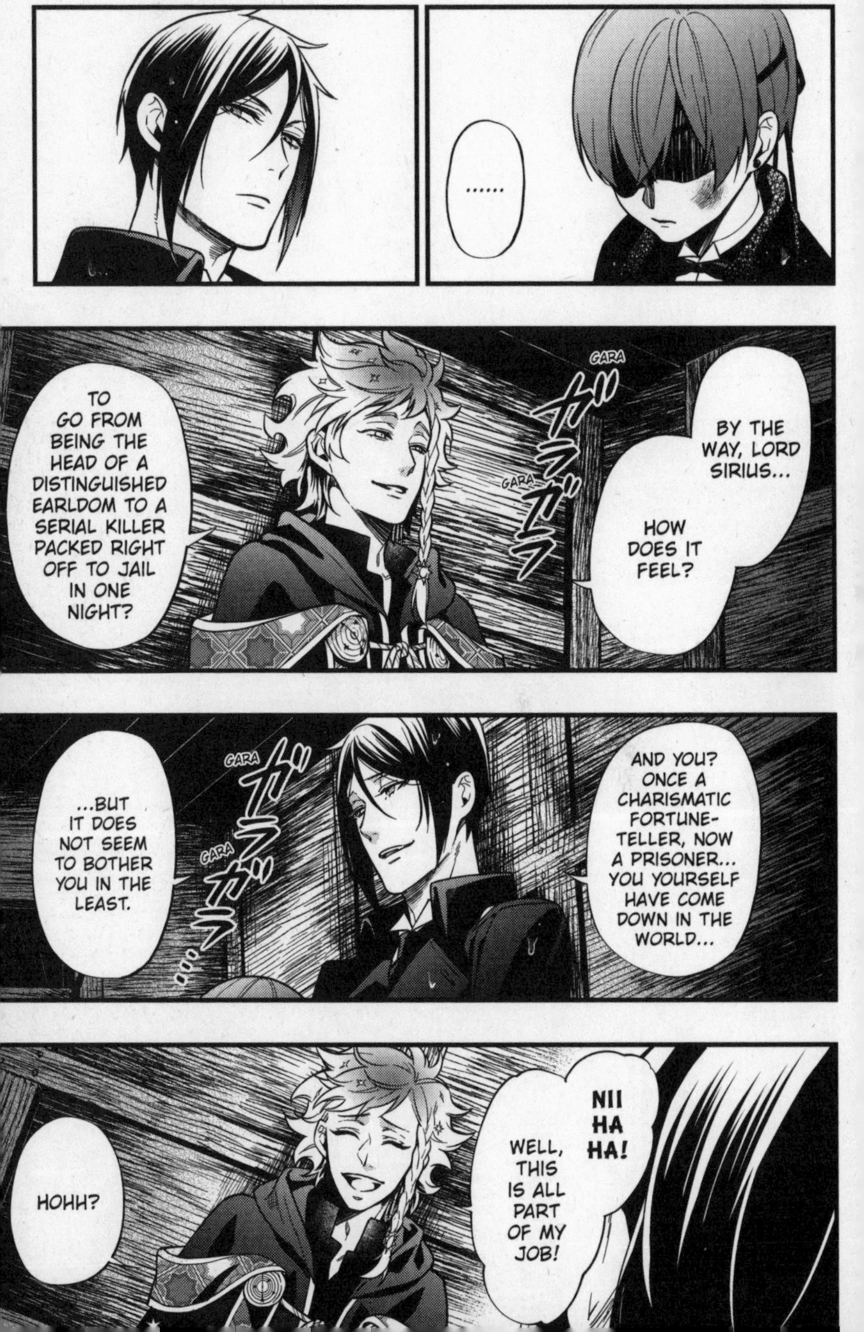
……
GARA
BY THE WAY, LORD SIRIUS...
HOW DOES IT FEEL?
GARA
TO GO FROM BEING THE HEAD OF A DISTINGUISHED EARLDOM TO A SERIAL KILLER PACKED RIGHT OFF TO JAIL IN ONE NIGHT?
AND YOU? ONCE A CHARISMATIC FORTUNE-TELLER, NOW A PRISONER... YOU YOURSELF HAVE COME DOWN IN THE WORLD...
GARA
GARA
...BUT IT DOES NOT SEEM TO BOTHER YOU IN THE LEAST.
NII HA HA!
WELL, THIS IS ALL PART OF MY JOB!
HOHH?

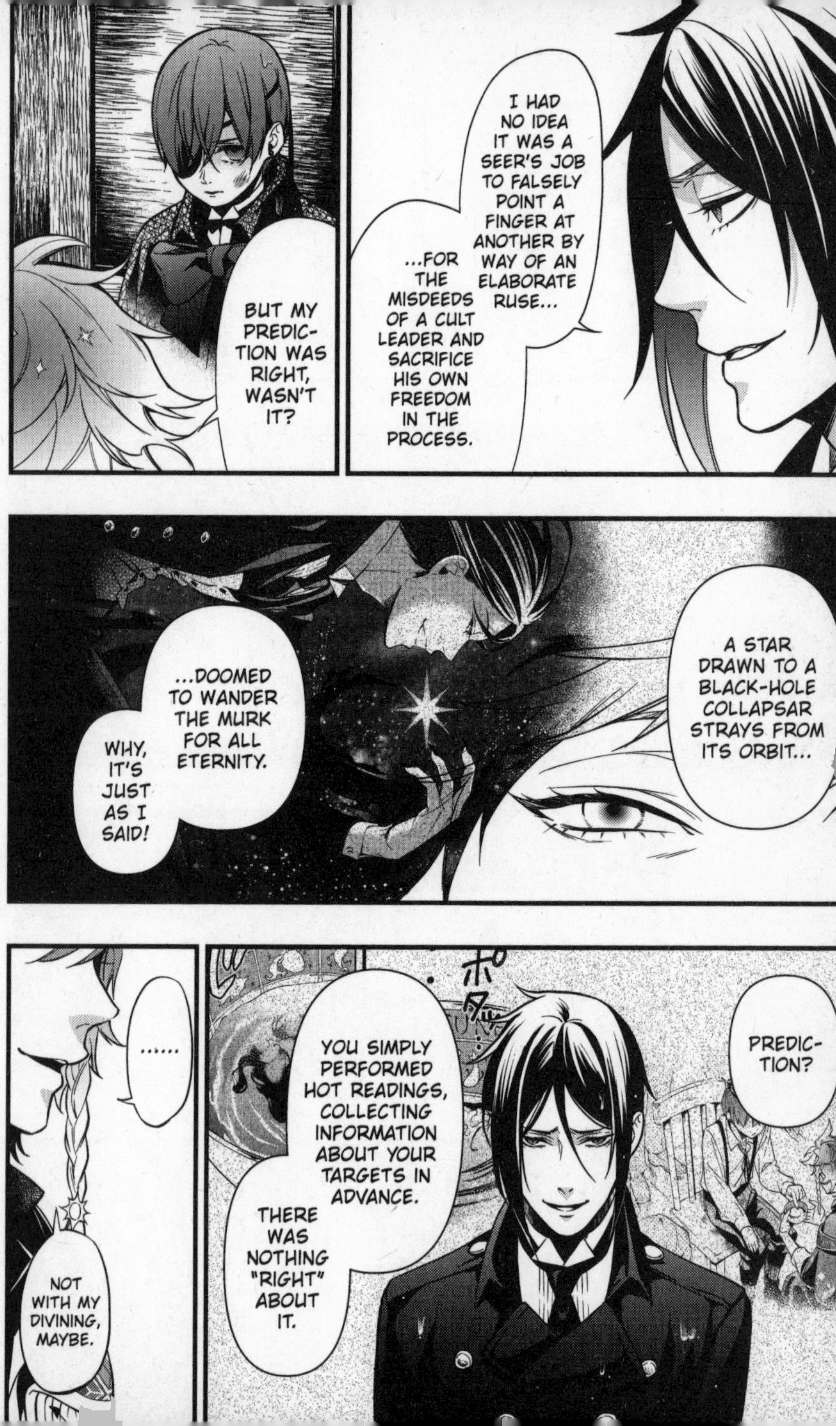
I HAD NO IDEA IT WAS A SEER'S JOB TO FALSELY POINT A FINGER AT ANOTHER BY WAY OF AN ELABORATE RUSE...
...FOR THE MISDEEDS OF A CULT LEADER AND SACRIFICE HIS OWN FREEDOM IN THE PROCESS.
BUT MY PREDICTION WAS RIGHT, WASN'T IT?
A STAR DRAWN TO A BLACK-HOLE COLLAPSAR STRAYS FROM ITS ORBIT...
...DOOMED TO WANDER THE MURK FOR ALL ETERNITY.
WHY, IT'S JUST AS I SAID!
PREDICTION?
ポタ
YOU SIMPLY PERFORMED HOT READINGS, COLLECTING INFORMATION ABOUT YOUR TARGETS IN ADVANCE.
THERE WAS NOTHING "RIGHT" ABOUT IT.
......
NOT WITH MY DIVINING, MAYBE.

GAN CBANG?

HEY!!

SHUT YER TRAPS!!

BUT THE MOMENT I LAID EYES ON YOU...

...I KNEW YOU WERE "DIFFERENT."

—?

OOH, SCARY.

WELL... I WONDER HOW MANY MORE HOURS OF GETTING THROWN AROUND THIS STINKY CARRIAGE WE HAVE TO ENDURE.

GARA GARA (CLATTER)

KNOW YOUR PLACE, YOU MURDEROUS LOT!

HEH...

NOT MUCH LONGER NOW, I WOULD SAY.

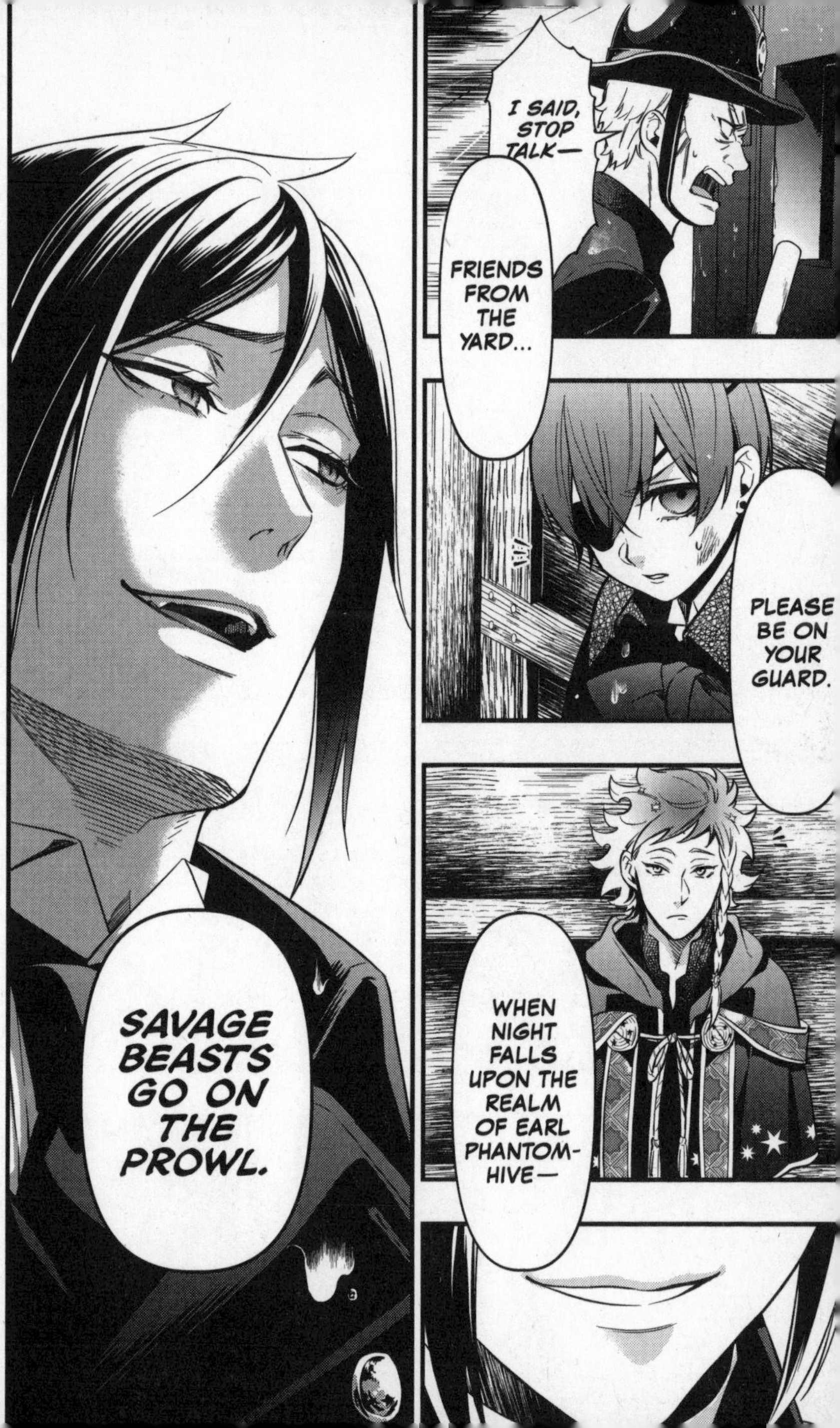
I SAID, STOP TALK—
FRIENDS FROM THE YARD...
PLEASE BE ON YOUR GUARD.
WHEN NIGHT FALLS UPON THE REALM OF EARL PHANTOM-HIVE—
SAVAGE BEASTS GO ON THE PROWL.

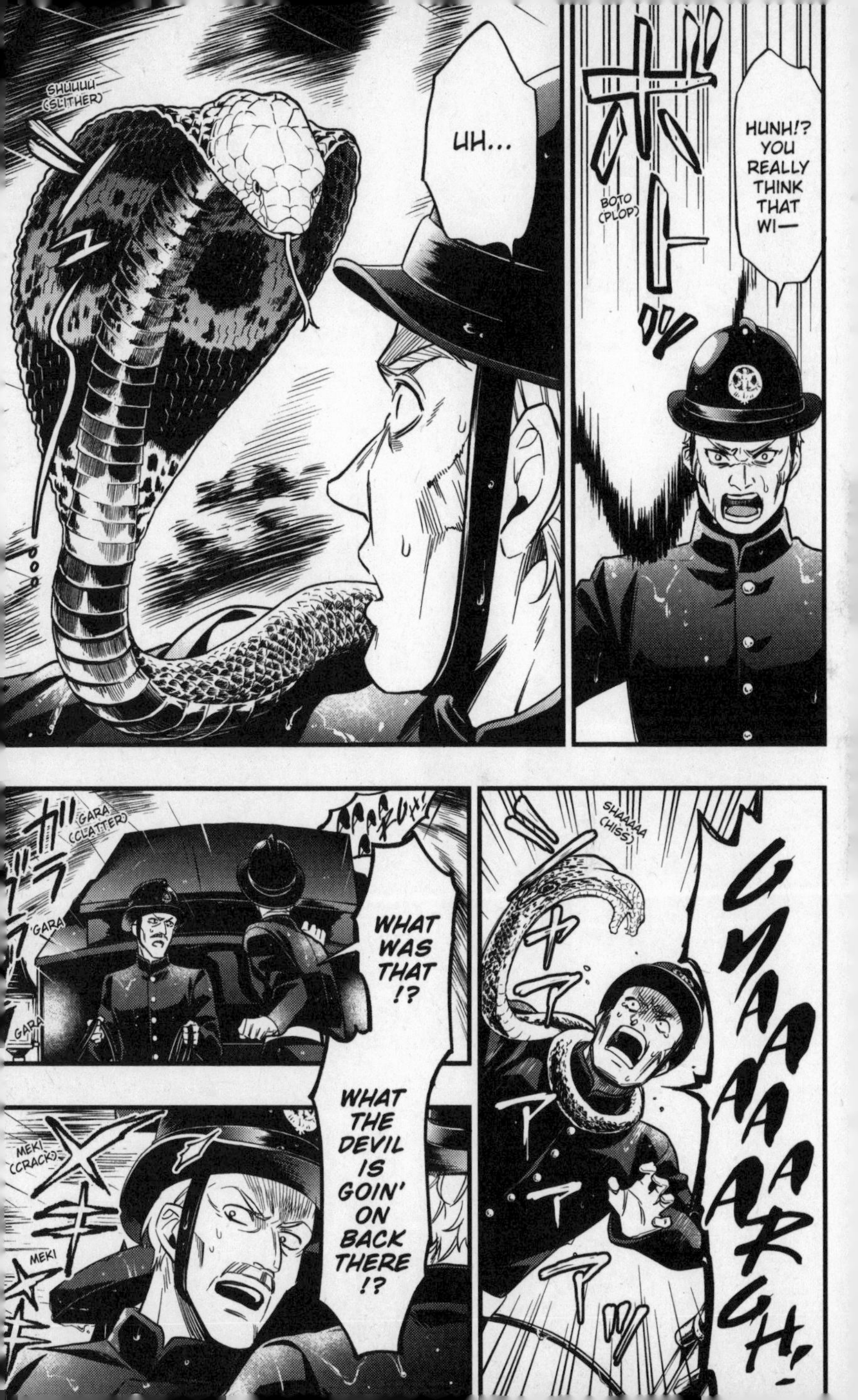
BOTO (PLOP)
HUNH!? YOU REALLY THINK THAT WI—
UH...
SHUUUU (SLITHER)
SHAAAAA (HISS)
UWAAAAAAARGH!
GARA (CLATTER)
GARA
GARA
WHAT WAS THAT!?
WHAT THE DEVIL IS GOIN' ON BACK THERE!?
MEKI (CRACK)
MEKI

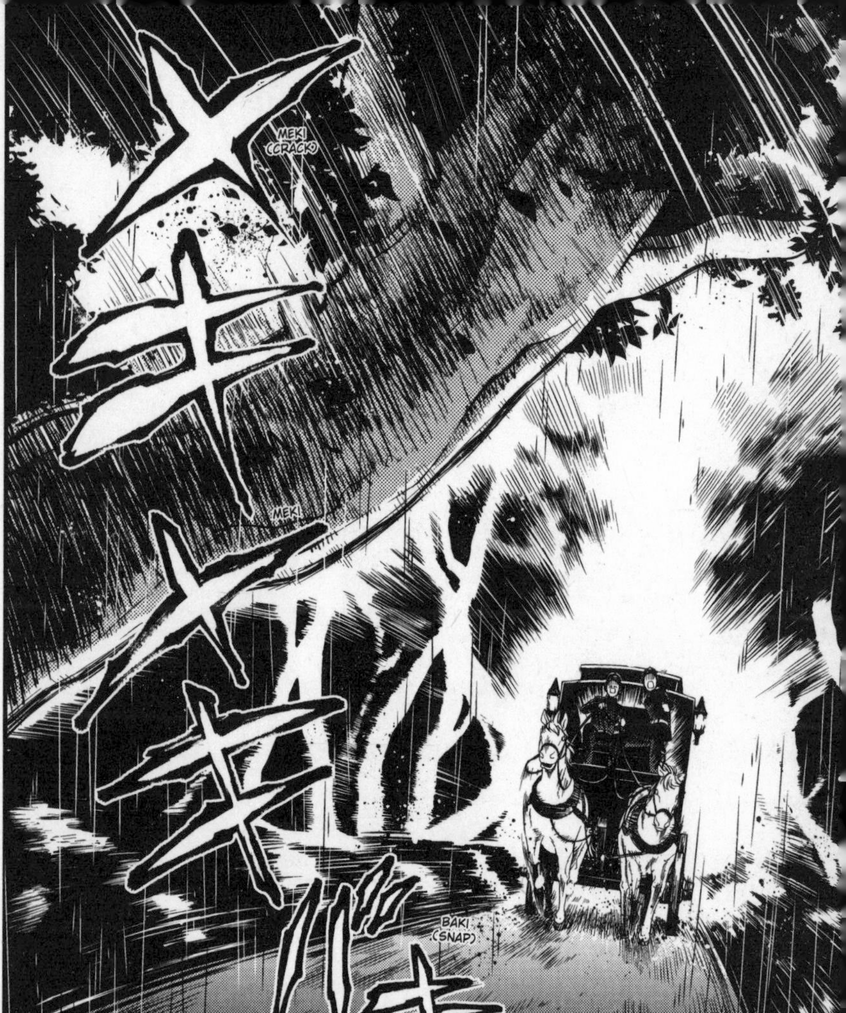
MEKI (CRACK)
MEKI
BAKI (SNAP)
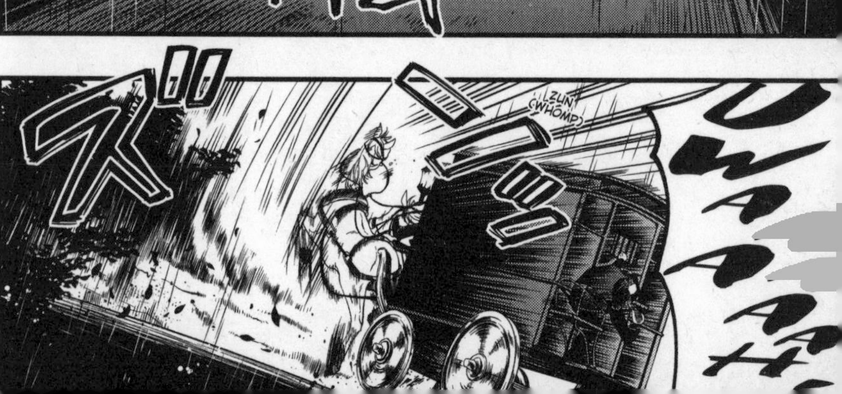
ZUN (WHOMP)
UWAAAAH

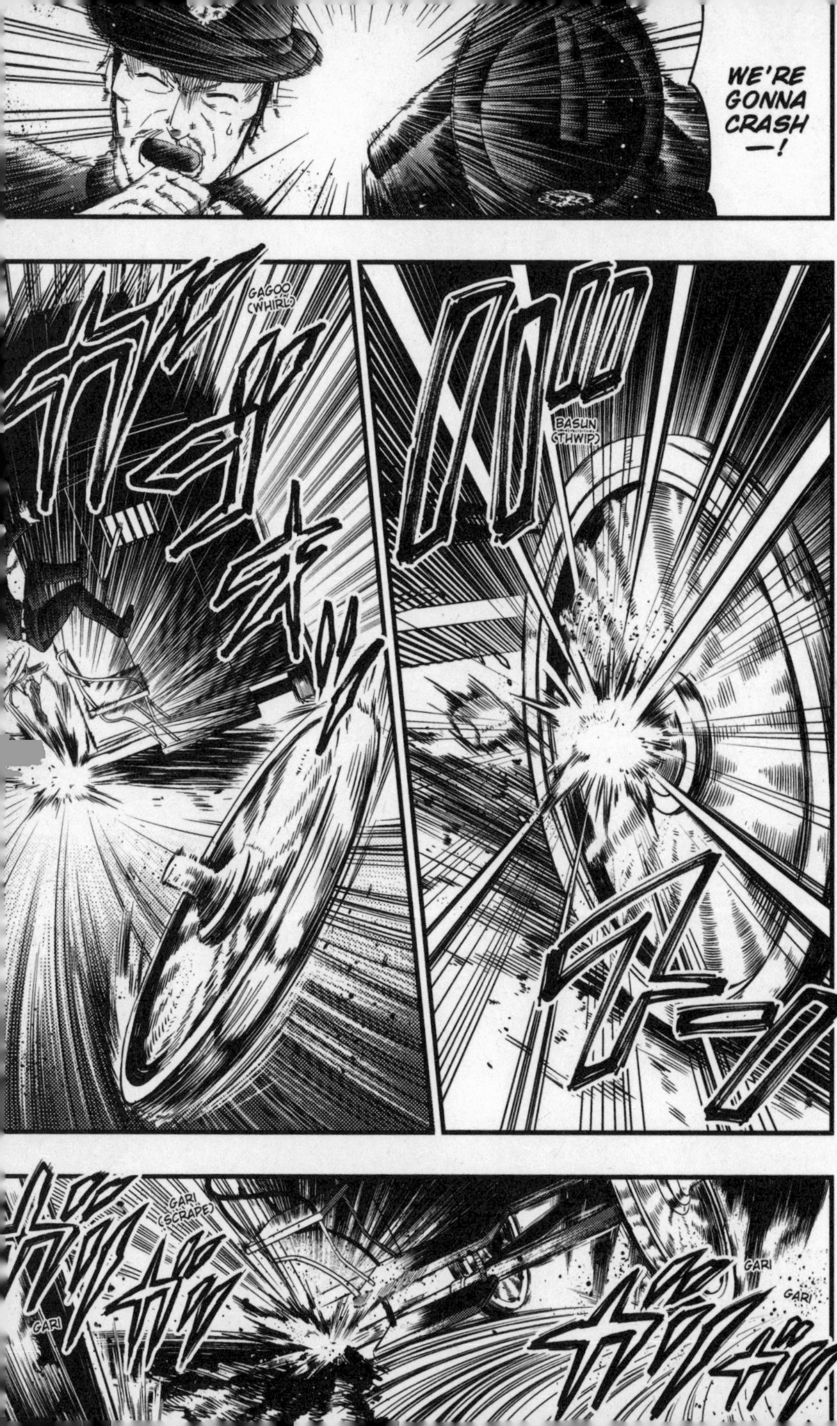
WE'RE GONNA CRASH—!
GAGOO (WHIRL)
BASUN (THWIP)
GARI (SCRAPE)
GARI
GARI
GARI

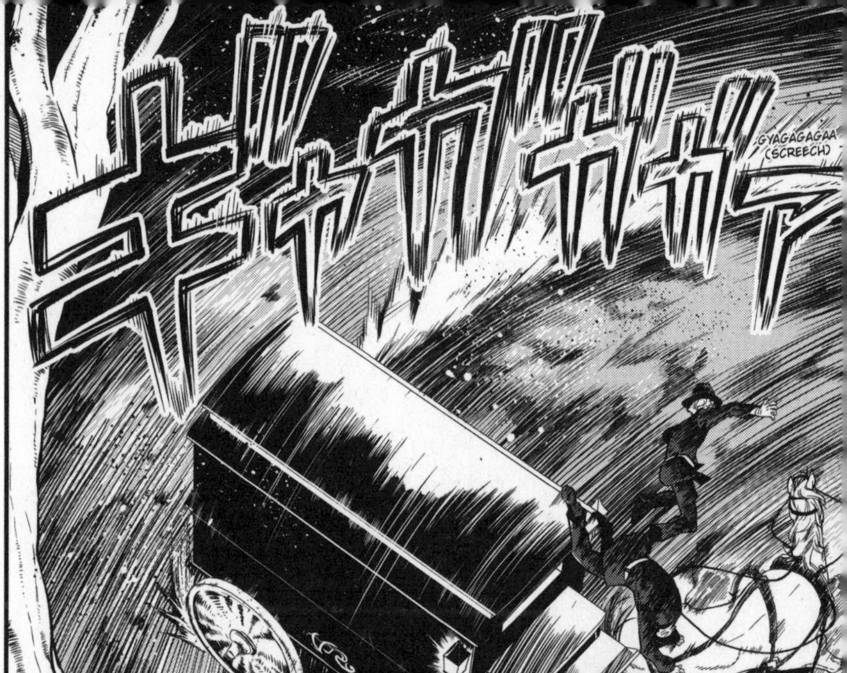
GYAGAGAGAA (SCREECH)
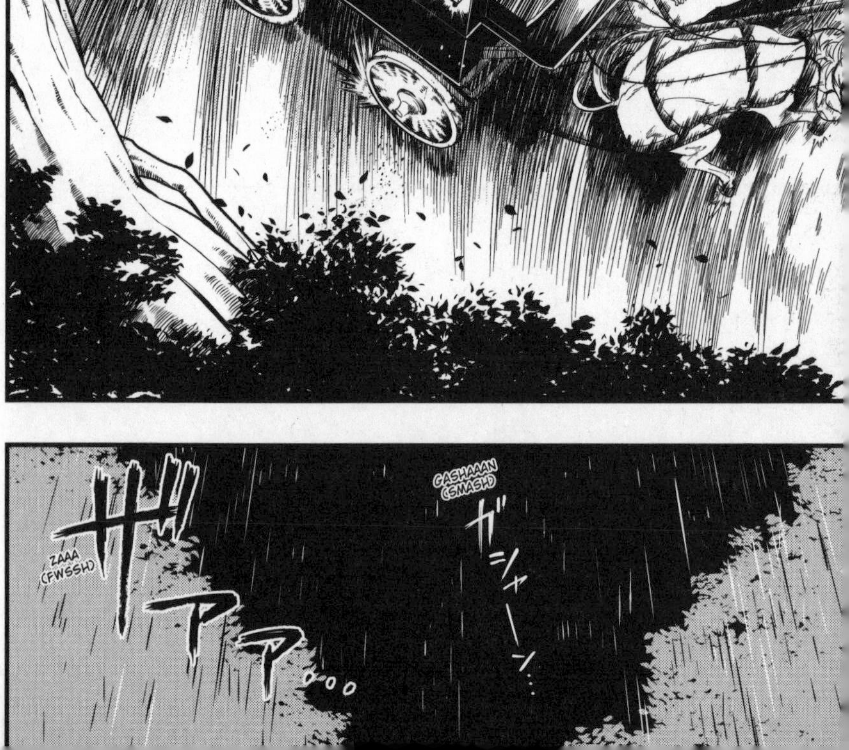
GASHAAAN (SMASH)
ZAAA (FWSSH)

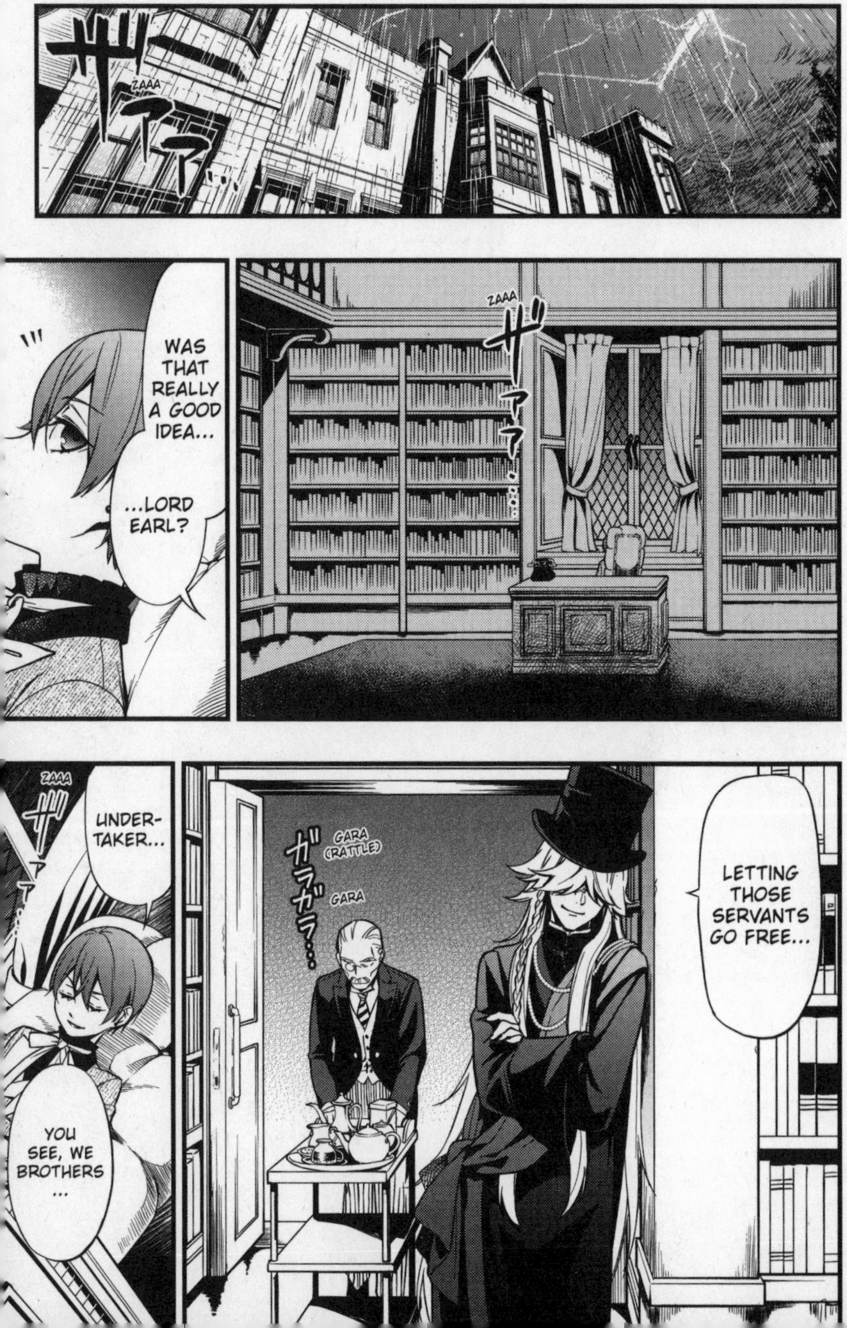
ZAAA
ZAAA
WAS THAT REALLY A GOOD IDEA...
...LORD EARL?
LETTING THOSE SERVANTS GO FREE...
GARA (RATTLE)
GARA
ZAAA
UNDER-TAKER...
YOU SEE, WE BROTHERS ...

HM?

...HAVE NEVER SO MUCH AS QUARRELLED.

WELL ...WE... HAVE HAD CHILDISH DISAGREEMENTS, OF COURSE, BUT...

KA (FLASH)

...AT THE IDEA OF...

...A SERIOUS FIGHT WITH MY LITTLE BROTHER.

GORO (CRUMBLE)

GORO

THAT'S WHY I'M BESIDE MYSELF WITH EXCITEMENT...

ZAAA (FWESH)

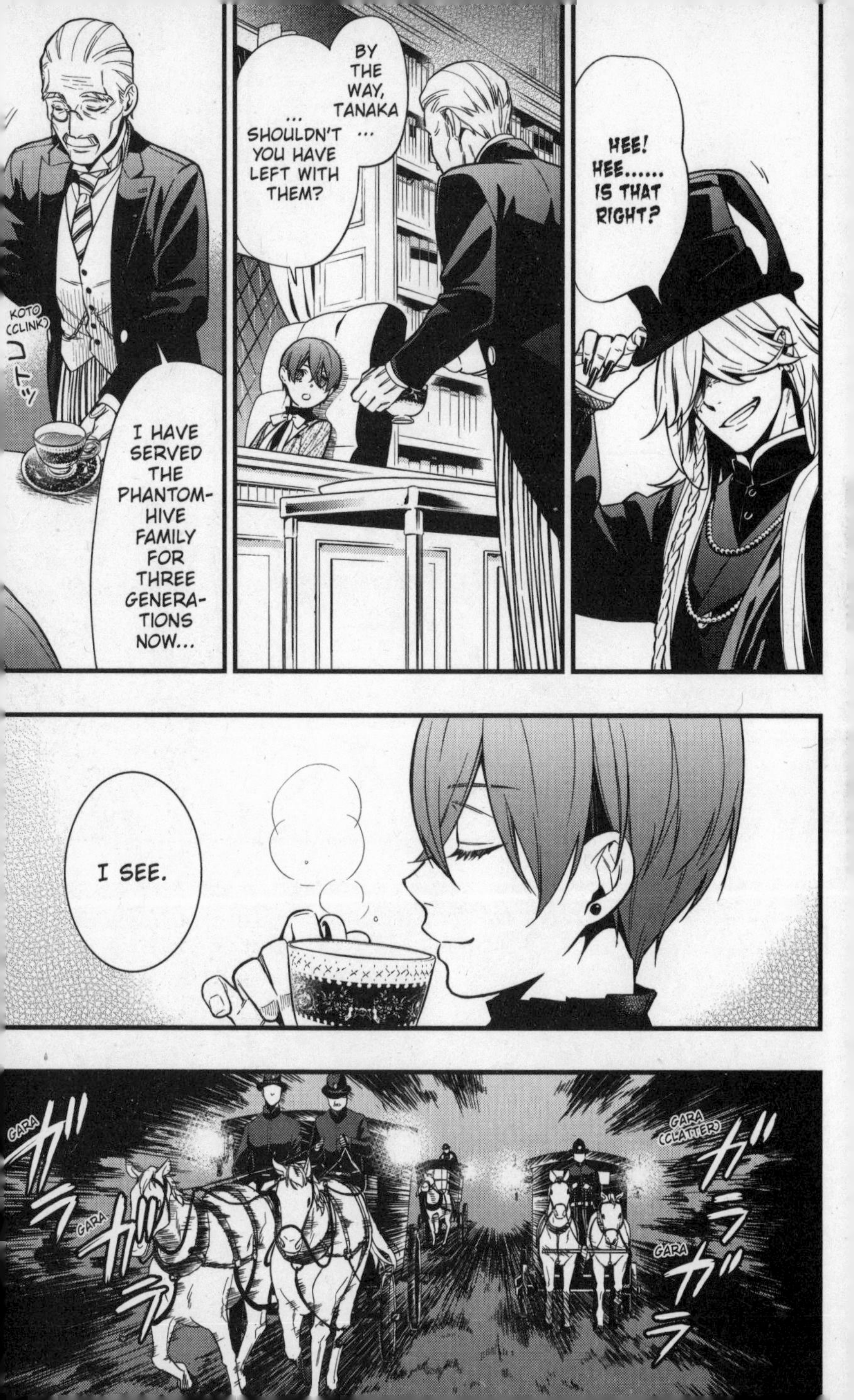
HEE! HEE...... IS THAT RIGHT?
BY THE WAY, TANAKA ... SHOULDN'T YOU HAVE LEFT WITH THEM?
KOTO (CLINK)
I HAVE SERVED THE PHANTOM-HIVE FAMILY FOR THREE GENERA-TIONS NOW...
I SEE.
GARA (CLATTER)
GARA
GARA
GARA

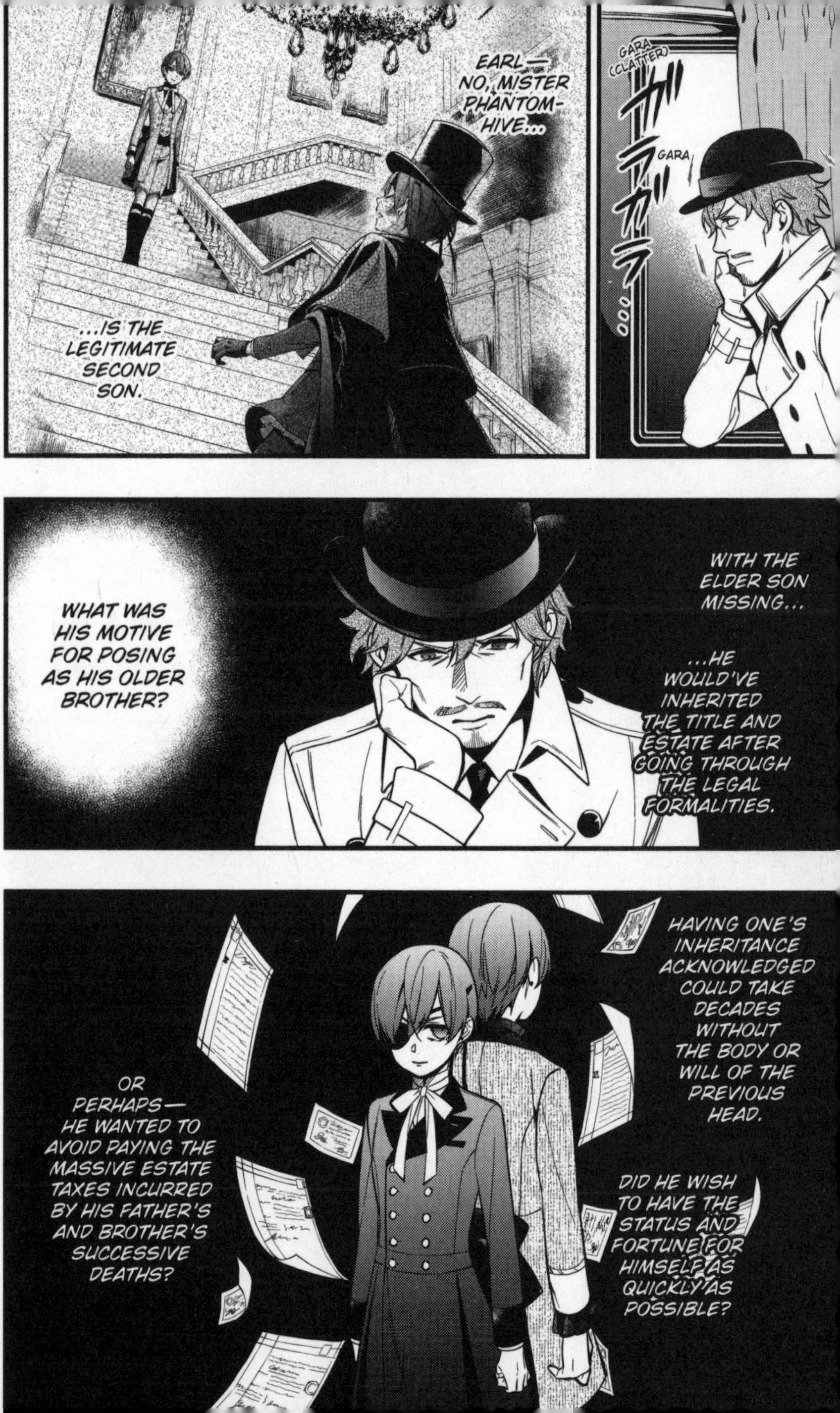
GARA (CLATTER)
ガラガラ…
GARA
EARL—NO, MISTER PHANTOMHIVE…
…IS THE LEGITIMATE SECOND SON.
WITH THE ELDER SON MISSING…
…HE WOULD'VE INHERITED THE TITLE AND ESTATE AFTER GOING THROUGH THE LEGAL FORMALITIES.
WHAT WAS HIS MOTIVE FOR POSING AS HIS OLDER BROTHER?
HAVING ONE'S INHERITANCE ACKNOWLEDGED COULD TAKE DECADES WITHOUT THE BODY OR WILL OF THE PREVIOUS HEAD.
DID HE WISH TO HAVE THE STATUS AND FORTUNE FOR HIMSELF AS QUICKLY AS POSSIBLE?
OR PERHAPS—HE WANTED TO AVOID PAYING THE MASSIVE ESTATE TAXES INCURRED BY HIS FATHER'S AND BROTHER'S SUCCESSIVE DEATHS?

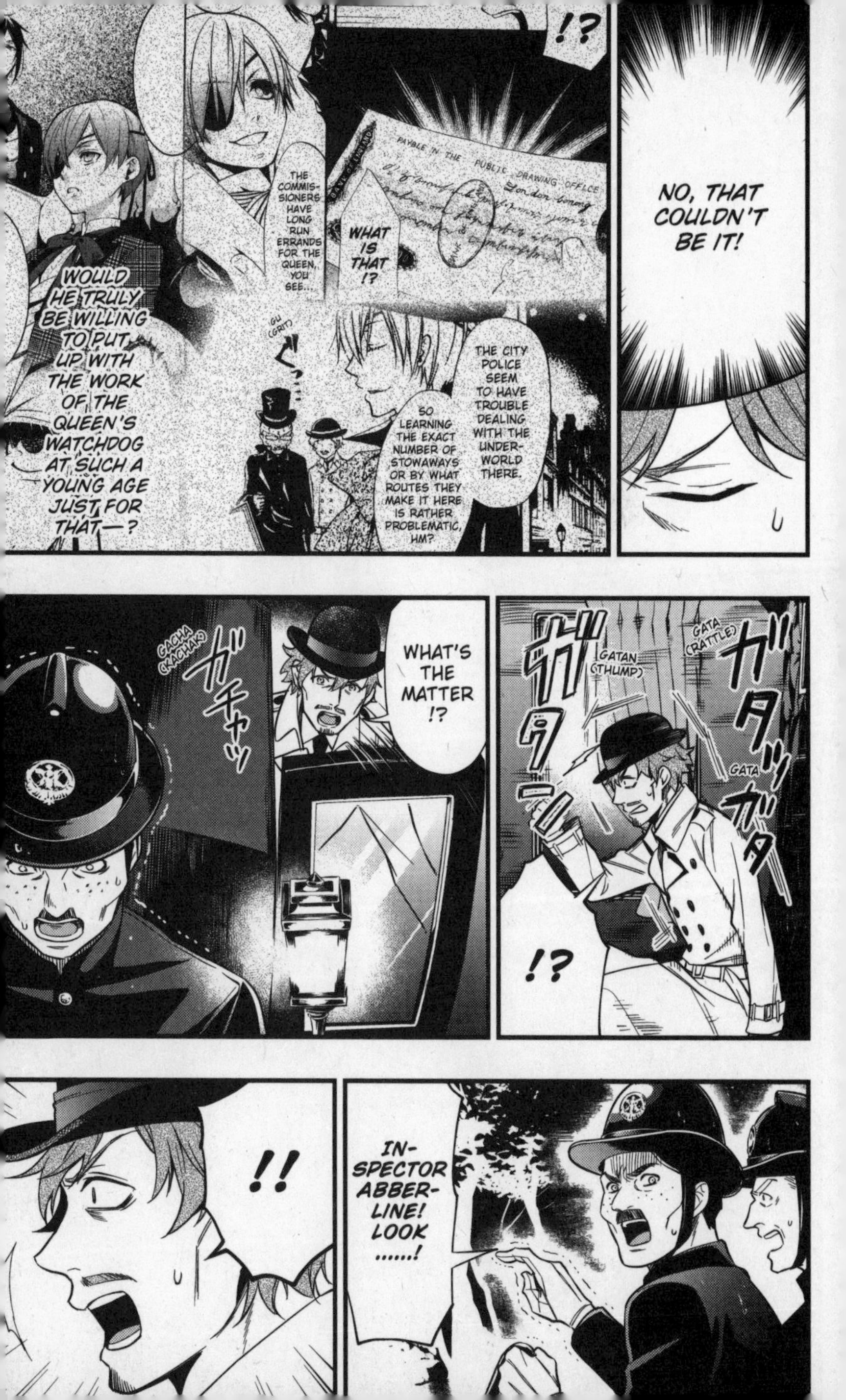
NO, THAT COULDN'T BE IT!
!?
PAYABLE IN THE PUBLIC DRAWING OFFICE
WHAT IS THAT !?
THE COMMISSIONERS HAVE LONG RUN ERRANDS FOR THE QUEEN, YOU SEE...
THE CITY POLICE SEEM TO HAVE TROUBLE DEALING WITH THE UNDERWORLD THERE.
SO LEARNING THE EXACT NUMBER OF STOWAWAYS OR BY WHAT ROUTES THEY MAKE IT HERE IS RATHER PROBLEMATIC, HM?
GU (GRIT)
WOULD HE TRULY BE WILLING TO PUT UP WITH THE WORK OF THE QUEEN'S WATCHDOG AT SUCH A YOUNG AGE JUST FOR THAT—?
GATA (RATTLE)
GATAN (THUMP)
GATA
!?
WHAT'S THE MATTER !?
GACHA (KACHAK)
INSPECTOR ABBERLINE! LOOK ......!
!!

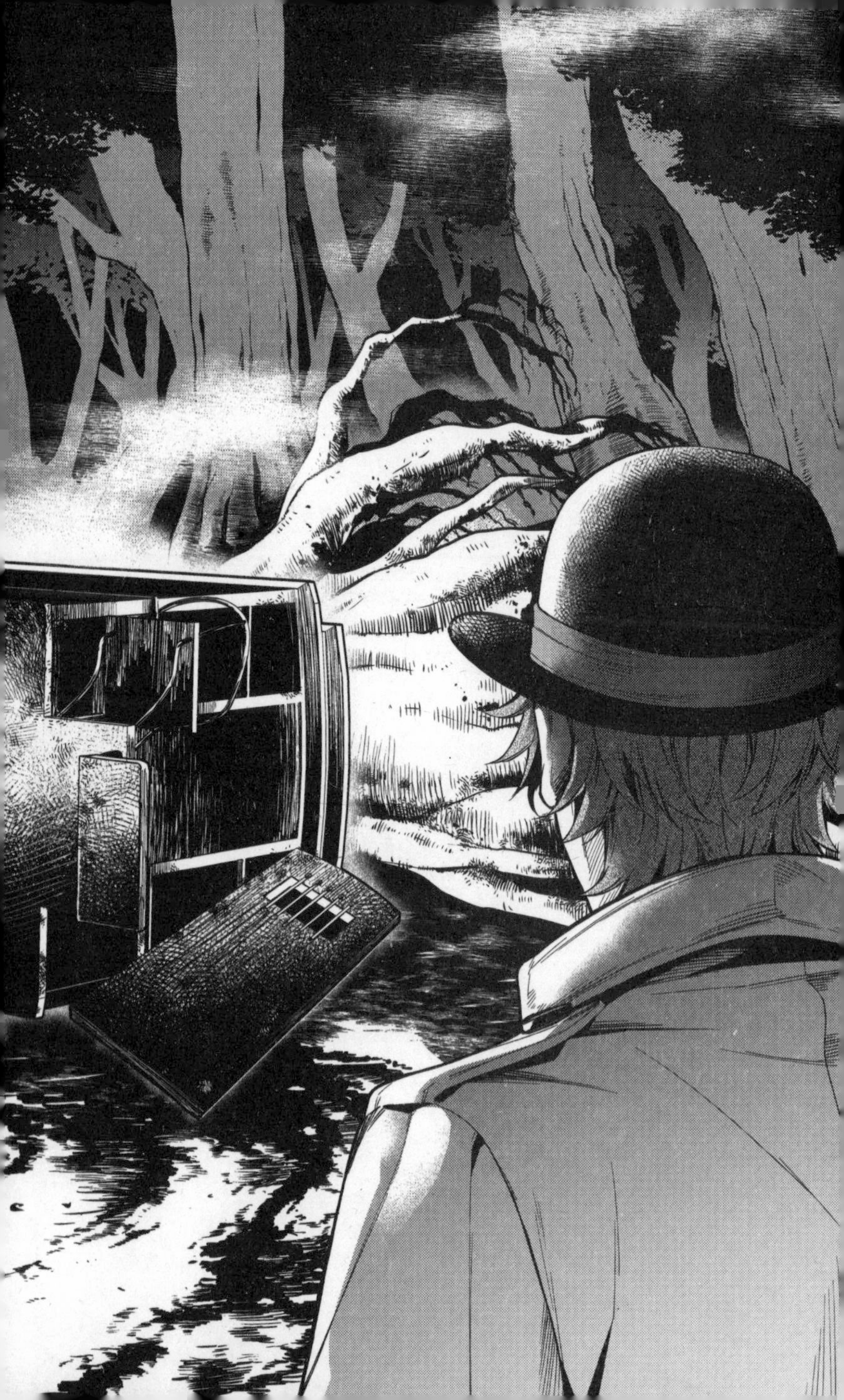

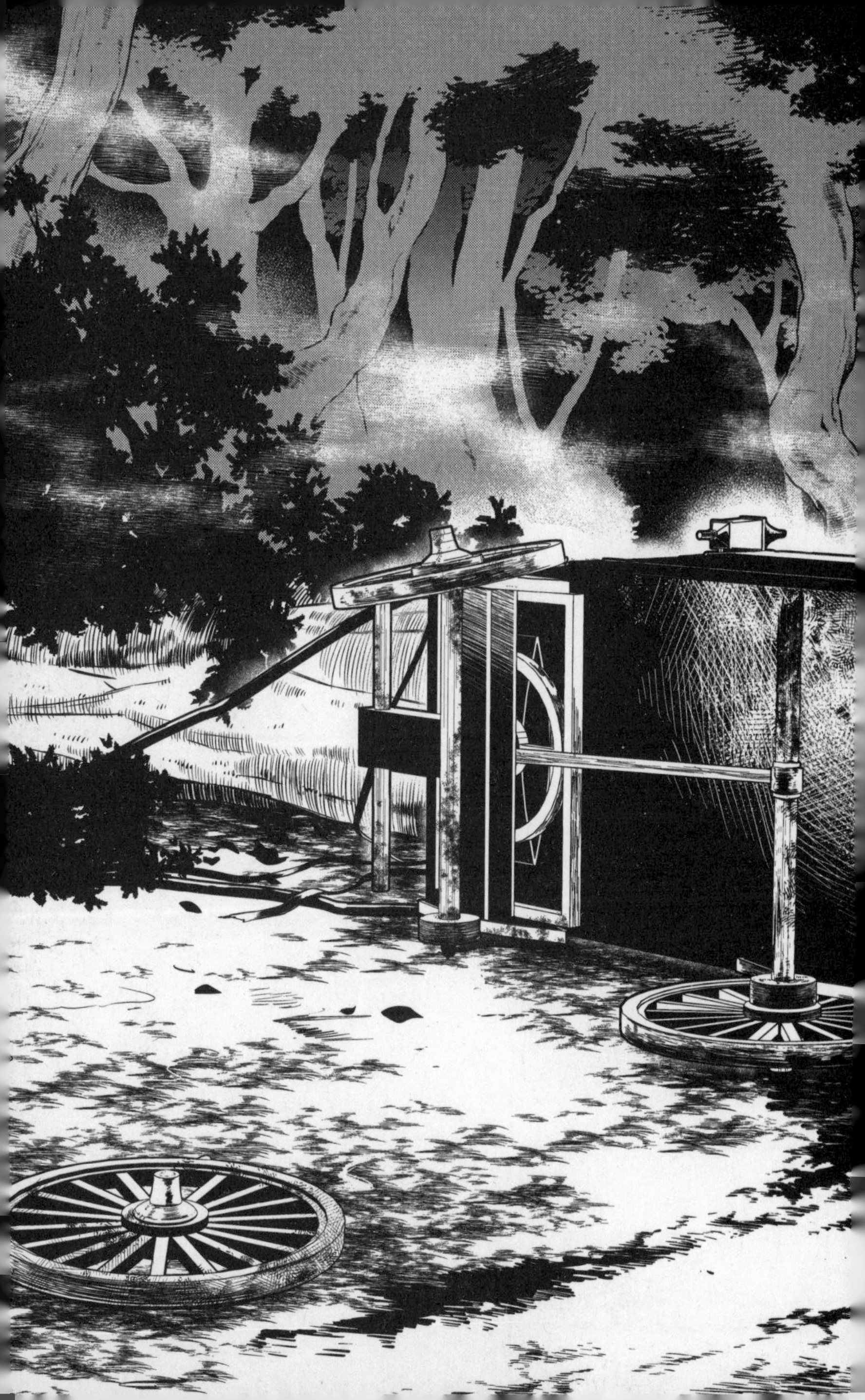

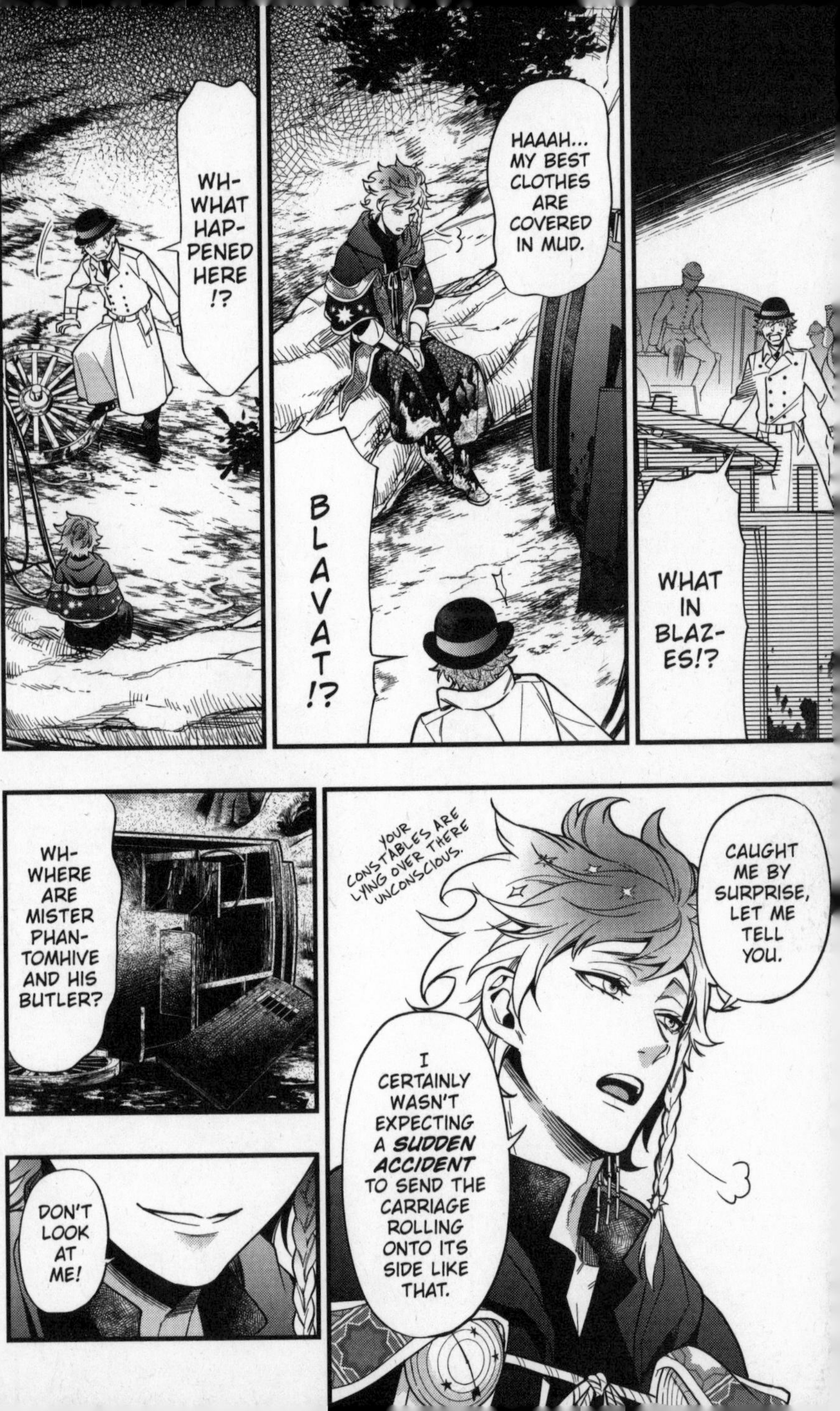
WHAT IN BLAZ-ES!?
HAAAH... MY BEST CLOTHES ARE COVERED IN MUD.
BLAVAT!?
WH-WHAT HAP-PENED HERE!?
CAUGHT ME BY SURPRISE, LET ME TELL YOU.
YOUR CONSTABLES ARE LYING OVER THERE UNCONSCIOUS.
I CERTAINLY WASN'T EXPECTING A SUDDEN ACCIDENT TO SEND THE CARRIAGE ROLLING ONTO ITS SIDE LIKE THAT.
WH-WHERE ARE MISTER PHAN-TOMHIVE AND HIS BUTLER?
DON'T LOOK AT ME!

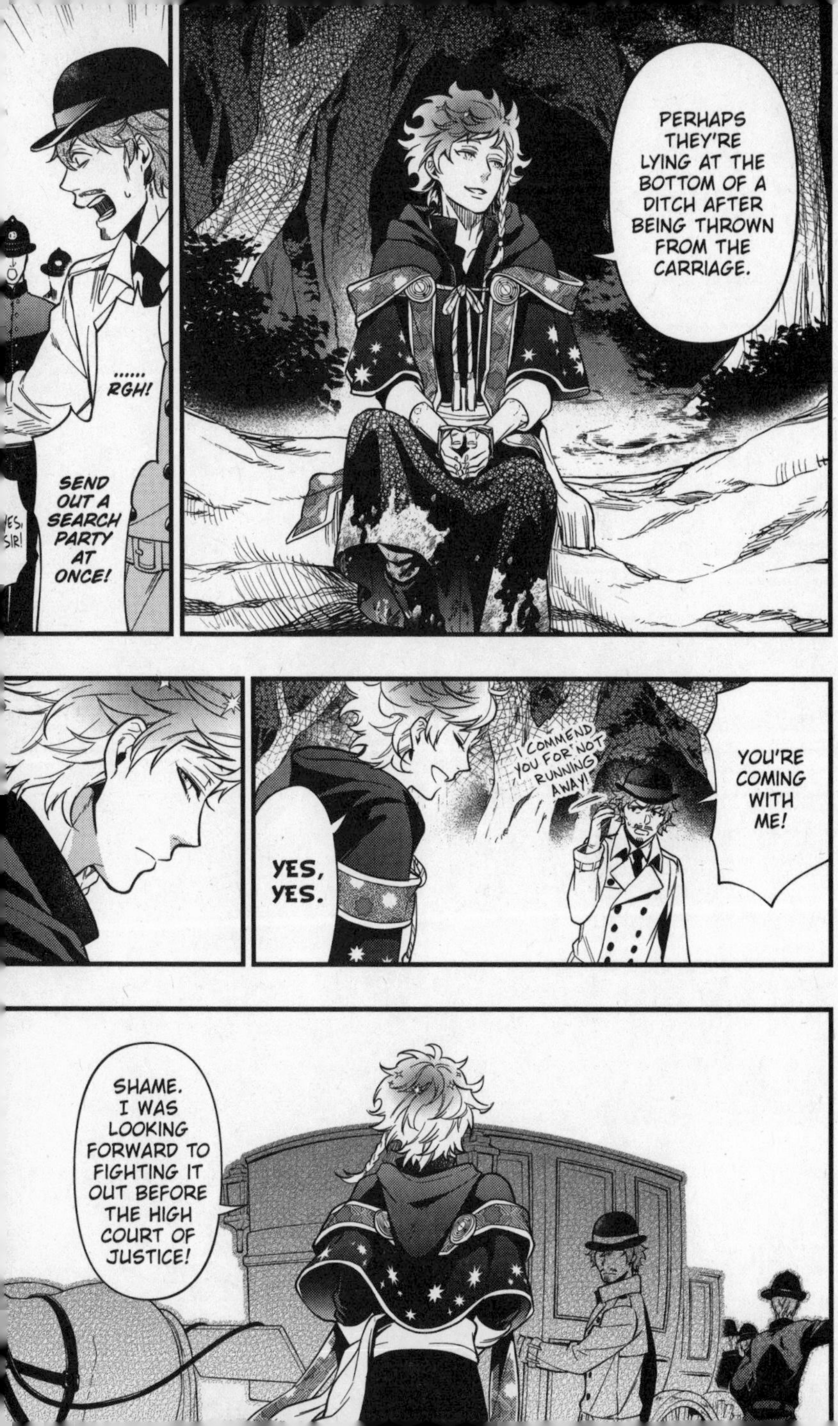
PERHAPS THEY'RE LYING AT THE BOTTOM OF A DITCH AFTER BEING THROWN FROM THE CARRIAGE.
......RGH!
SEND OUT A SEARCH PARTY AT ONCE!
YES, SIR!
YOU'RE COMING WITH ME!
I COMMEND YOU FOR NOT RUNNING AWAY!
YES, YES.
SHAME. I WAS LOOKING FORWARD TO FIGHTING IT OUT BEFORE THE HIGH COURT OF JUSTICE!

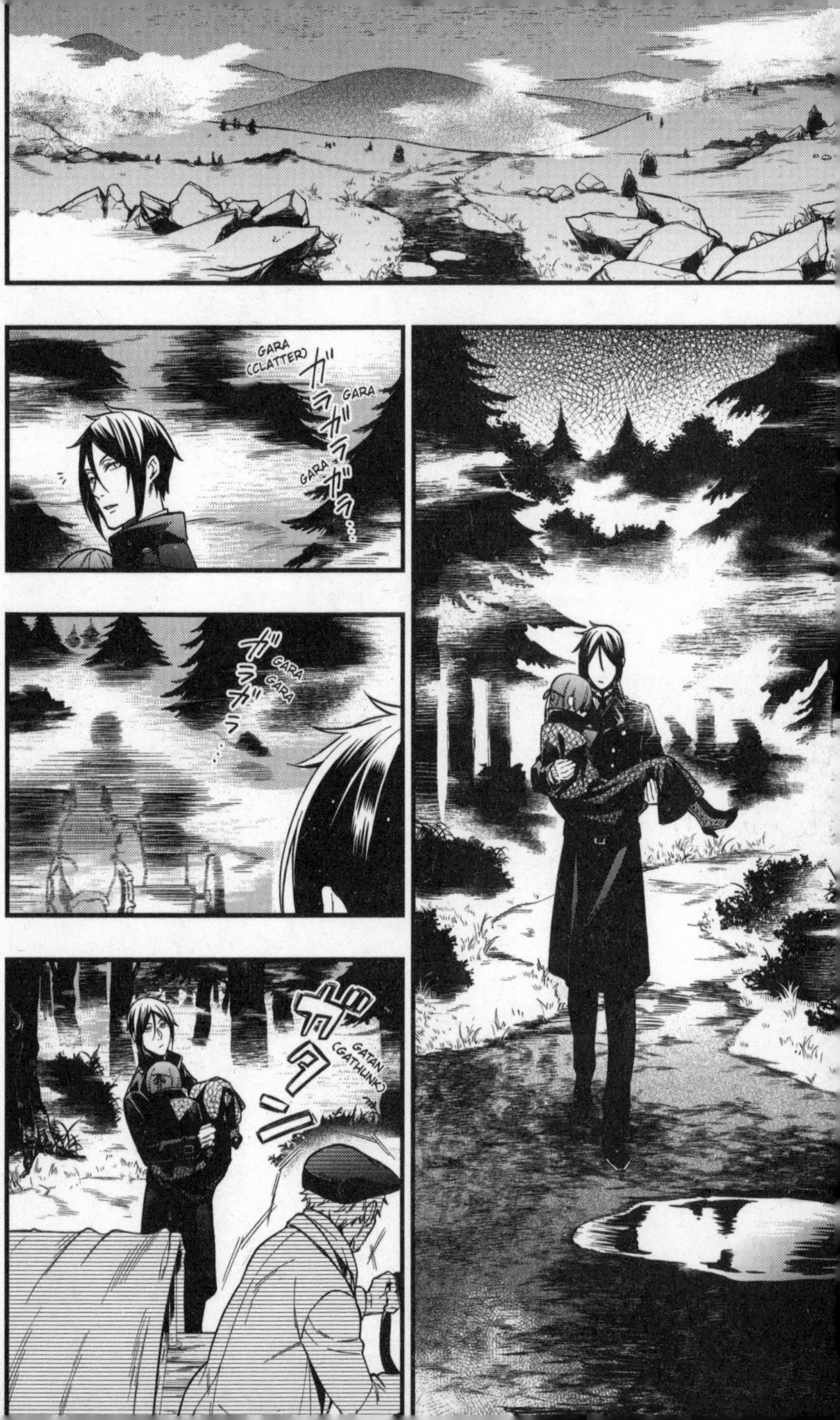
GARA (CLATTER)
GARA
GARA
GARA
GARA
GATAN (GATHUNK)

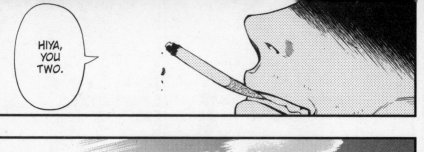

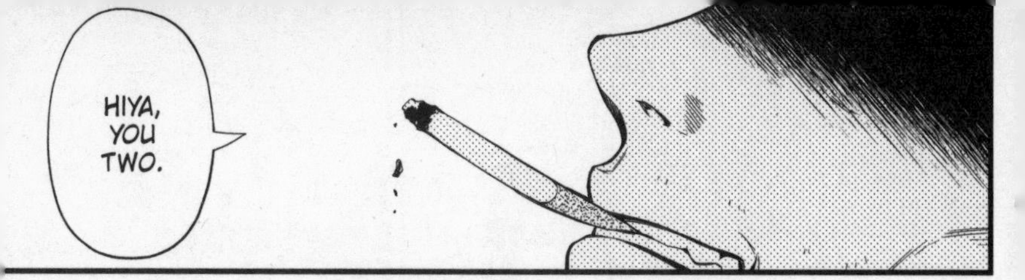
HIYA, YOU TWO.

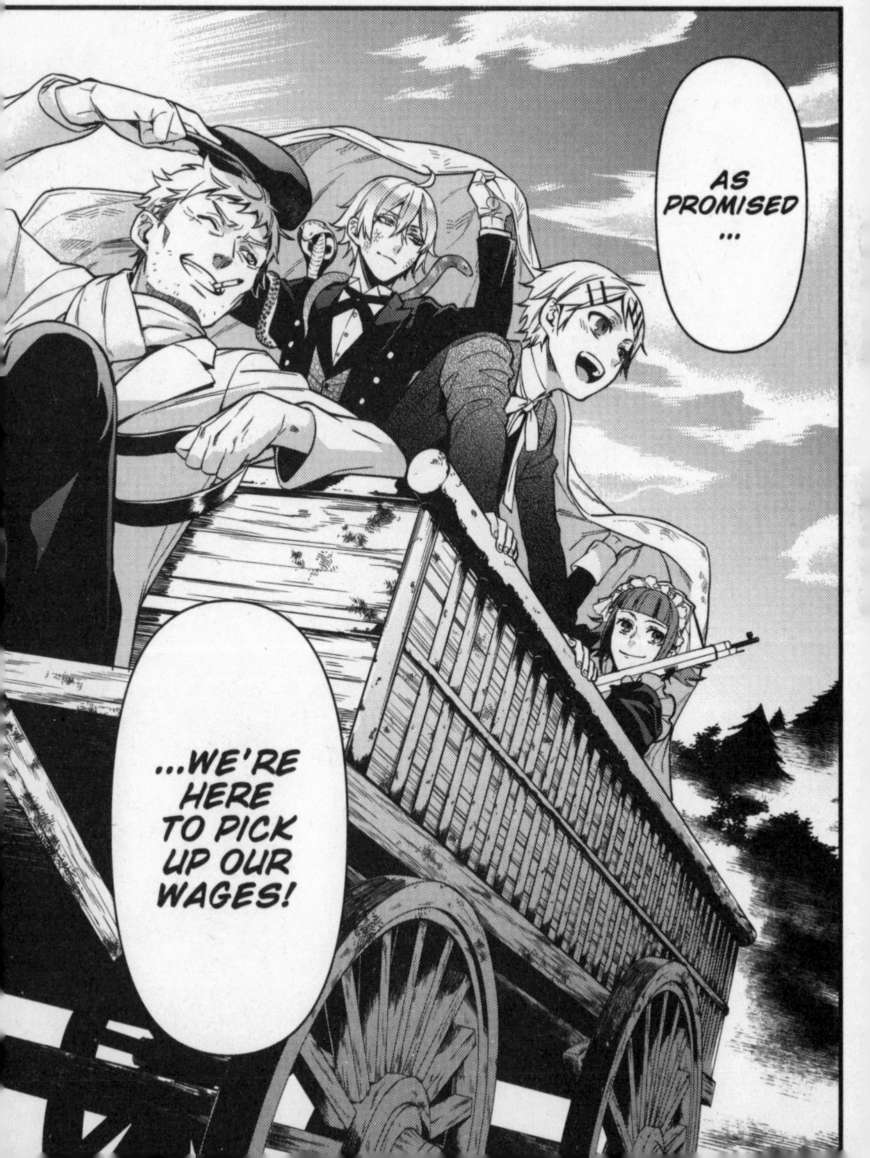
AS PROMISED...
...WE'RE HERE TO PICK UP OUR WAGES!

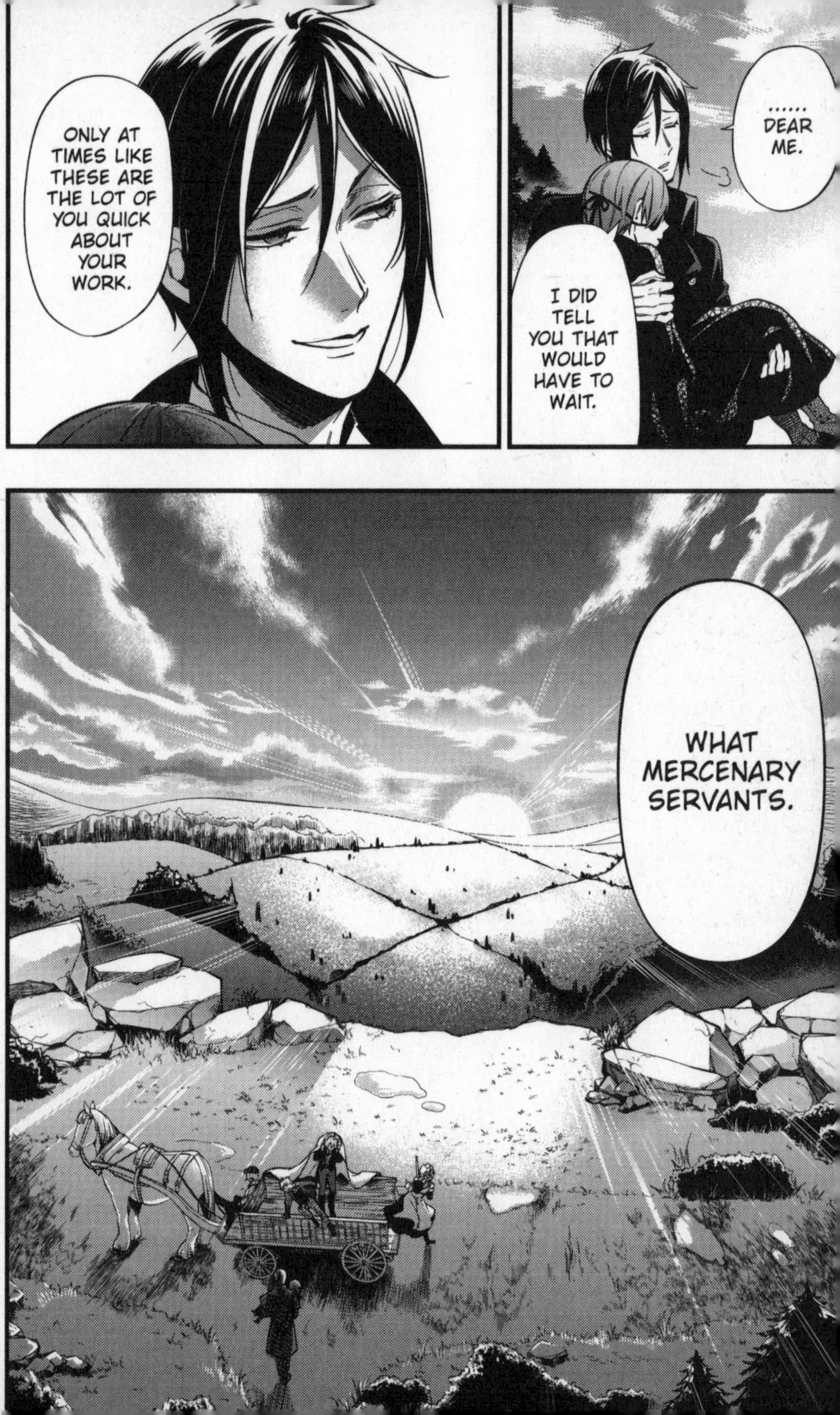
...... DEAR ME.
I DID TELL YOU THAT WOULD HAVE TO WAIT.
ONLY AT TIMES LIKE THESE ARE THE LOT OF YOU QUICK ABOUT YOUR WORK.
WHAT MERCENARY SERVANTS.

Black Butler

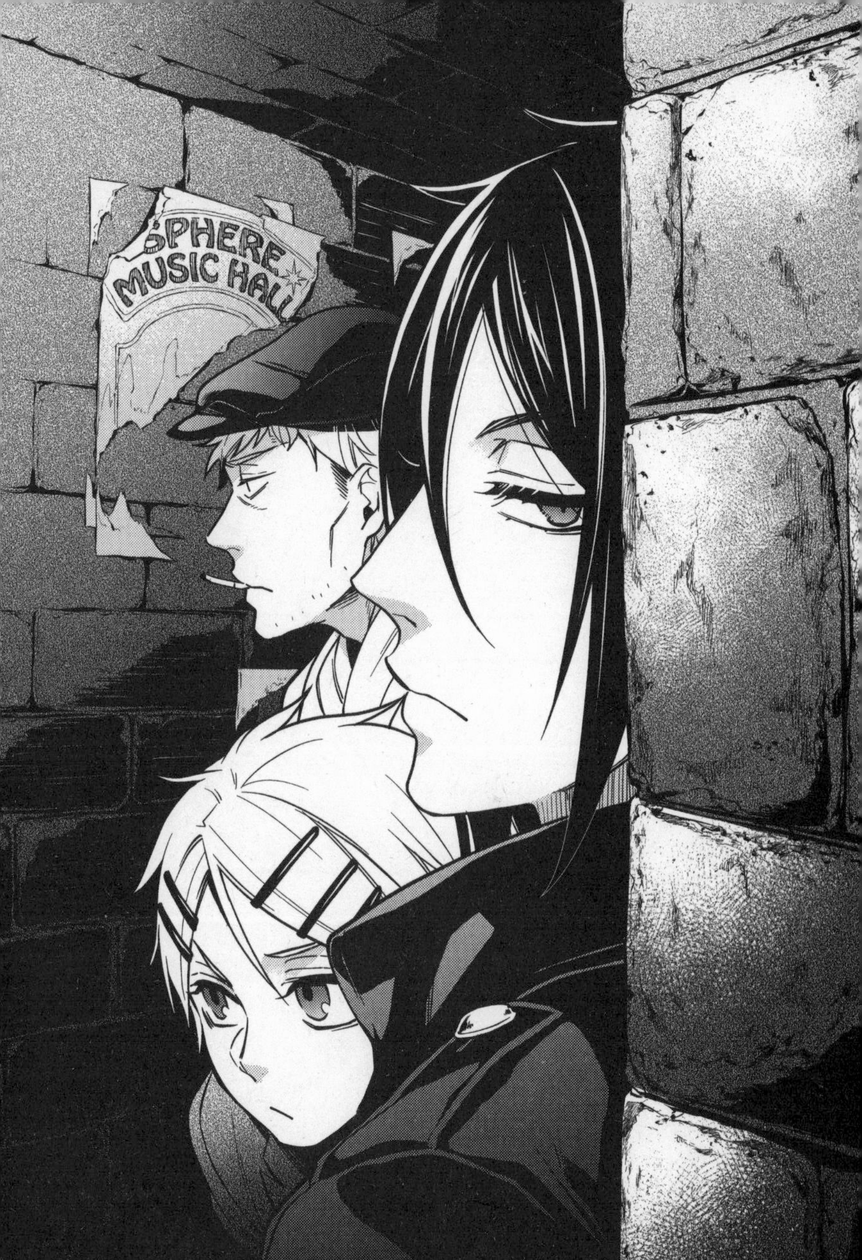
SPHERE MUSIC HALL

Chapter 146
At night: The Butler, On the Run

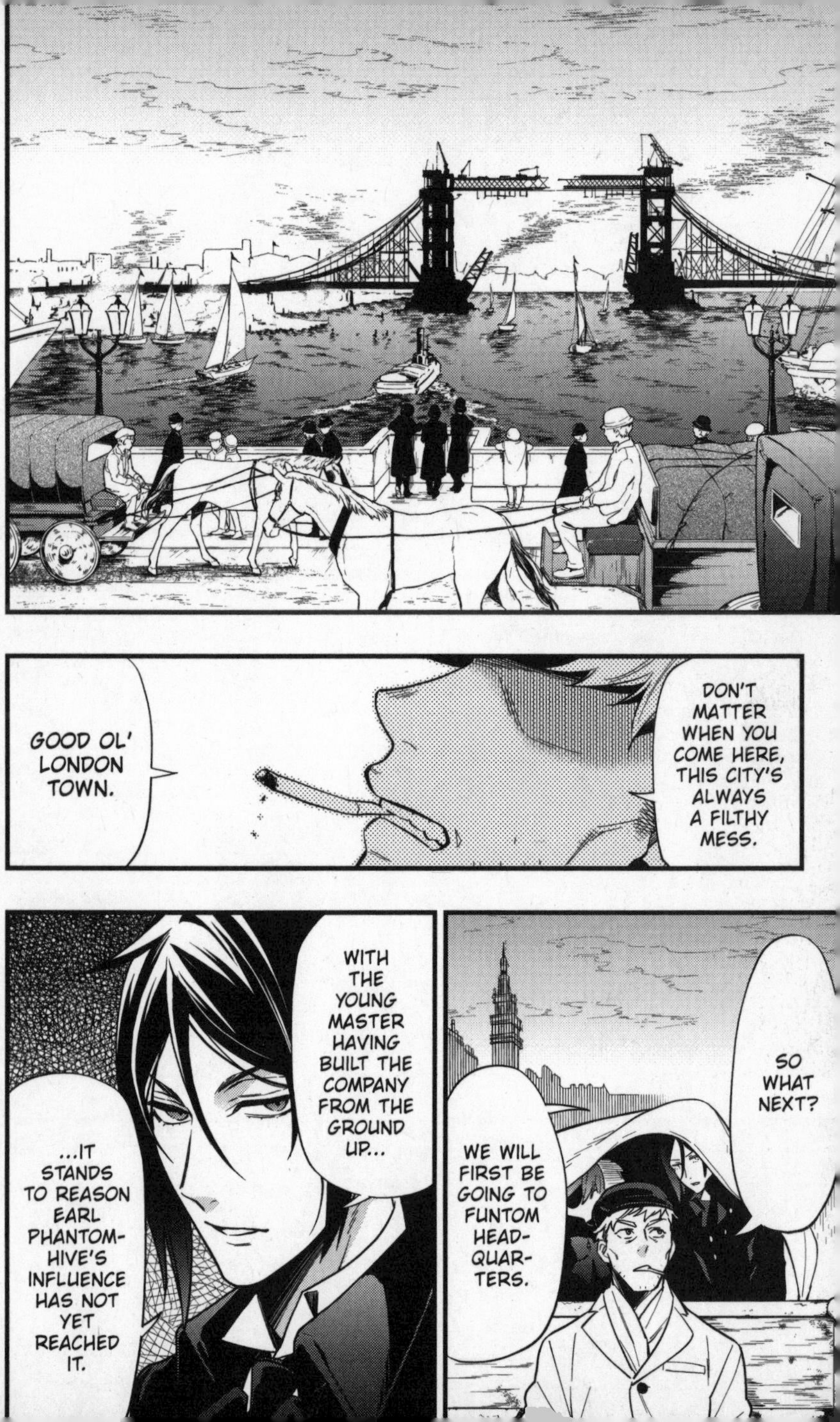
DON'T MATTER WHEN YOU COME HERE, THIS CITY'S ALWAYS A FILTHY MESS.
GOOD OL' LONDON TOWN.
SO WHAT NEXT?
WE WILL FIRST BE GOING TO FUNTOM HEAD-QUAR-TERS.
WITH THE YOUNG MASTER HAVING BUILT THE COMPANY FROM THE GROUND UP...
...IT STANDS TO REASON EARL PHANTOM-HIVE'S INFLUENCE HAS NOT YET REACHED IT.

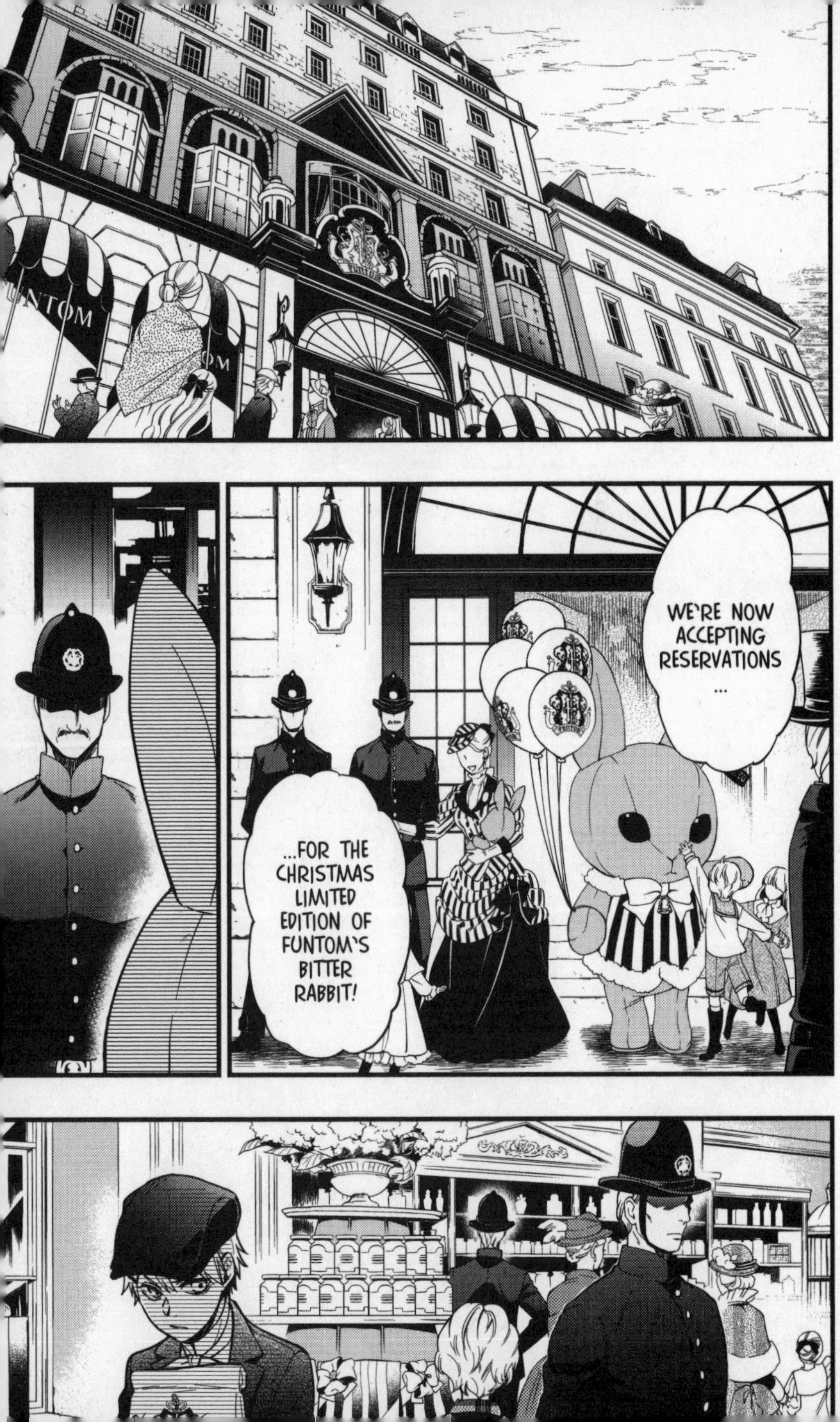
WE'RE NOW ACCEPTING RESERVATIONS ...
...FOR THE CHRISTMAS LIMITED EDITION OF FUNTOM'S BITTER RABBIT!

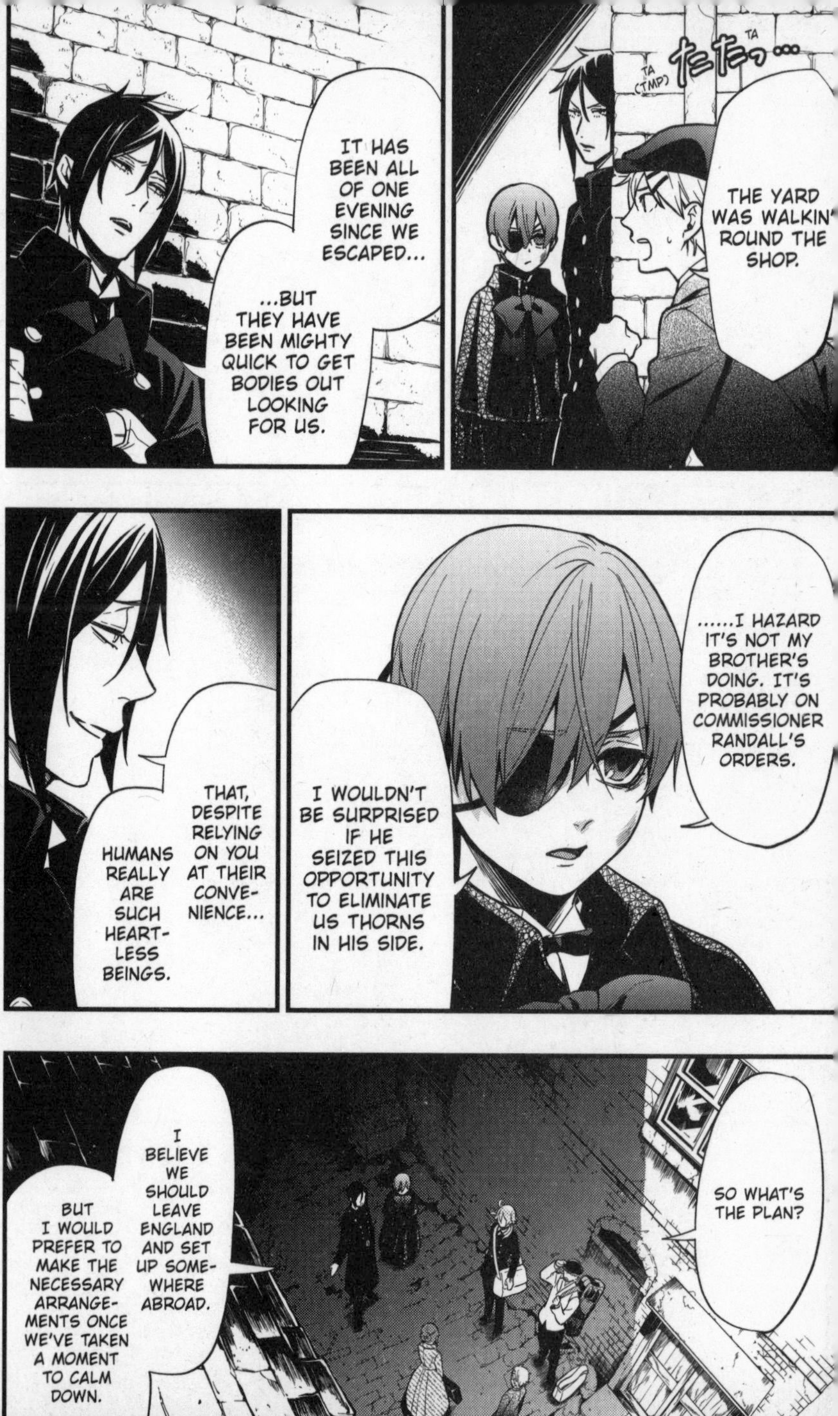
たたっ…
TA TA (TMP)
THE YARD WAS WALKIN' ROUND THE SHOP.
IT HAS BEEN ALL OF ONE EVENING SINCE WE ESCAPED...
...BUT THEY HAVE BEEN MIGHTY QUICK TO GET BODIES OUT LOOKING FOR US.
......I HAZARD IT'S NOT MY BROTHER'S DOING. IT'S PROBABLY ON COMMISSIONER RANDALL'S ORDERS.
I WOULDN'T BE SURPRISED IF HE SEIZED THIS OPPORTUNITY TO ELIMINATE US THORNS IN HIS SIDE.
THAT, DESPITE RELYING ON YOU AT THEIR CONVE-NIENCE...
HUMANS REALLY ARE SUCH HEART-LESS BEINGS.
SO WHAT'S THE PLAN?
I BELIEVE WE SHOULD LEAVE ENGLAND AND SET UP SOME-WHERE ABROAD.
BUT I WOULD PREFER TO MAKE THE NECESSARY ARRANGE-MENTS ONCE WE'VE TAKEN A MOMENT TO CALM DOWN.

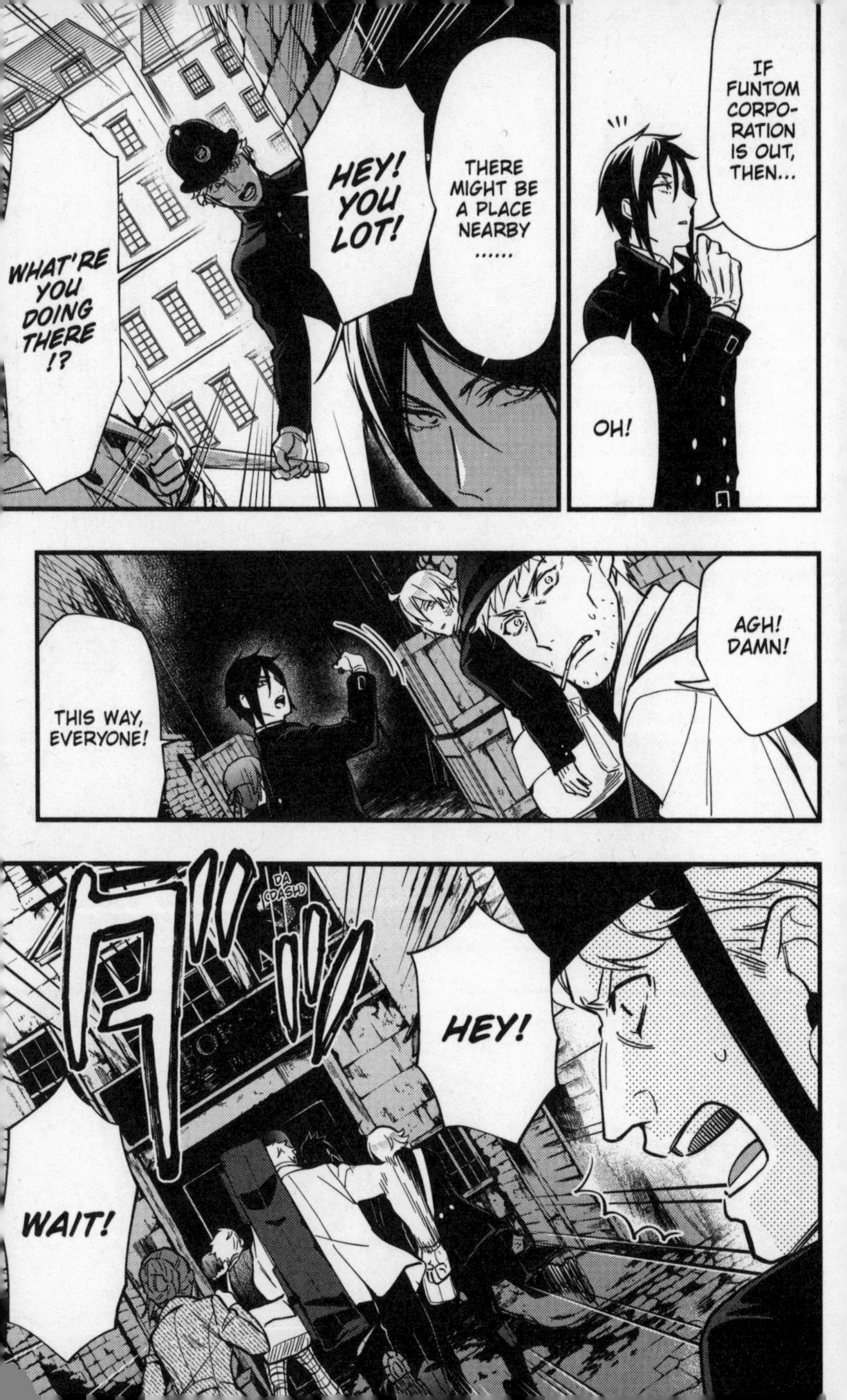
IF FUNTOM CORPORATION IS OUT, THEN...
OH!
THERE MIGHT BE A PLACE NEARBY ......
HEY! YOU LOT!
WHAT'RE YOU DOING THERE!?
AGH! DAMN!
THIS WAY, EVERYONE!
DA (DASH)
HEY!
WAIT!

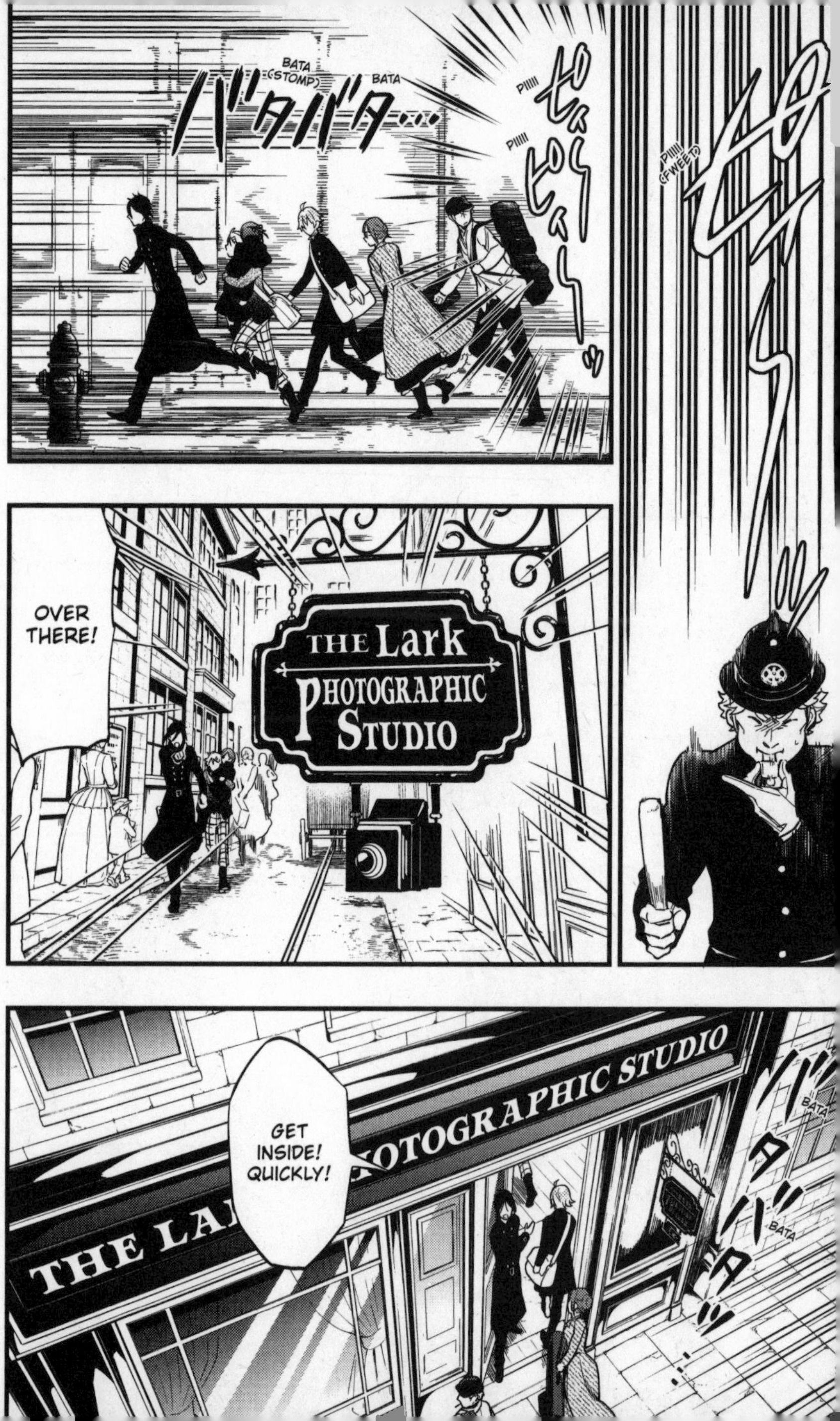
PIIIII (FWEET)
PIIIII
PIIIII
BATA (STOMP)
BATA
OVER THERE!
THE Lark PHOTOGRAPHIC STUDIO
BATA
BATA
GET INSIDE! QUICKLY!

THE LARK

PHOTOGRAPHIC STUDIO

THEY RAN DOWN A BACK ALLEY!

AFTER 'EM!

BATA BATA BATA

バタバタバタ

PHOTOGRAPHIC STUDIO

PHEW...!

しほっ・・・。

BASHA (FLASH)

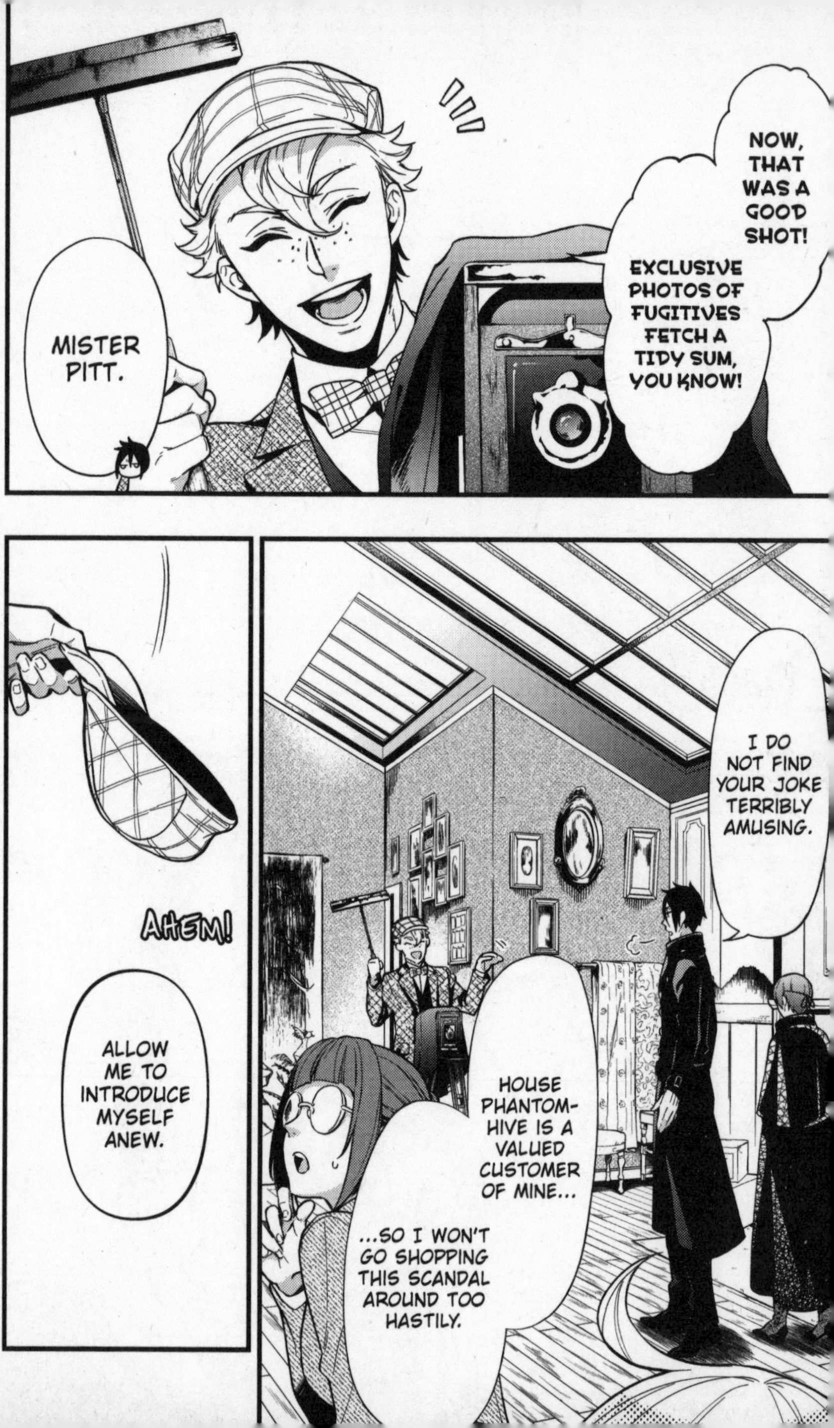
NOW, THAT WAS A GOOD SHOT!
EXCLUSIVE PHOTOS OF FUGITIVES FETCH A TIDY SUM, YOU KNOW!
MISTER PITT.
I DO NOT FIND YOUR JOKE TERRIBLY AMUSING.
HOUSE PHANTOM-HIVE IS A VALUED CUSTOMER OF MINE...
...SO I WON'T GO SHOPPING THIS SCANDAL AROUND TOO HASTILY.
AHEM!
ALLOW ME TO INTRODUCE MYSELF ANEW.

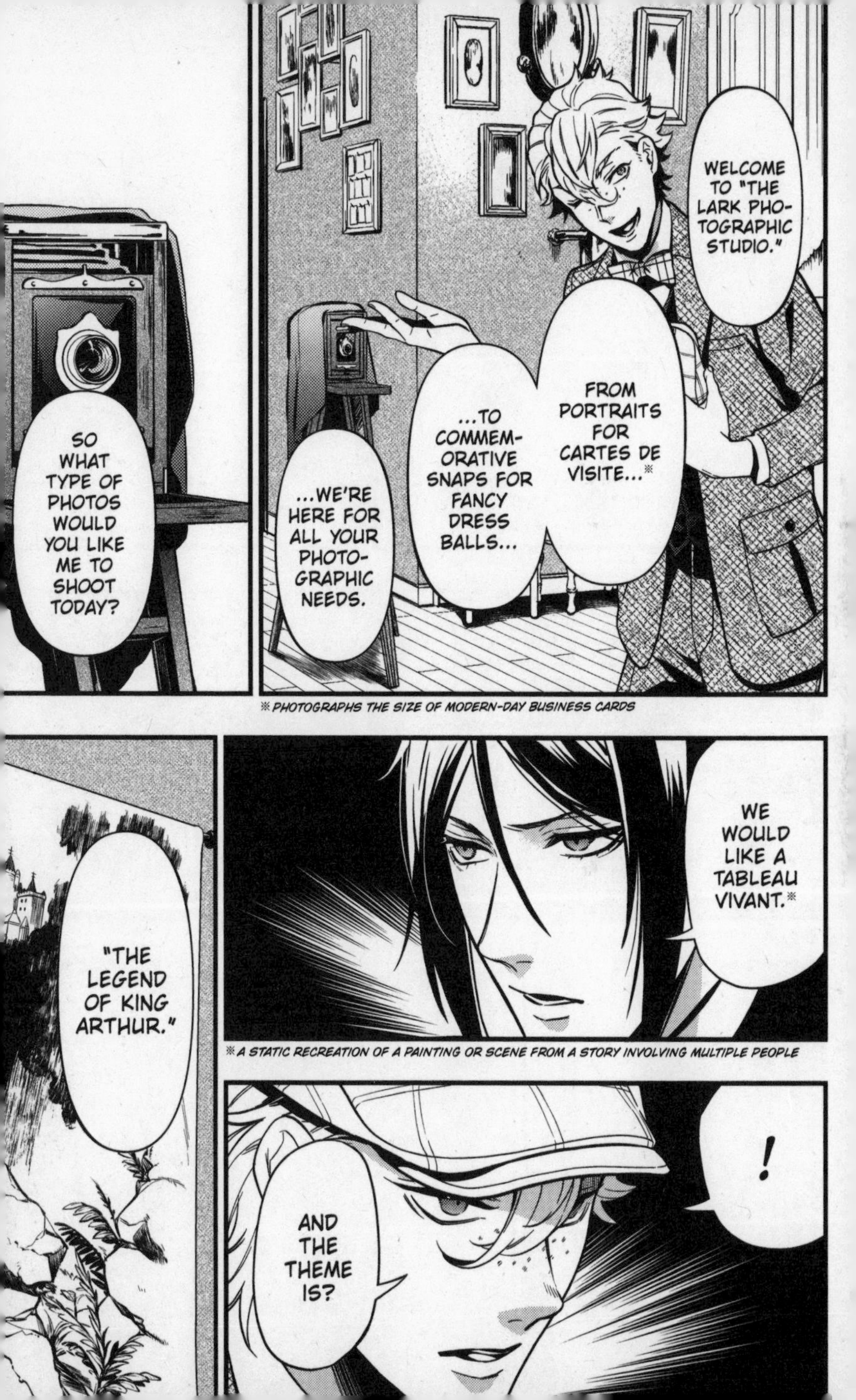
WELCOME TO "THE LARK PHOTOGRAPHIC STUDIO."
FROM PORTRAITS FOR CARTES DE VISITE...※
...TO COMMEMORATIVE SNAPS FOR FANCY DRESS BALLS...
...WE'RE HERE FOR ALL YOUR PHOTOGRAPHIC NEEDS.
SO WHAT TYPE OF PHOTOS WOULD YOU LIKE ME TO SHOOT TODAY?
WE WOULD LIKE A TABLEAU VIVANT.※
!
AND THE THEME IS?
"THE LEGEND OF KING ARTHUR."
※ PHOTOGRAPHS THE SIZE OF MODERN-DAY BUSINESS CARDS

※ A STATIC RECREATION OF A PAINTING OR SCENE FROM A STORY INVOLVING MULTIPLE PEOPLE

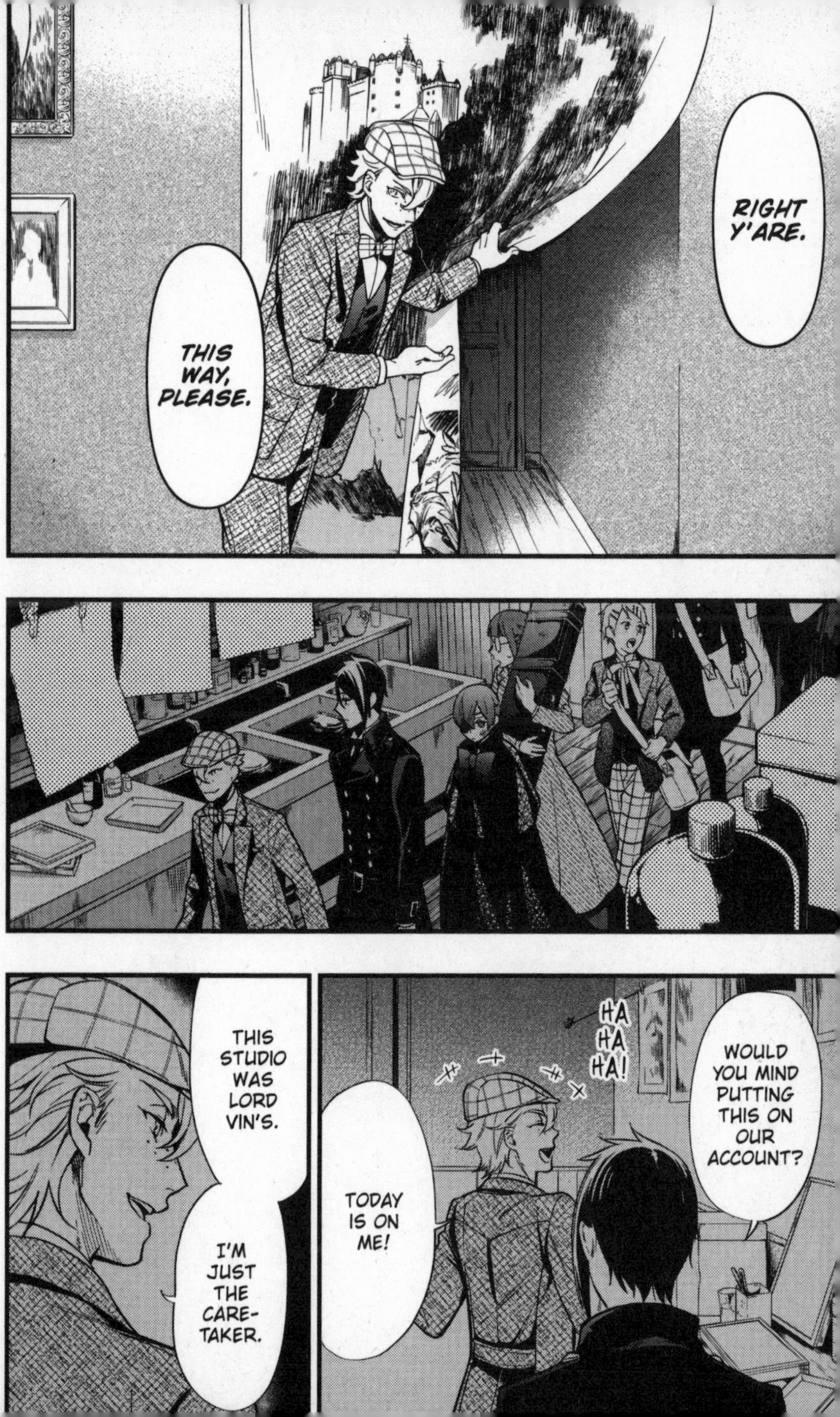
RIGHT Y'ARE.
THIS WAY, PLEASE.
WOULD YOU MIND PUTTING THIS ON OUR ACCOUNT?
HA HA HA!
TODAY IS ON ME!
THIS STUDIO WAS LORD VIN'S.
I'M JUST THE CARE-TAKER.

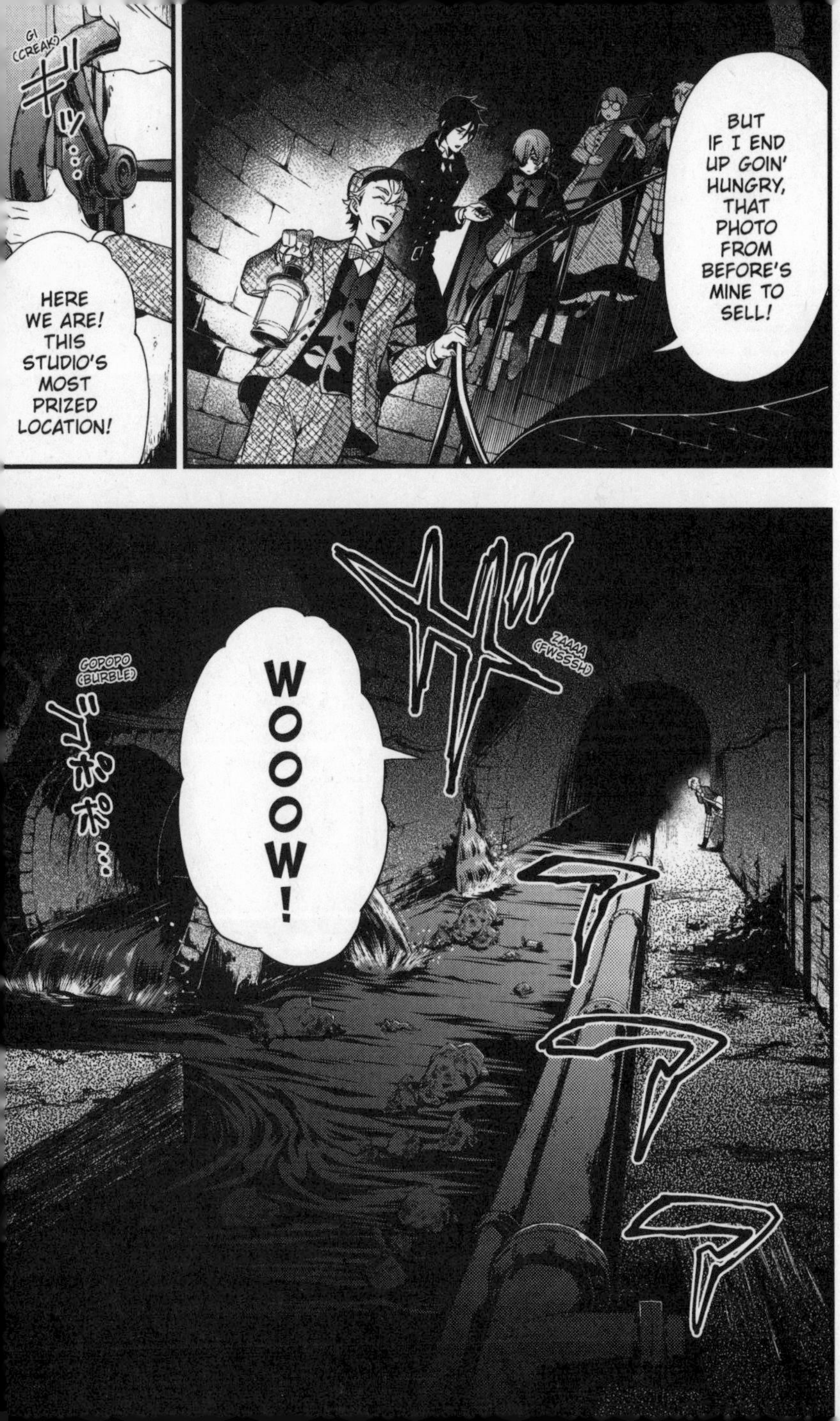
BUT IF I END UP GOIN' HUNGRY, THAT PHOTO FROM BEFORE'S MINE TO SELL!
GI (CREAK)
HERE WE ARE! THIS STUDIO'S MOST PRIZED LOCATION!
ZAAAA (FWSSSH)
WOOOW!
GOPOPO (BURBLE)

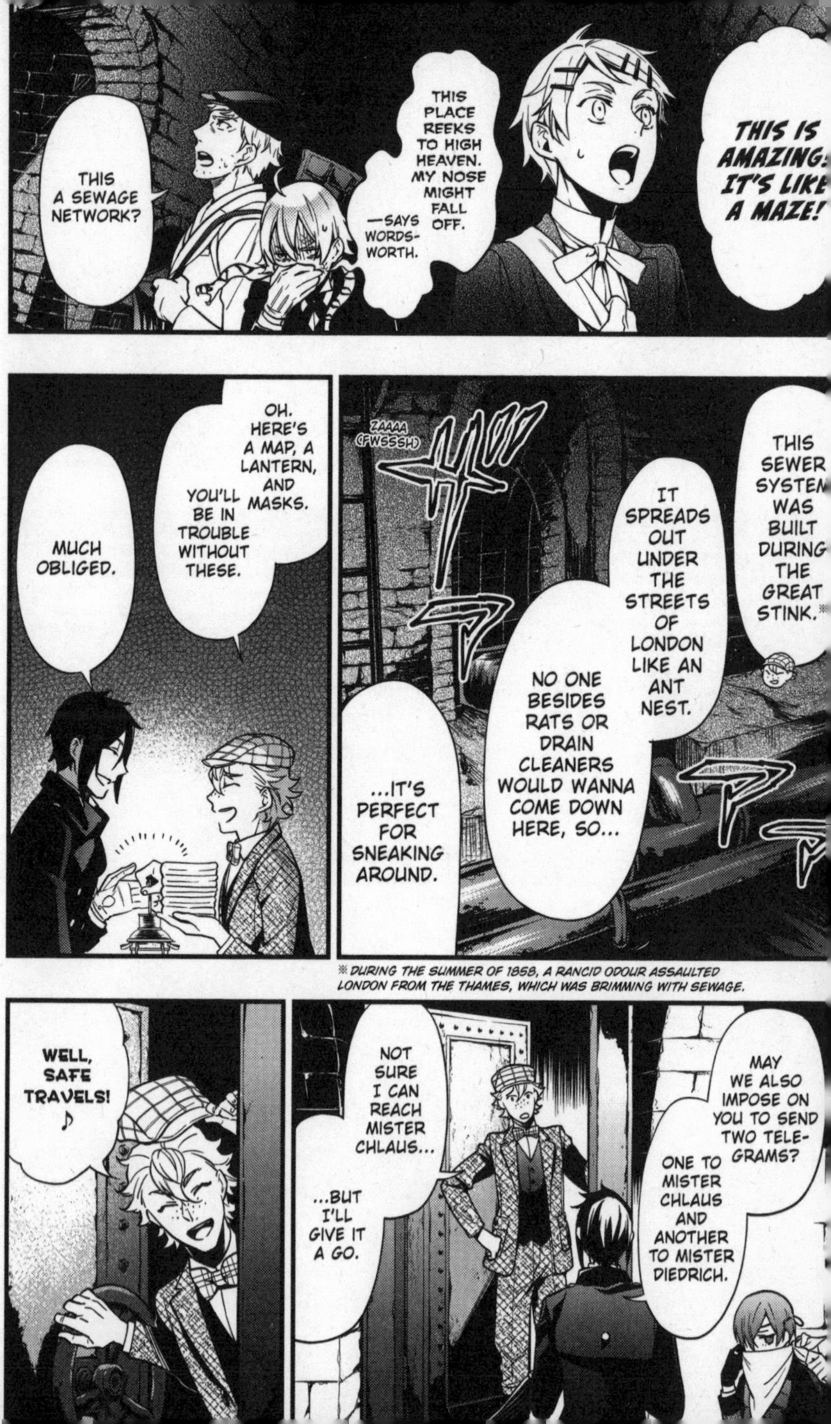
THIS IS AMAZING! IT'S LIKE A MAZE!
THIS PLACE REEKS TO HIGH HEAVEN. MY NOSE MIGHT FALL OFF.
—SAYS WORDSWORTH.
THIS A SEWAGE NETWORK?
THIS SEWER SYSTEM WAS BUILT DURING THE GREAT STINK.※
IT SPREADS OUT UNDER THE STREETS OF LONDON LIKE AN ANT NEST.
NO ONE BESIDES RATS OR DRAIN CLEANERS WOULD WANNA COME DOWN HERE, SO...
...IT'S PERFECT FOR SNEAKING AROUND.
ZAAAA (FWSSSH)
OH. HERE'S A MAP, A LANTERN, AND MASKS.
YOU'LL BE IN TROUBLE WITHOUT THESE.
MUCH OBLIGED.
MAY WE ALSO IMPOSE ON YOU TO SEND TWO TELEGRAMS?
ONE TO MISTER CHLAUS AND ANOTHER TO MISTER DIEDRICH.
NOT SURE I CAN REACH MISTER CHLAUS...
...BUT I'LL GIVE IT A GO.
WELL, SAFE TRAVELS! ♪

※ *DURING THE SUMMER OF 1858, A RANCID ODOUR ASSAULTED LONDON FROM THE THAMES, WHICH WAS BRIMMING WITH SEWAGE.*

OOO
(WHOOSH)

LET US
CONTINUE
ONWARD.

オオオ...

KACHI
CKACHAK)

FREEZE.

♪

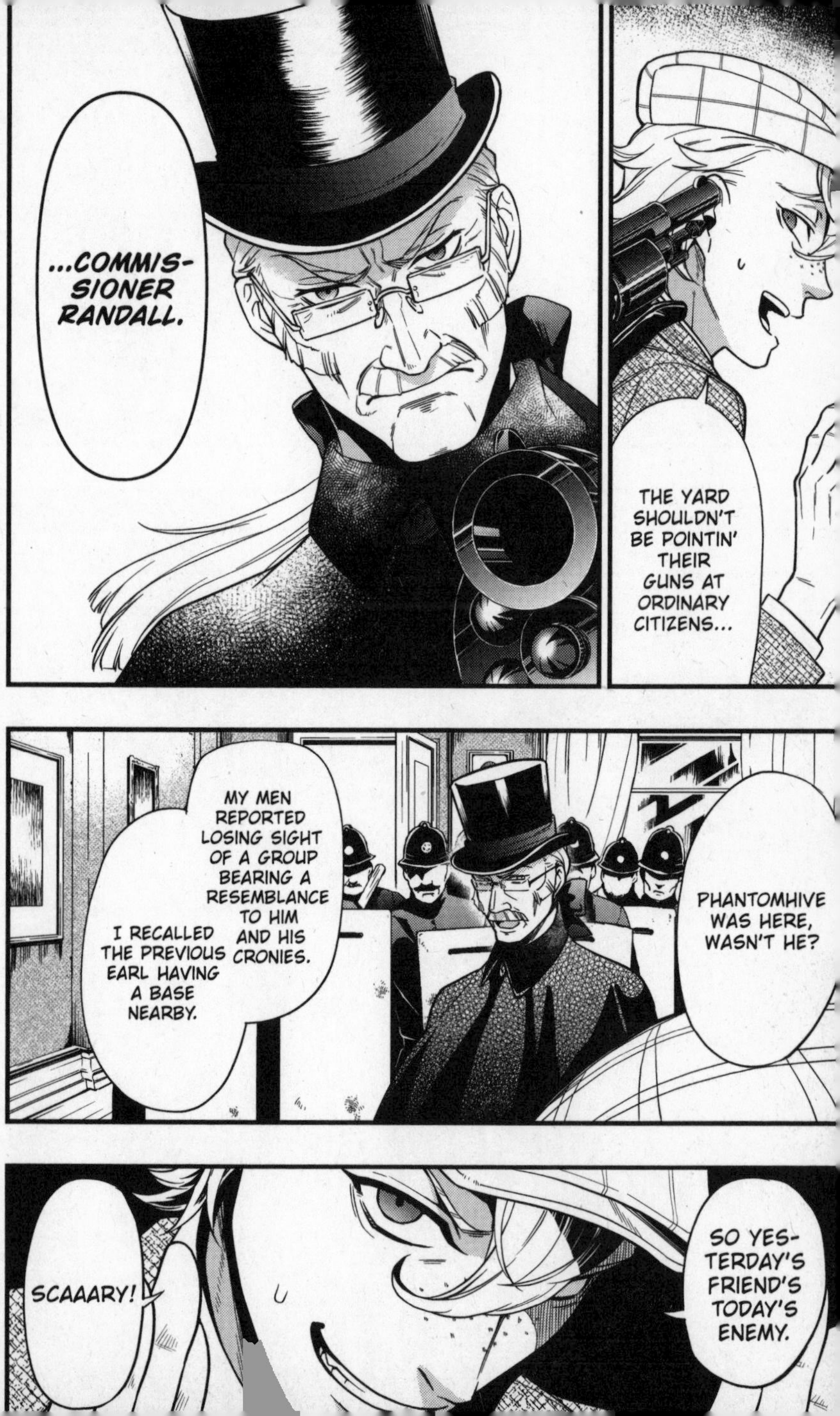
THE YARD SHOULDN'T BE POINTIN' THEIR GUNS AT ORDINARY CITIZENS...
...COMMISSIONER RANDALL.
PHANTOMHIVE WAS HERE, WASN'T HE?
MY MEN REPORTED LOSING SIGHT OF A GROUP BEARING A RESEMBLANCE TO HIM AND HIS CRONIES.
I RECALLED THE PREVIOUS EARL HAVING A BASE NEARBY.
SO YESTERDAY'S FRIEND'S TODAY'S ENEMY.
SCAAARY!

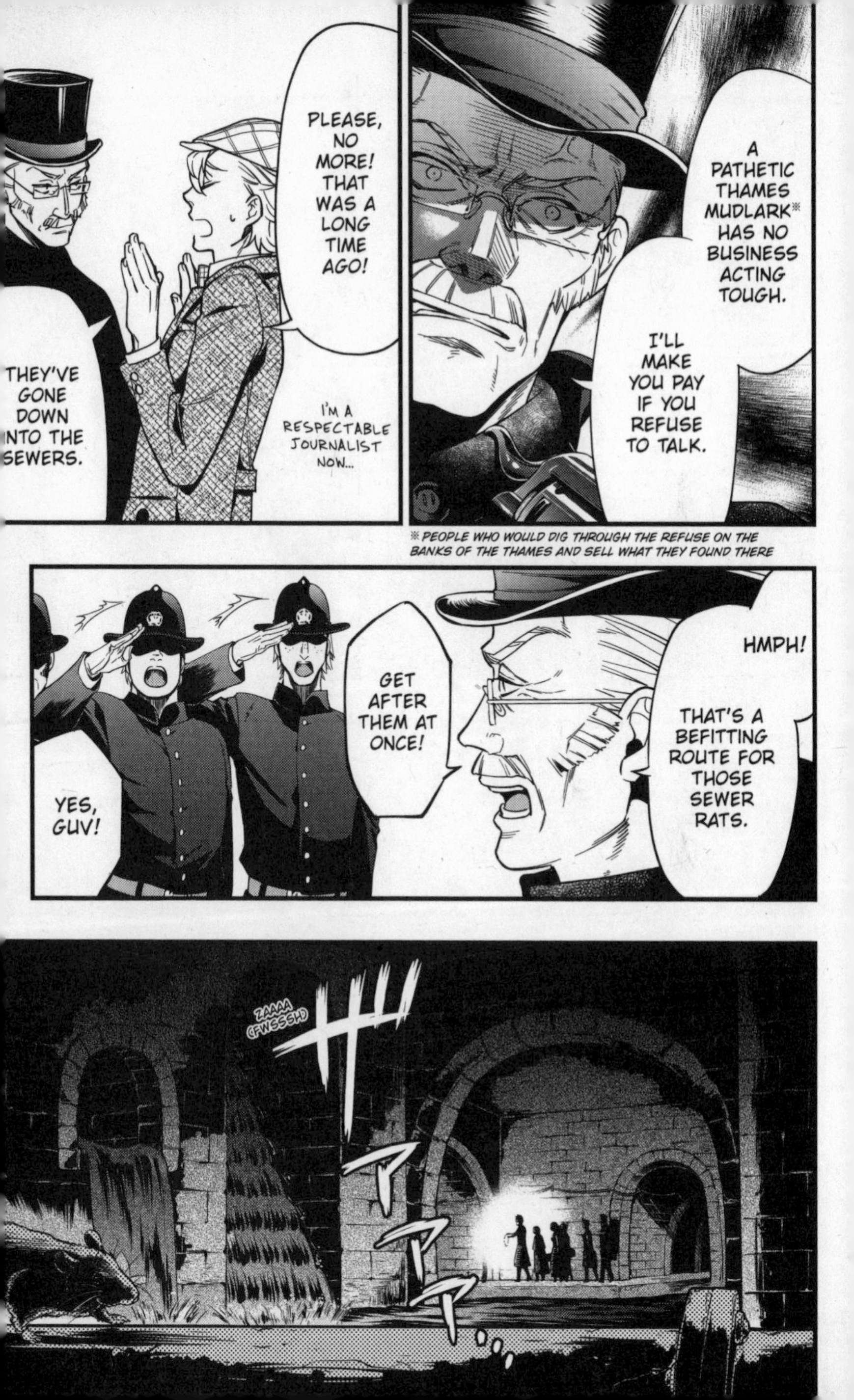
A PATHETIC THAMES MUDLARK※ HAS NO BUSINESS ACTING TOUGH.
I'LL MAKE YOU PAY IF YOU REFUSE TO TALK.
PLEASE, NO MORE! THAT WAS A LONG TIME AGO!
I'M A RESPECTABLE JOURNALIST NOW...
THEY'VE GONE DOWN INTO THE SEWERS.
HMPH!
THAT'S A BEFITTING ROUTE FOR THOSE SEWER RATS.
GET AFTER THEM AT ONCE!
YES, GUV!
ZAAAA (FWSSSH)

※ *PEOPLE WHO WOULD DIG THROUGH THE REFUSE ON THE BANKS OF THE THAMES AND SELL WHAT THEY FOUND THERE*

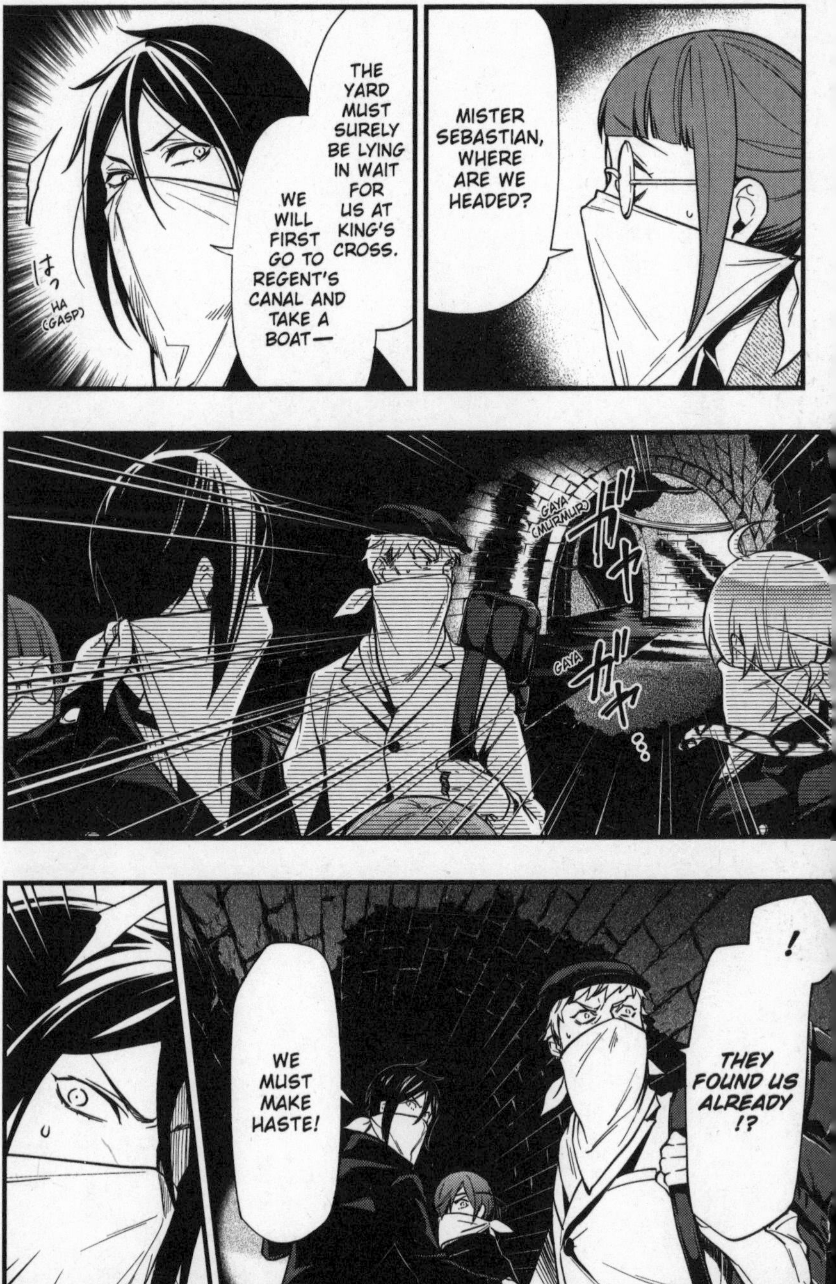
MISTER SEBASTIAN, WHERE ARE WE HEADED?
THE YARD MUST SURELY BE LYING IN WAIT FOR US AT KING'S CROSS.
WE WILL FIRST GO TO REGENT'S CANAL AND TAKE A BOAT—
はっ
HA (GASP)
ガヤ
GAYA (MURMUR)
ガヤ
GAYA
!
THEY FOUND US ALREADY!?
WE MUST MAKE HASTE!

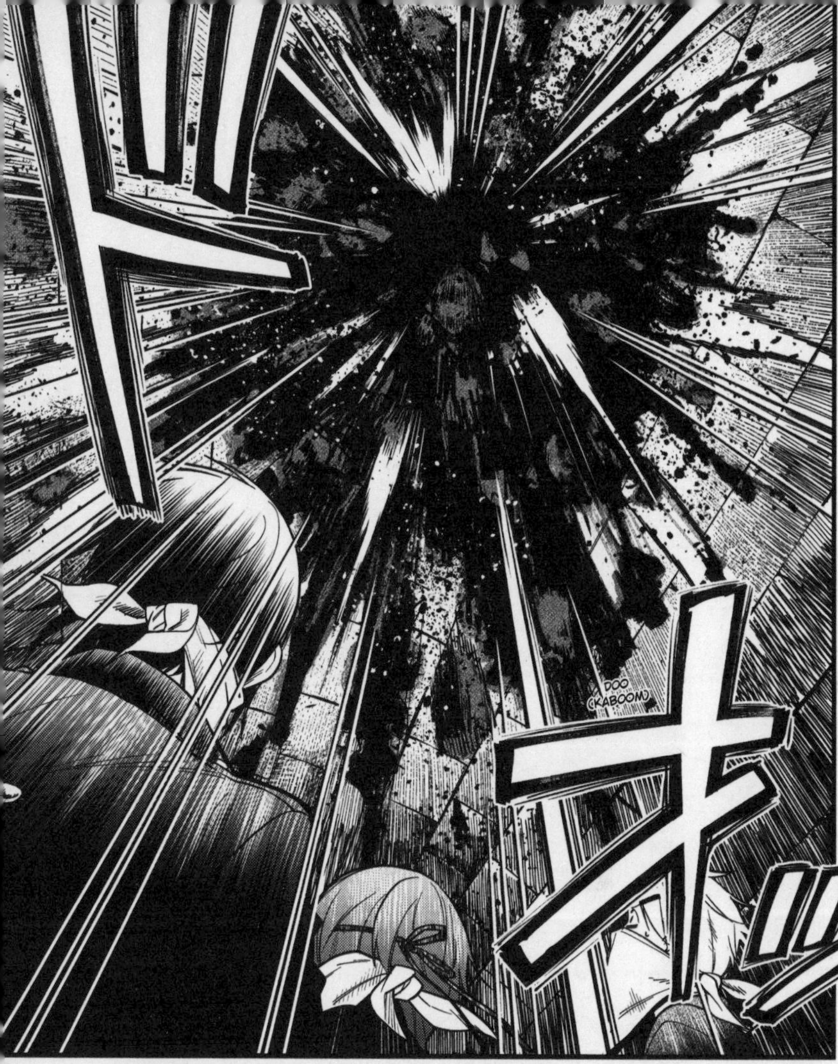
DOO
(KABOOM)

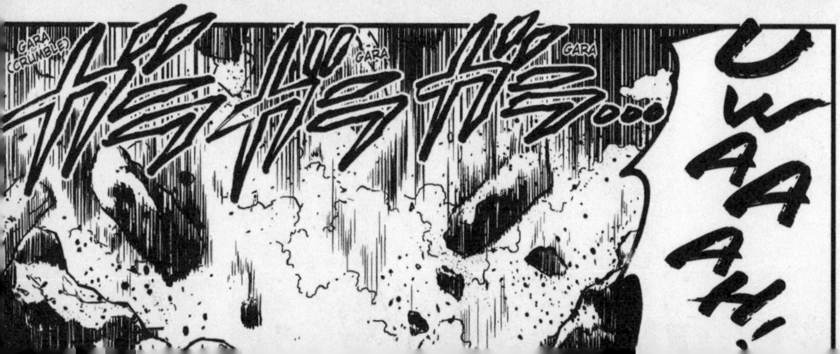
UWAAAAH!
GARA
GARA
GARA
(CRUMBLE)

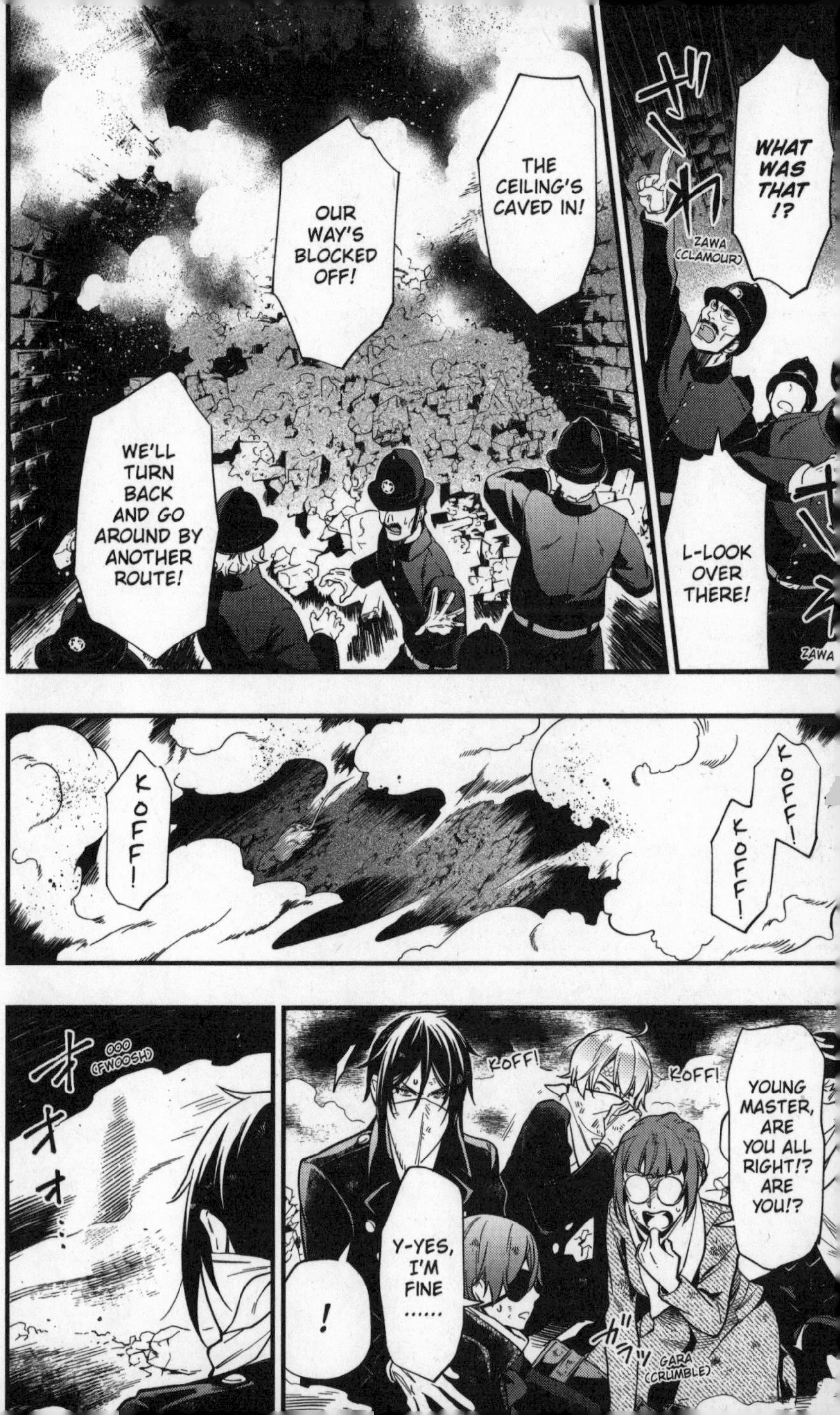
WHAT WAS THAT!?
ZAWA (CLAMOUR)
L-LOOK OVER THERE!
ZAWA
THE CEILING'S CAVED IN!
OUR WAY'S BLOCKED OFF!
WE'LL TURN BACK AND GO AROUND BY ANOTHER ROUTE!
KOFF! KOFF!
KOFF!
YOUNG MASTER, ARE YOU ALL RIGHT!? ARE YOU!?
KOFF!
KOFF!
Y-YES, I'M FINE ......
GARA (CRUMBLE)
!
OOO (FWOOSH)

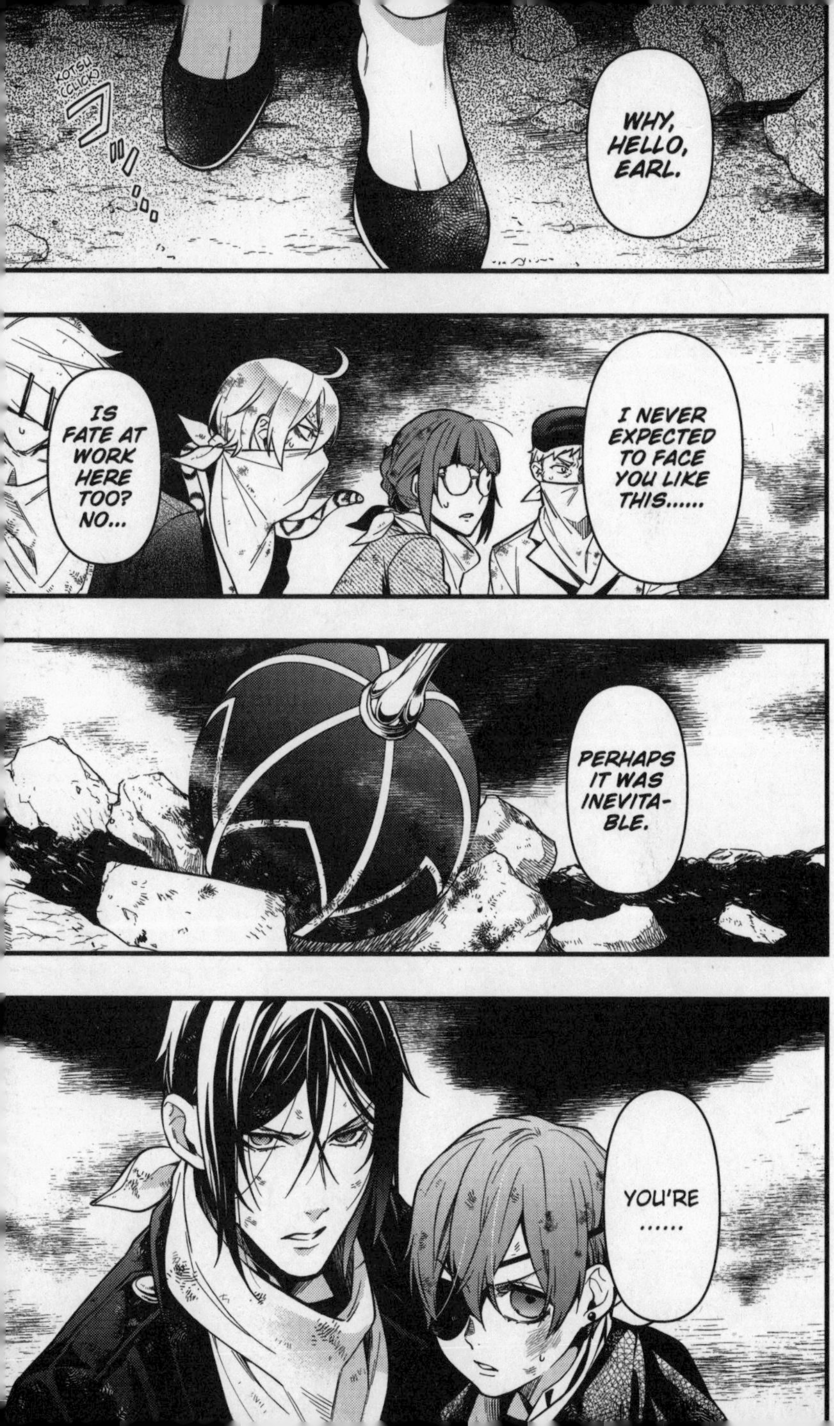
WHY, HELLO, EARL.
KOTSU (CLICK)
I NEVER EXPECTED TO FACE YOU LIKE THIS......
IS FATE AT WORK HERE TOO? NO...
PERHAPS IT WAS INEVITA-BLE.
YOU'RE ......

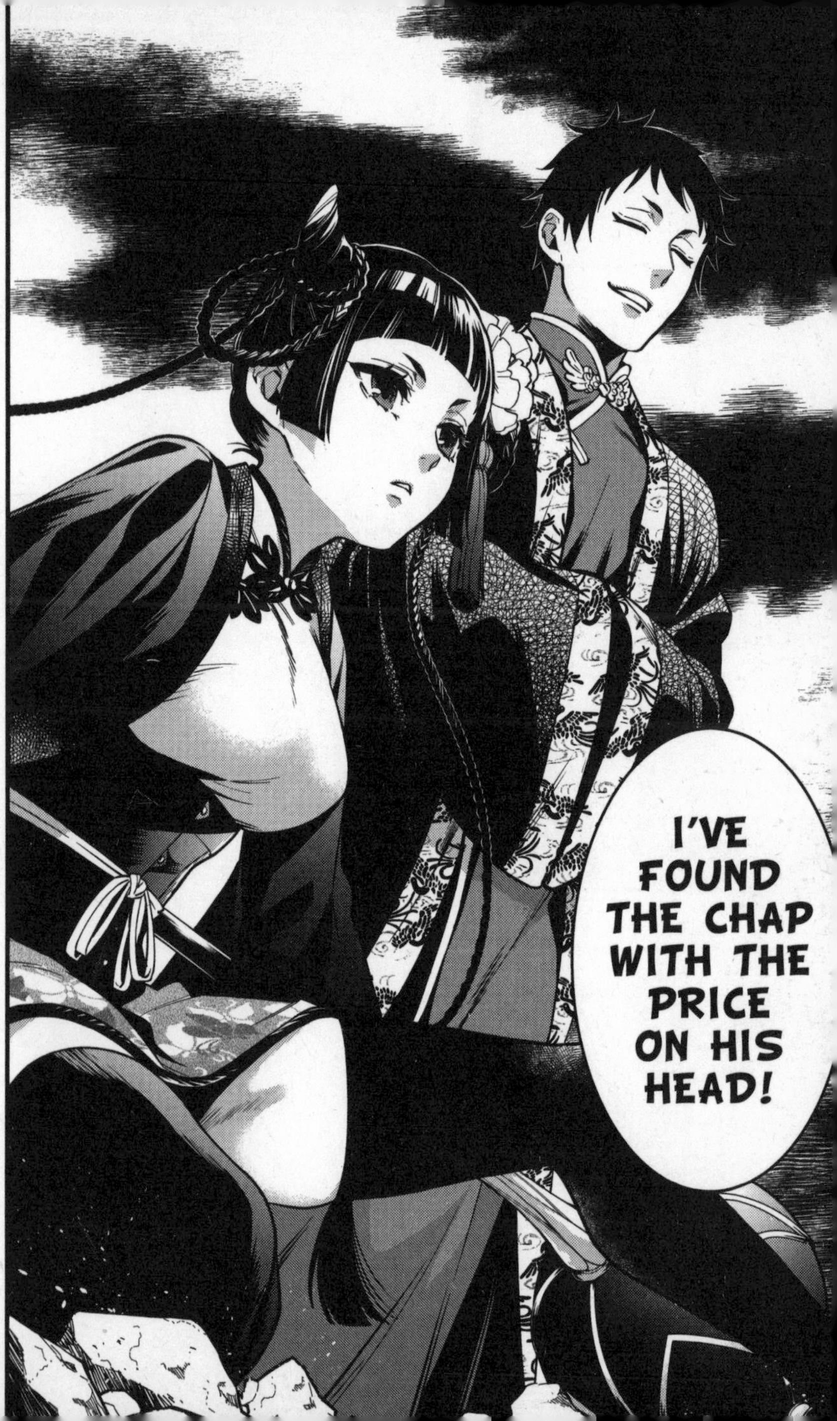
I'VE FOUND THE CHAP WITH THE PRICE ON HIS HEAD!

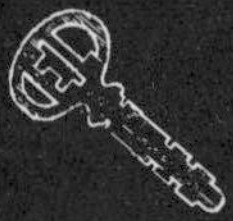

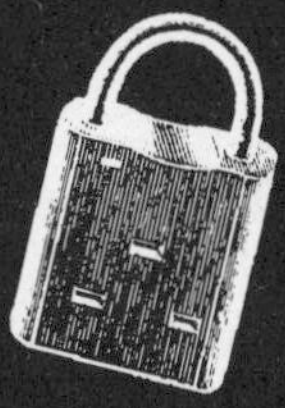

Black Butler

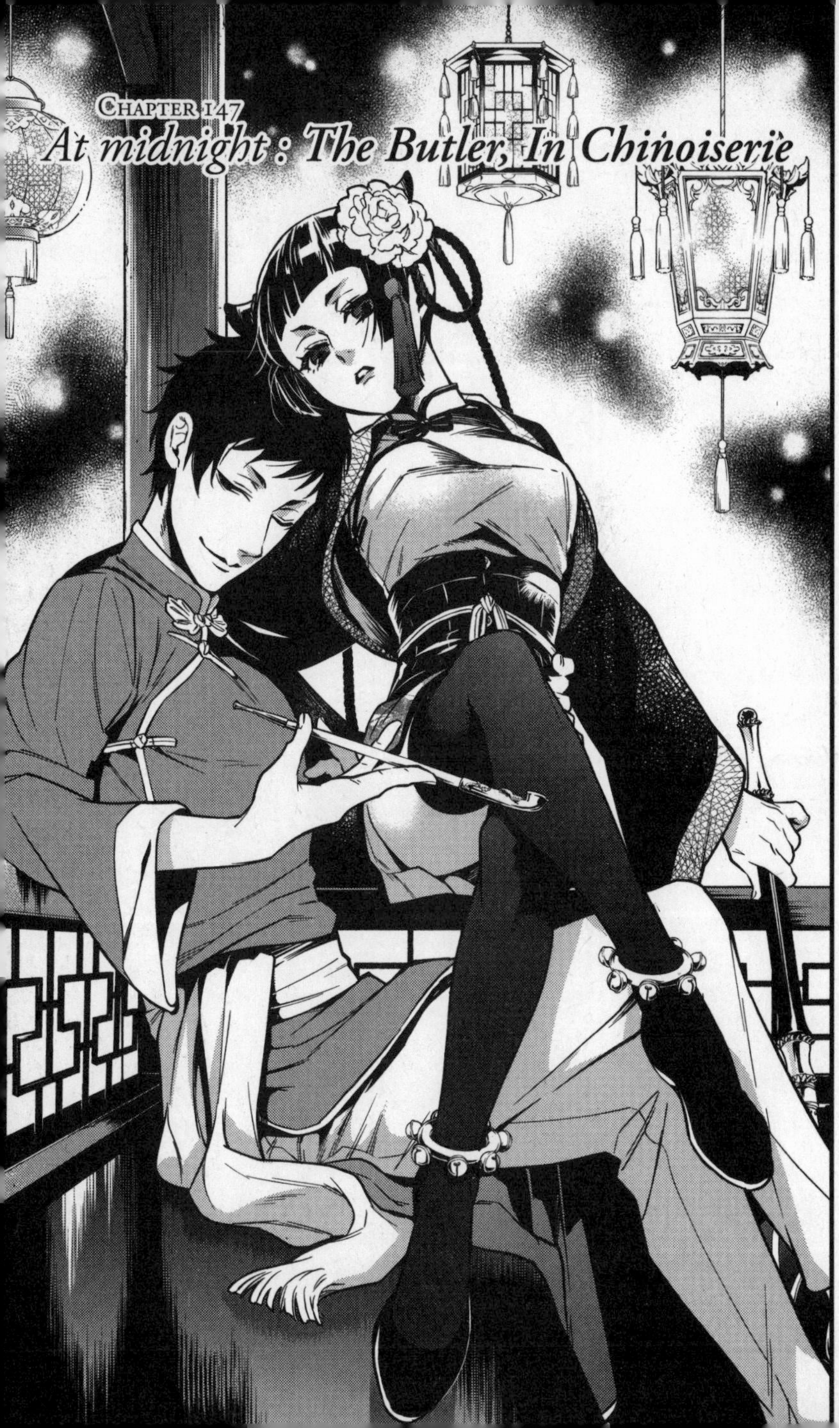
Chapter 147
At midnight : The Butler, In Chinoiserie

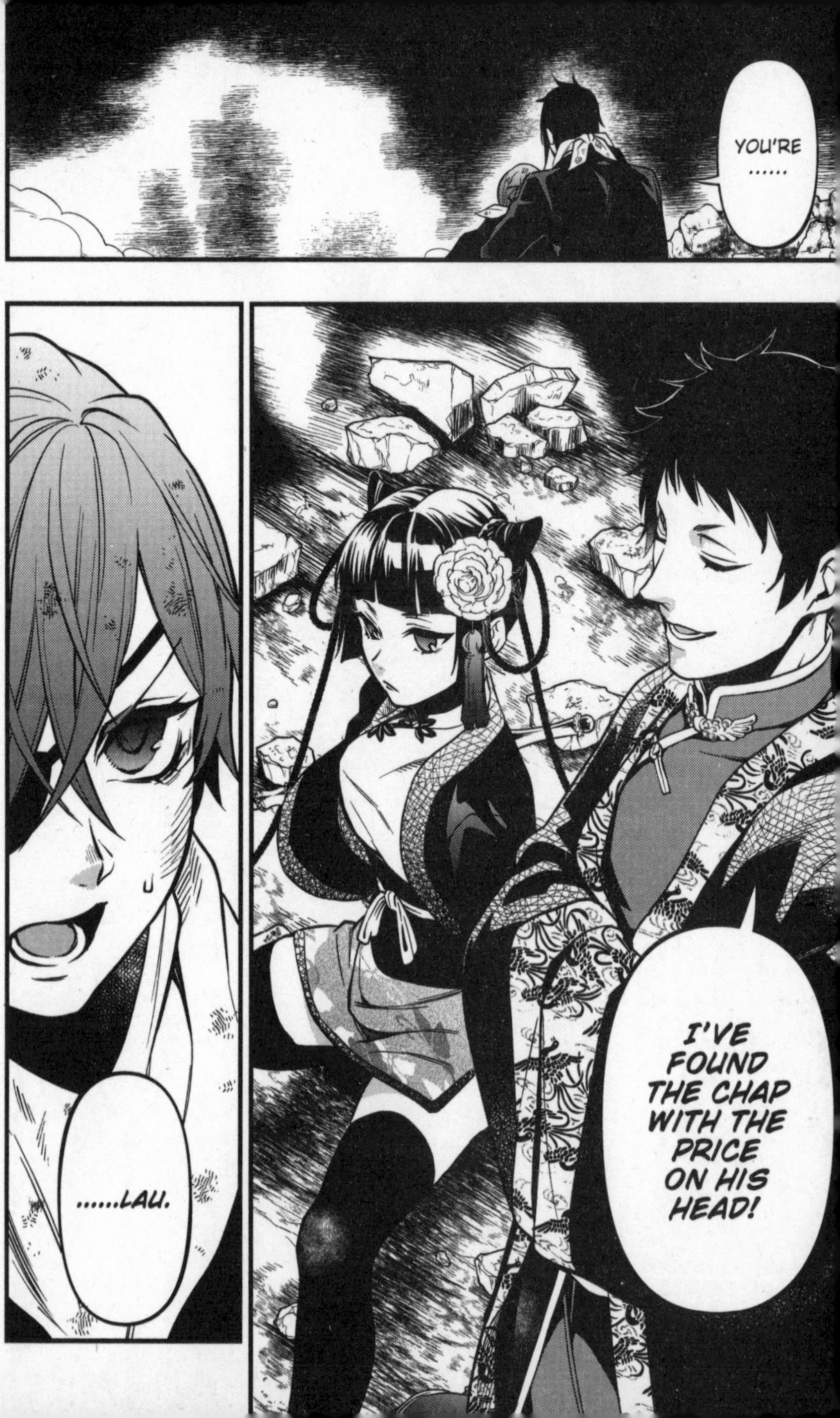
YOU'RE ......
I'VE FOUND THE CHAP WITH THE PRICE ON HIS HEAD!
......LAU.

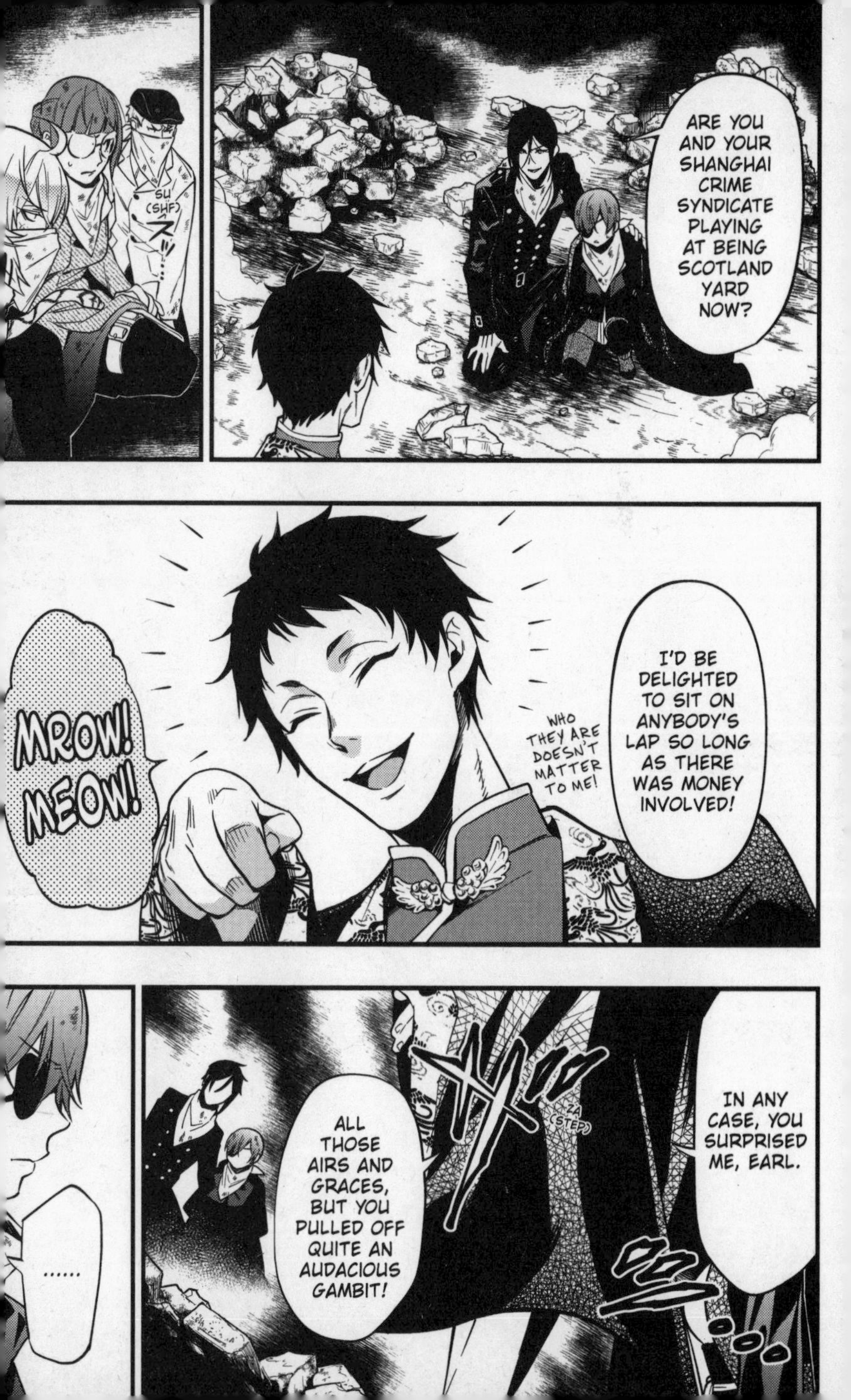
ARE YOU AND YOUR SHANGHAI CRIME SYNDICATE PLAYING AT BEING SCOTLAND YARD NOW?
SU (SHF)
I'D BE DELIGHTED TO SIT ON ANYBODY'S LAP SO LONG AS THERE WAS MONEY INVOLVED!
WHO THEY ARE DOESN'T MATTER TO ME!
MROW! MEOW!
IN ANY CASE, YOU SURPRISED ME, EARL.
ZA (STEP)
ALL THOSE AIRS AND GRACES, BUT YOU PULLED OFF QUITE AN AUDACIOUS GAMBIT!
......

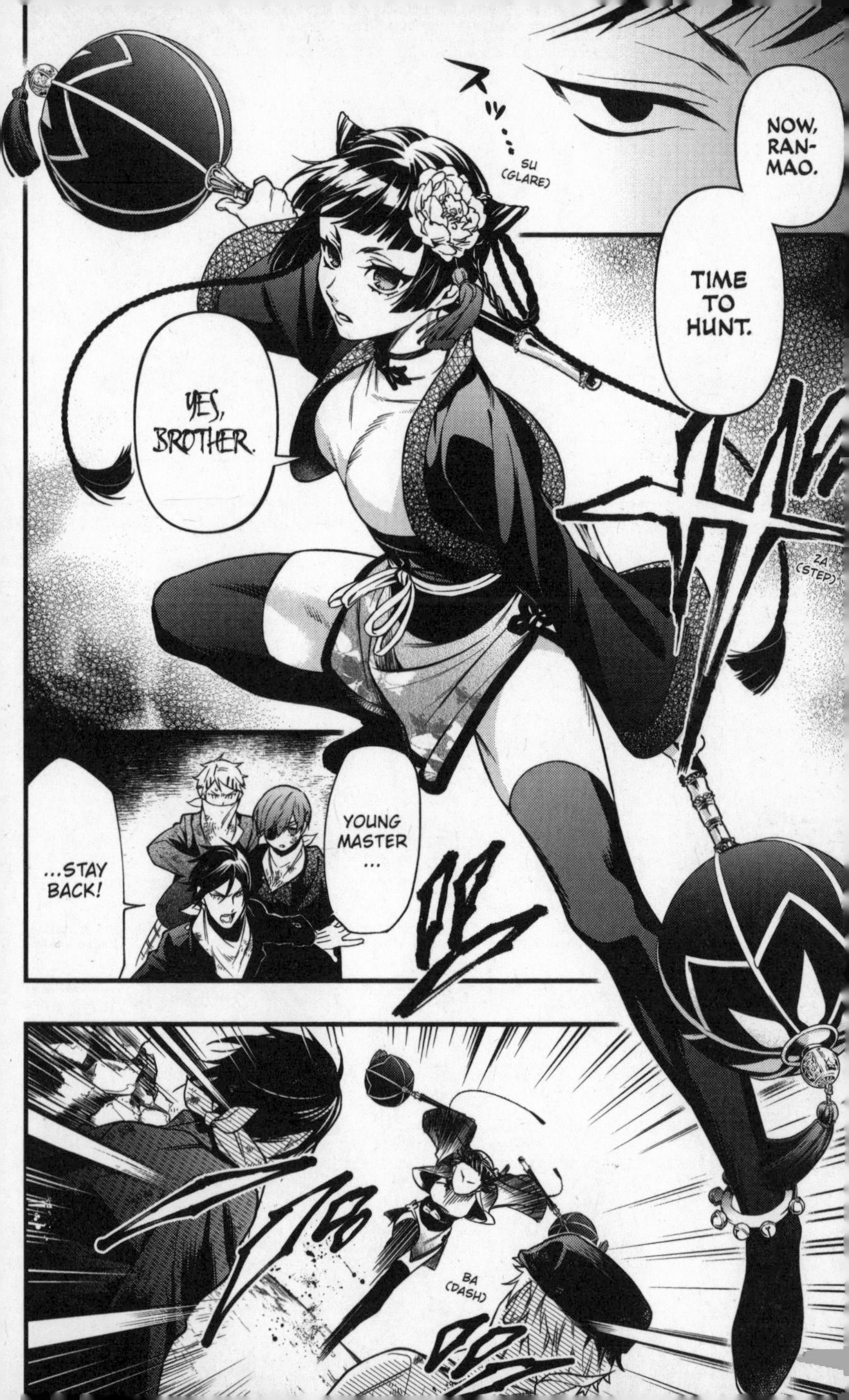
NOW, RAN-MAO.
TIME TO HUNT.
スッ…
SU (GLARE)
YES, BROTHER.
ZA (STEP)
YOUNG MASTER ...
...STAY BACK!
BA (DASH)

H!!
ラ

GARA
(CRUMBLE)

DOGGO
(BOOM)

GARA

YOU'RE A LOOKER, LI'L LADY, BUT YOU'RE CRAZY-STRONG!

SHAN
(JANGLE)

GYUN
(ZOOM)

SO FAST ......

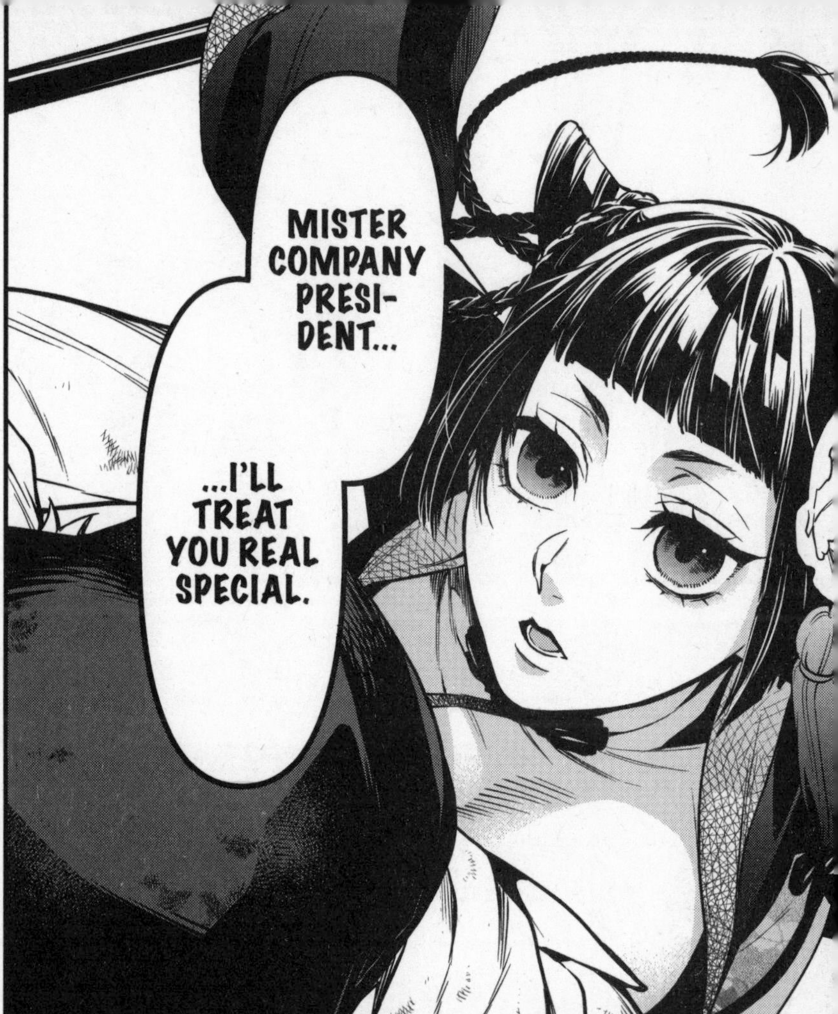
MISTER COMPANY PRESI-DENT...
...I'LL TREAT YOU REAL SPECIAL.
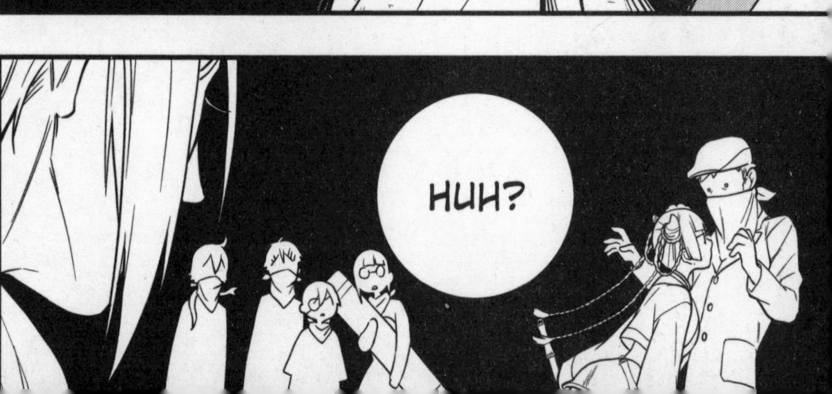
HUH?

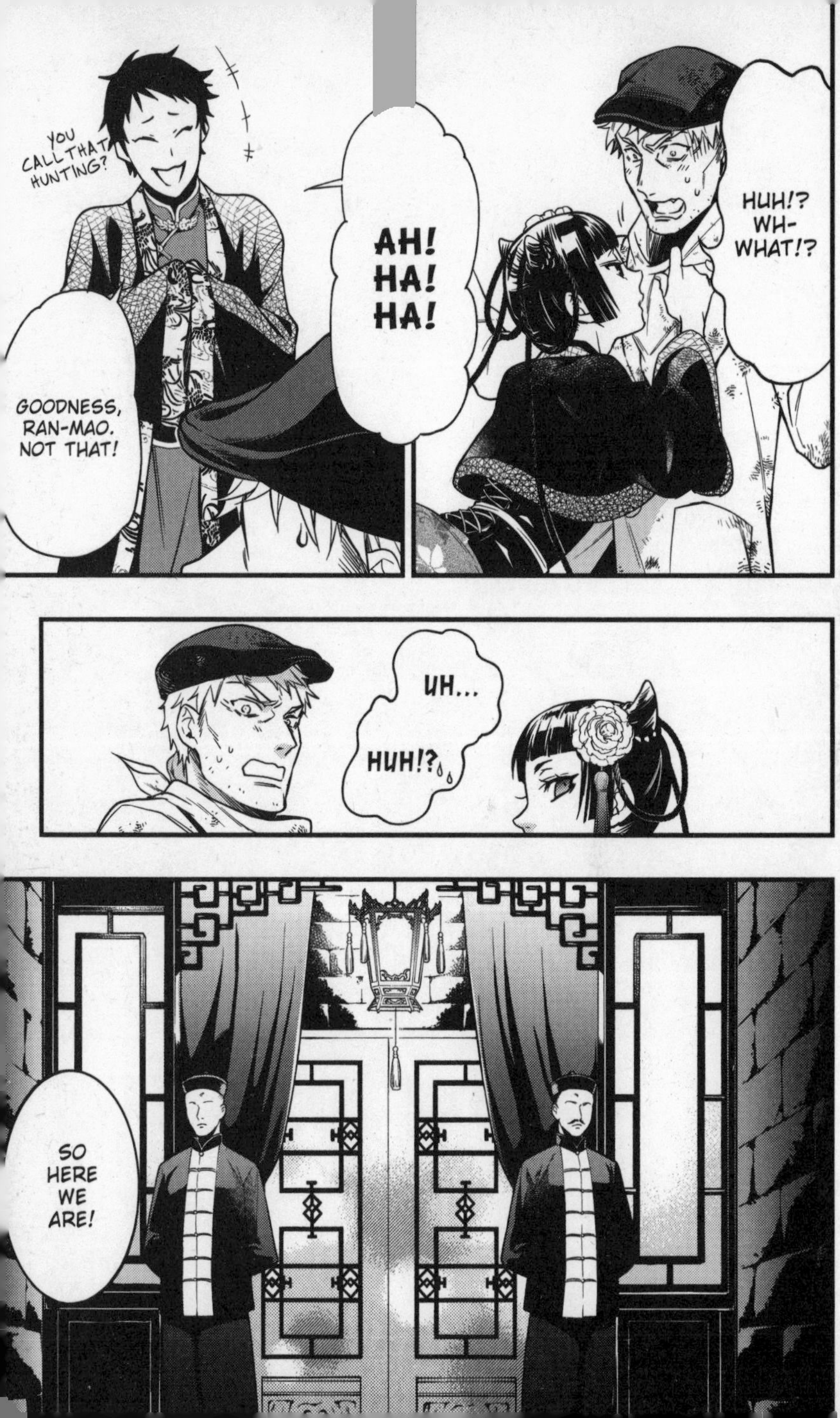
HUH!? WH-WHAT!?
AH! HA! HA!
YOU CALL THAT HUNTING?
GOODNESS, RAN-MAO. NOT THAT!
UH... HUH!?
SO HERE WE ARE!

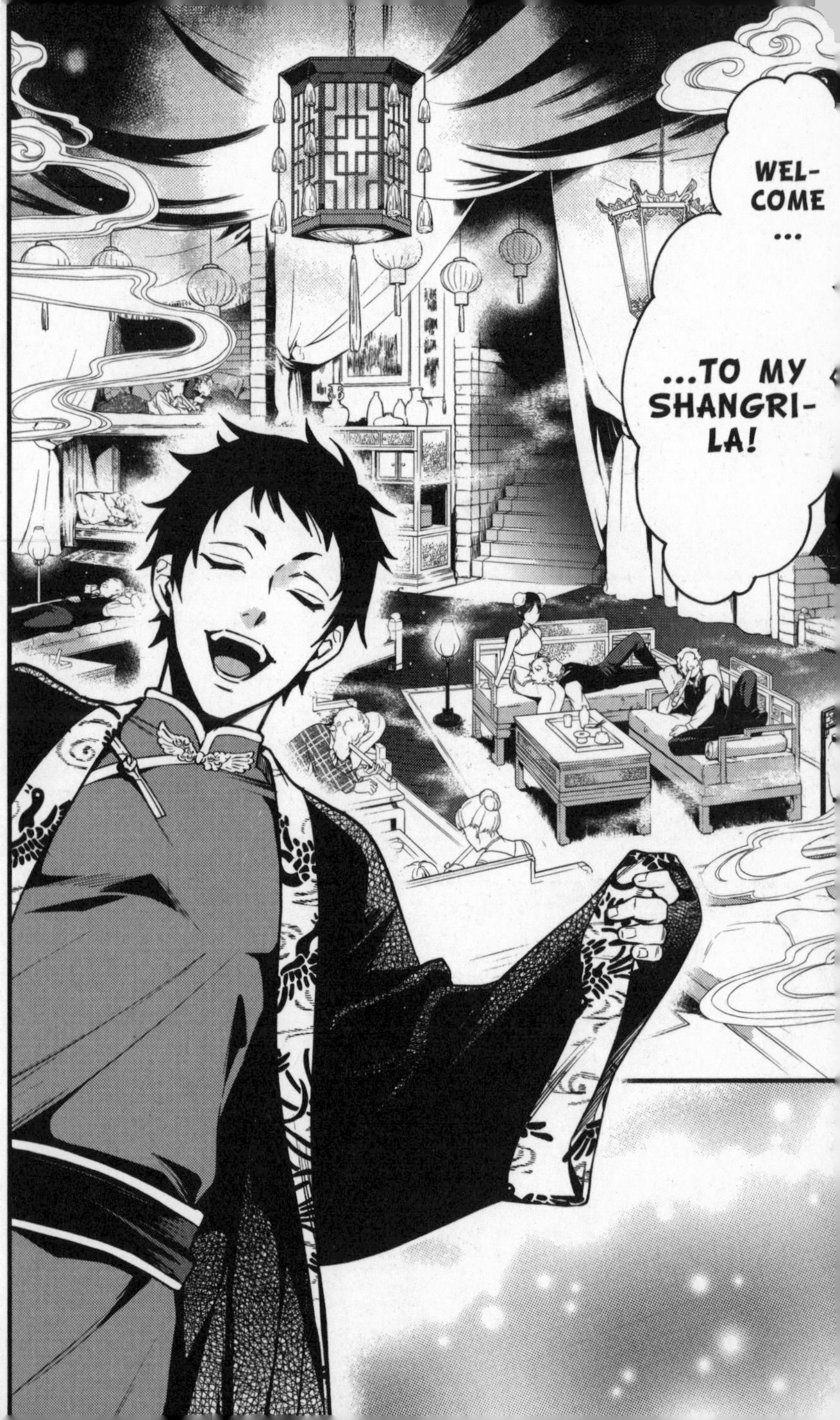
WEL-
COME
...
...TO MY
SHANGRI-
LA!

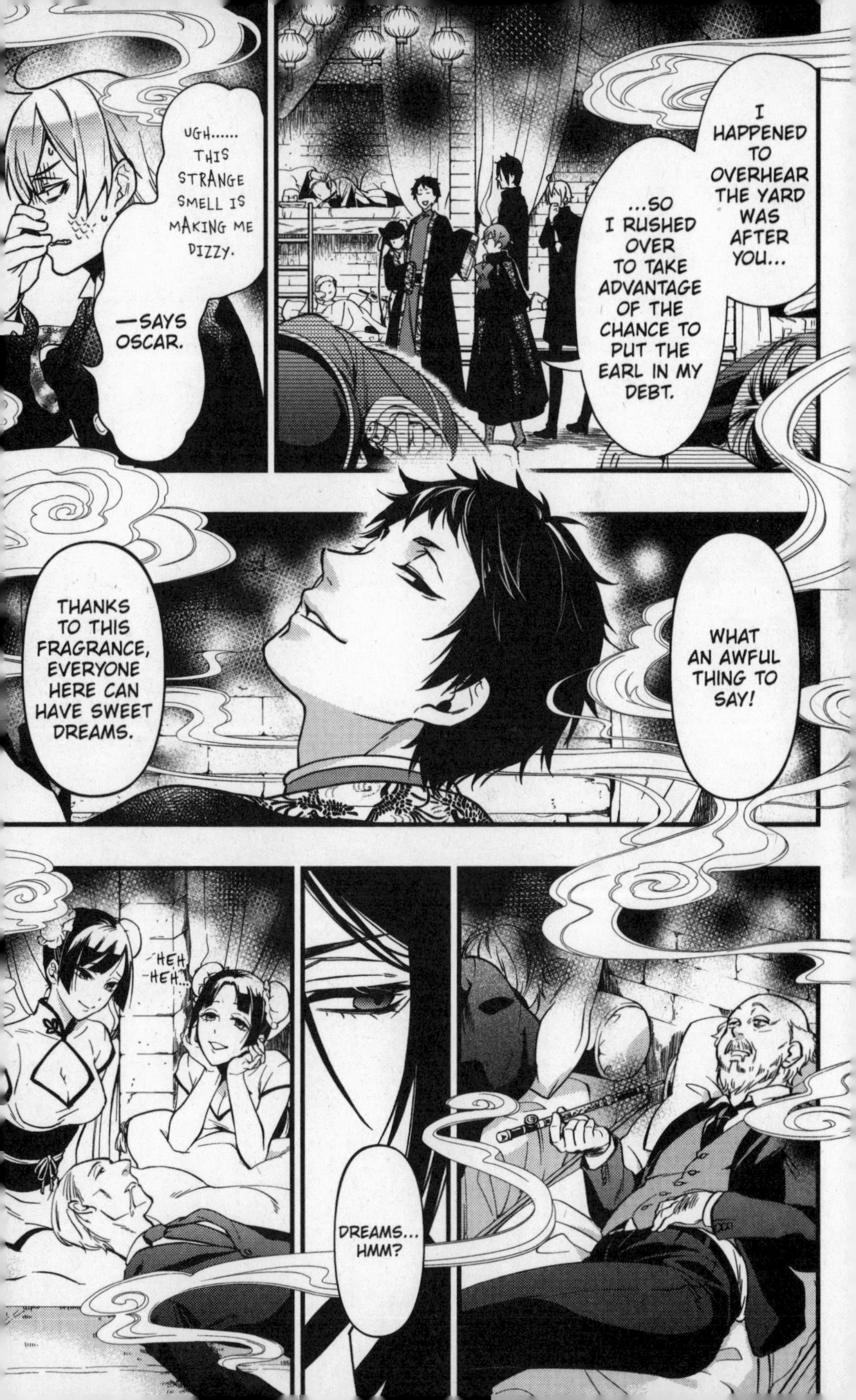
I HAPPENED TO OVERHEAR THE YARD WAS AFTER YOU...
...SO I RUSHED OVER TO TAKE ADVANTAGE OF THE CHANCE TO PUT THE EARL IN MY DEBT.
UGH...... THIS STRANGE SMELL IS MAKING ME DIZZY.
—SAYS OSCAR.
WHAT AN AWFUL THING TO SAY!
THANKS TO THIS FRAGRANCE, EVERYONE HERE CAN HAVE SWEET DREAMS.
DREAMS... HMM?
HEH HEH...

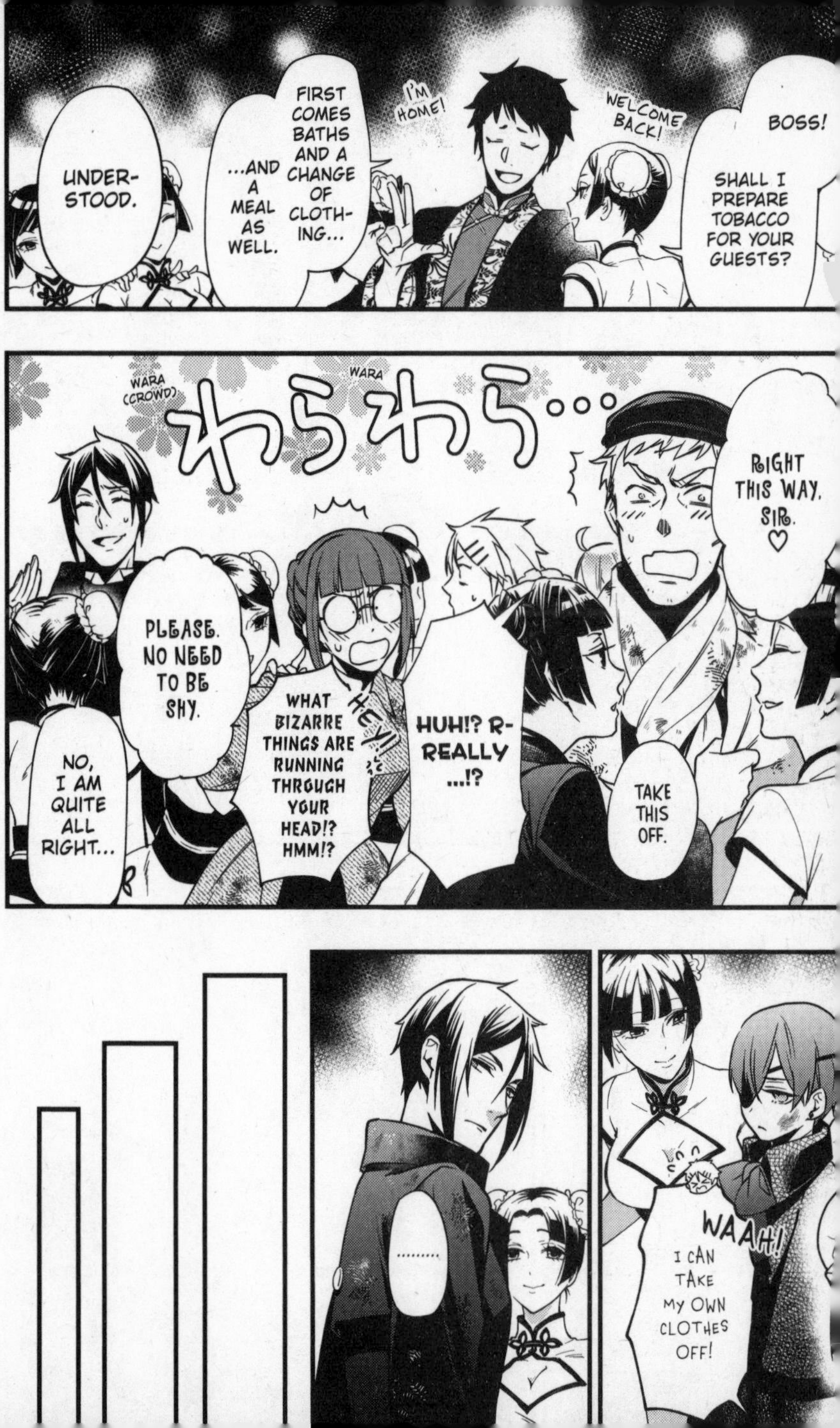
BOSS!
SHALL I PREPARE TOBACCO FOR YOUR GUESTS?
WELCOME BACK!
I'M HOME!
FIRST COMES BATHS AND A CHANGE OF CLOTHING...
...AND A MEAL AS WELL.
UNDERSTOOD.
WARA (CROWD)
WARA
わらわら…
RIGHT THIS WAY, SIR. ♡
TAKE THIS OFF.
HUH!? R-REALLY ...!?
HEY!!
WHAT BIZARRE THINGS ARE RUNNING THROUGH YOUR HEAD!? HMM!?
PLEASE. NO NEED TO BE SHY.
NO, I AM QUITE ALL RIGHT...
WAAH!
I CAN TAKE MY OWN CLOTHES OFF!
....

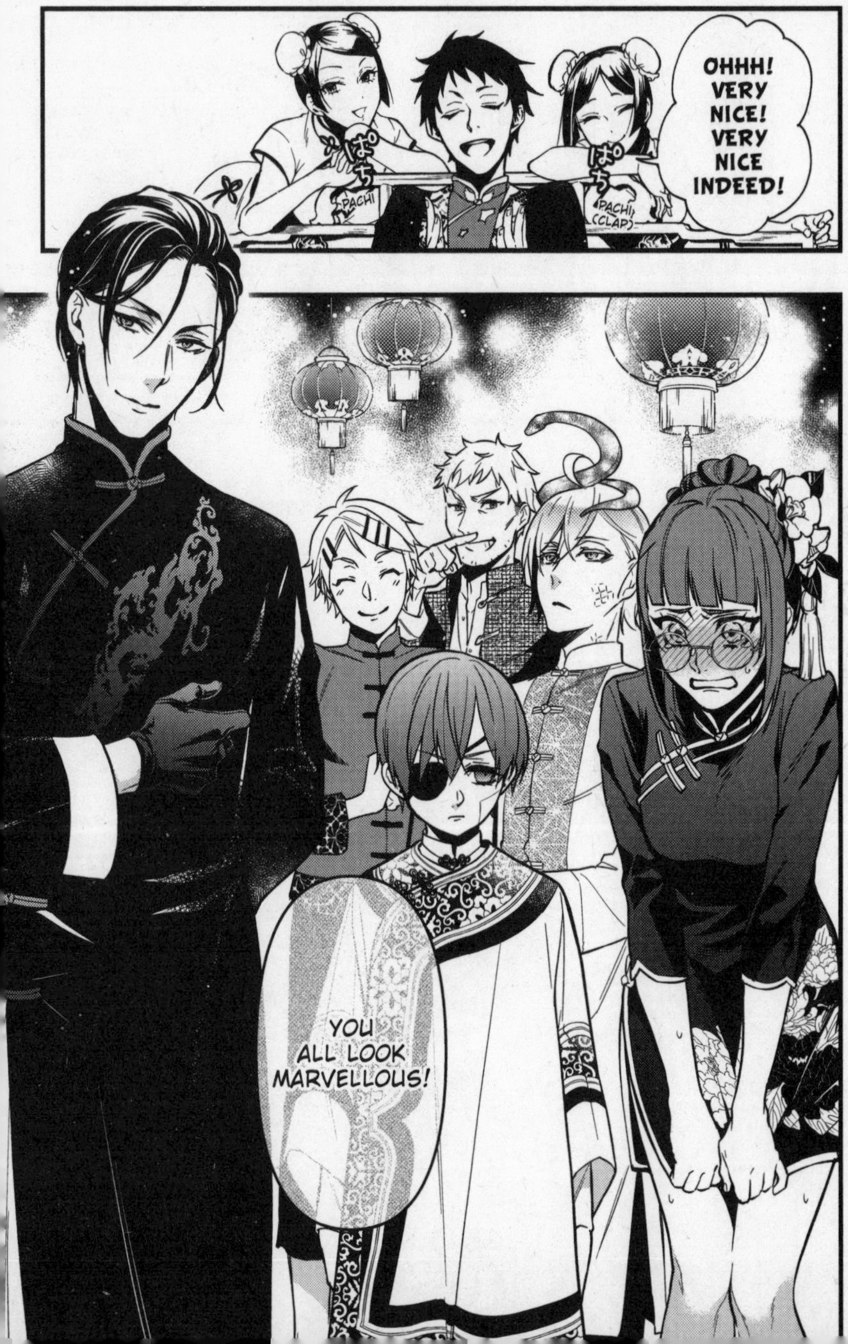
OHHH! VERY NICE! VERY NICE INDEED!
ぱち
PACHI (CLAP)
ぱち
PACHI
YOU ALL LOOK MARVELLOUS!

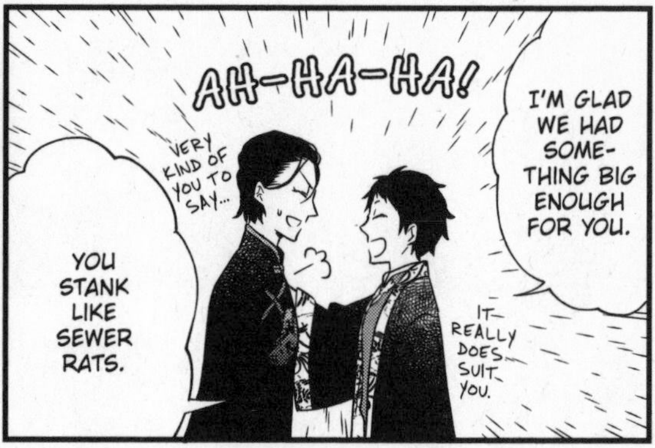
I'M GLAD WE HAD SOME-THING BIG ENOUGH FOR YOU.
AH-HA-HA!
IT REALLY DOES SUIT YOU.
VERY KIND OF YOU TO SAY...
YOU STANK LIKE SEWER RATS.
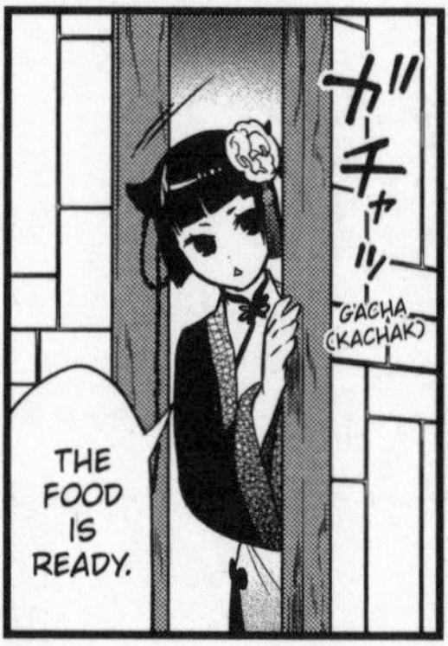
ガチャッ
GACHA (KACHAK)
THE FOOD IS READY.
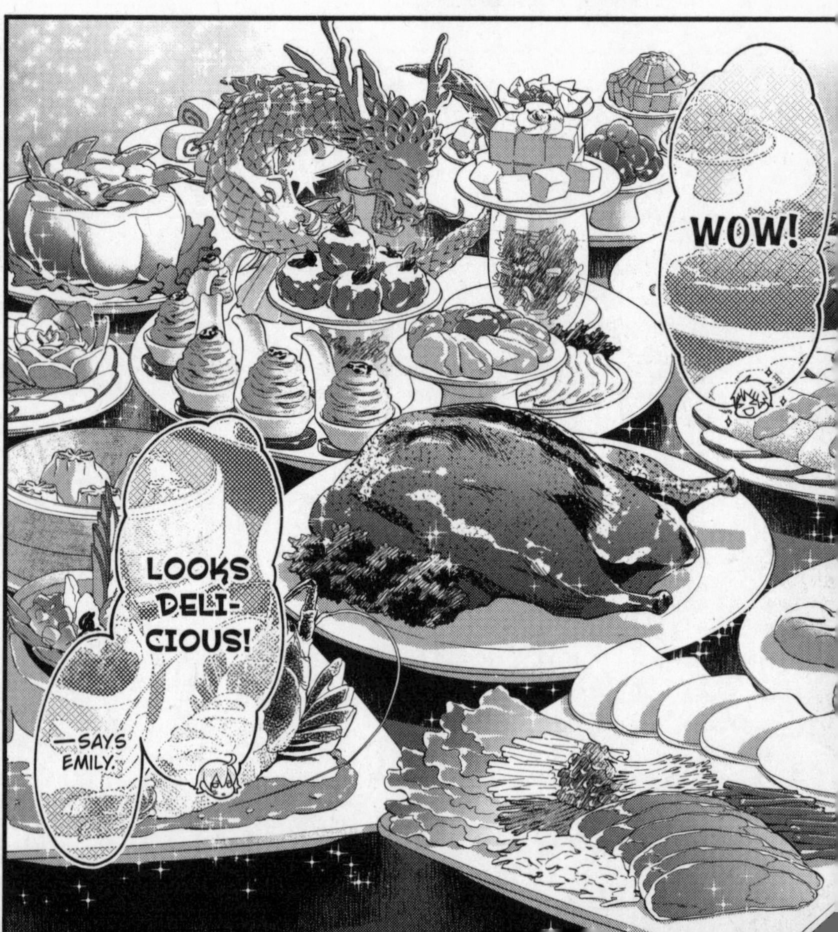
WOW!
LOOKS DELI-CIOUS!
—SAYS EMILY.

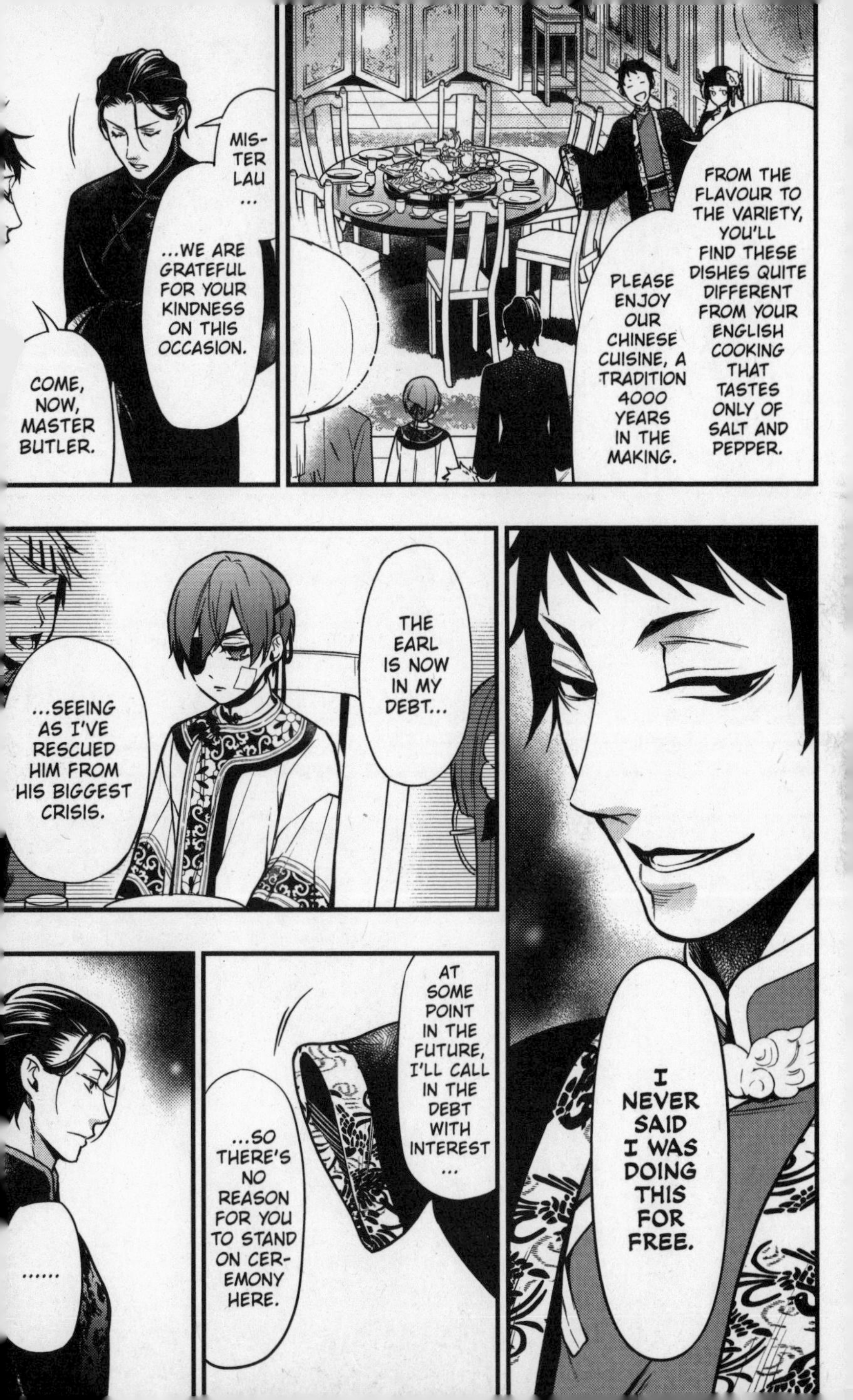
FROM THE FLAVOUR TO THE VARIETY, YOU'LL FIND THESE DISHES QUITE DIFFERENT FROM YOUR ENGLISH COOKING THAT TASTES ONLY OF SALT AND PEPPER.
PLEASE ENJOY OUR CHINESE CUISINE, A TRADITION 4000 YEARS IN THE MAKING.
MISTER LAU...
...WE ARE GRATEFUL FOR YOUR KINDNESS ON THIS OCCASION.
COME, NOW, MASTER BUTLER.
I NEVER SAID I WAS DOING THIS FOR FREE.
THE EARL IS NOW IN MY DEBT...
...SEEING AS I'VE RESCUED HIM FROM HIS BIGGEST CRISIS.
AT SOME POINT IN THE FUTURE, I'LL CALL IN THE DEBT WITH INTEREST...
...SO THERE'S NO REASON FOR YOU TO STAND ON CEREMONY HERE.
......

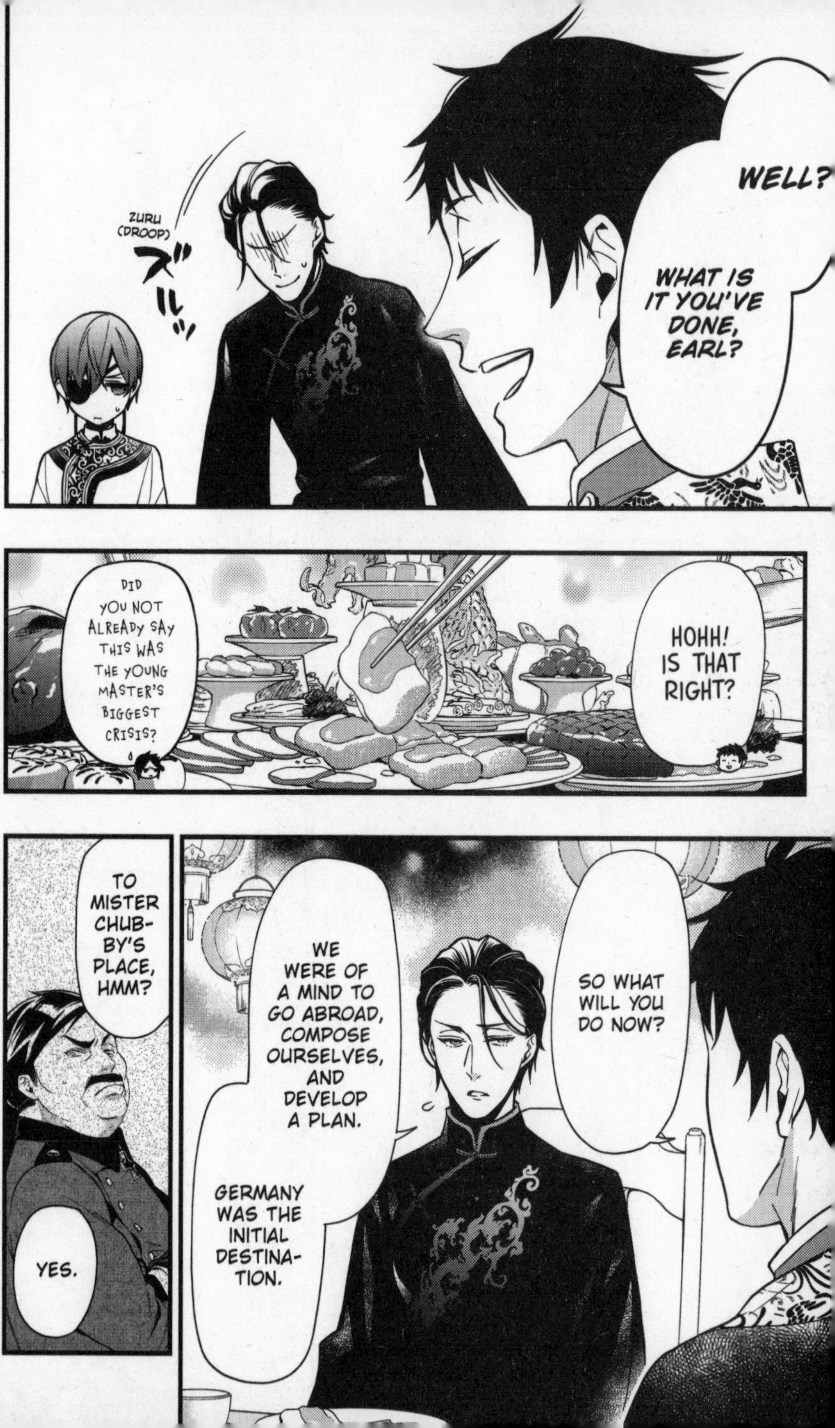
WELL?
WHAT IS IT YOU'VE DONE, EARL?
ZURU (DROOP)
ズルッ
HOHH! IS THAT RIGHT?
DID YOU NOT ALREADY SAY THIS WAS THE YOUNG MASTER'S BIGGEST CRISIS?
SO WHAT WILL YOU DO NOW?
WE WERE OF A MIND TO GO ABROAD, COMPOSE OURSELVES, AND DEVELOP A PLAN.
GERMANY WAS THE INITIAL DESTINATION.
TO MISTER CHUBBY'S PLACE, HMM?
YES.

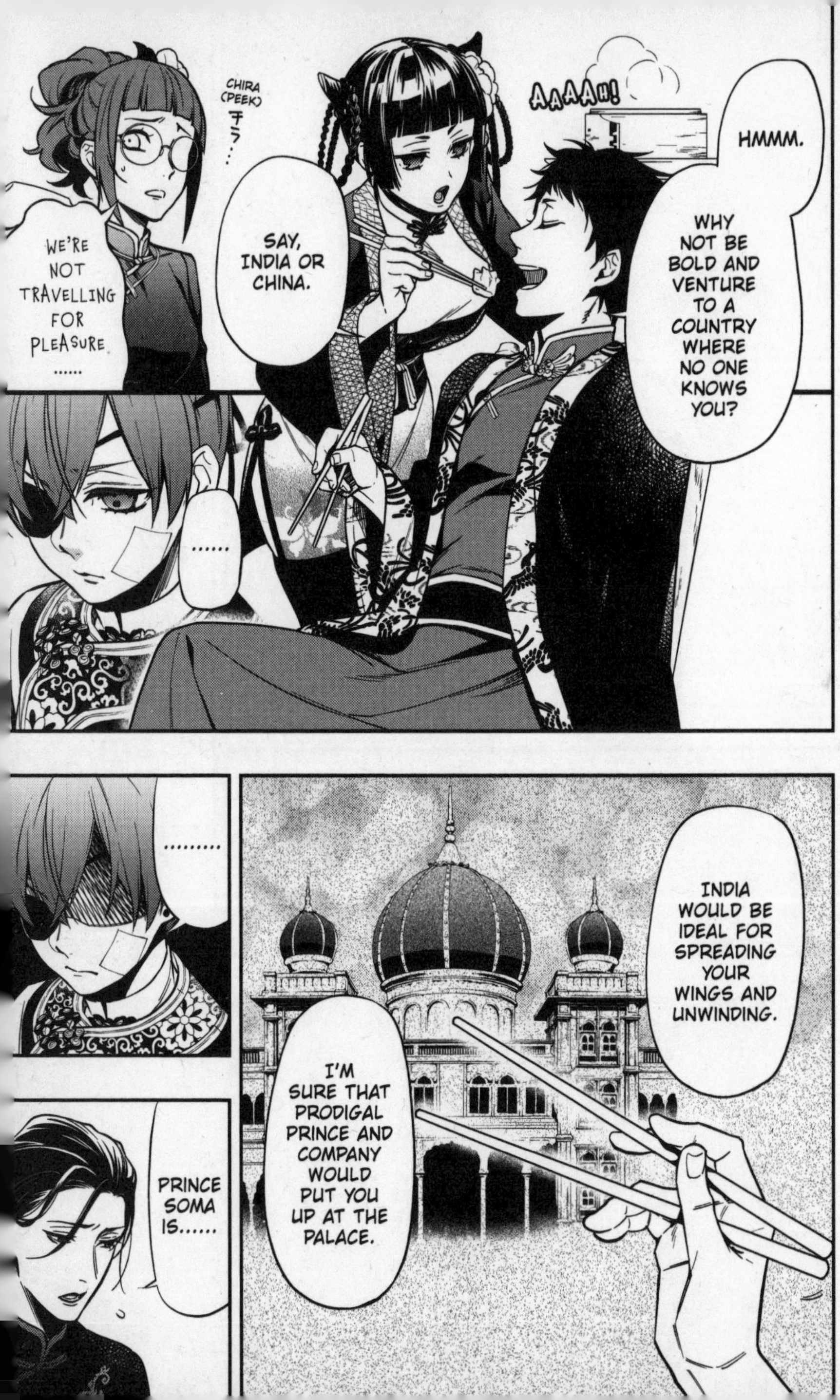
HMMM.
AAAAH!
WHY NOT BE BOLD AND VENTURE TO A COUNTRY WHERE NO ONE KNOWS YOU?
SAY, INDIA OR CHINA.
CHIRA (PEEK)
チラ…
WE'RE NOT TRAVELLING FOR PLEASURE ......
......
INDIA WOULD BE IDEAL FOR SPREADING YOUR WINGS AND UNWINDING.
I'M SURE THAT PRODIGAL PRINCE AND COMPANY WOULD PUT YOU UP AT THE PALACE.
....
PRINCE SOMA IS......

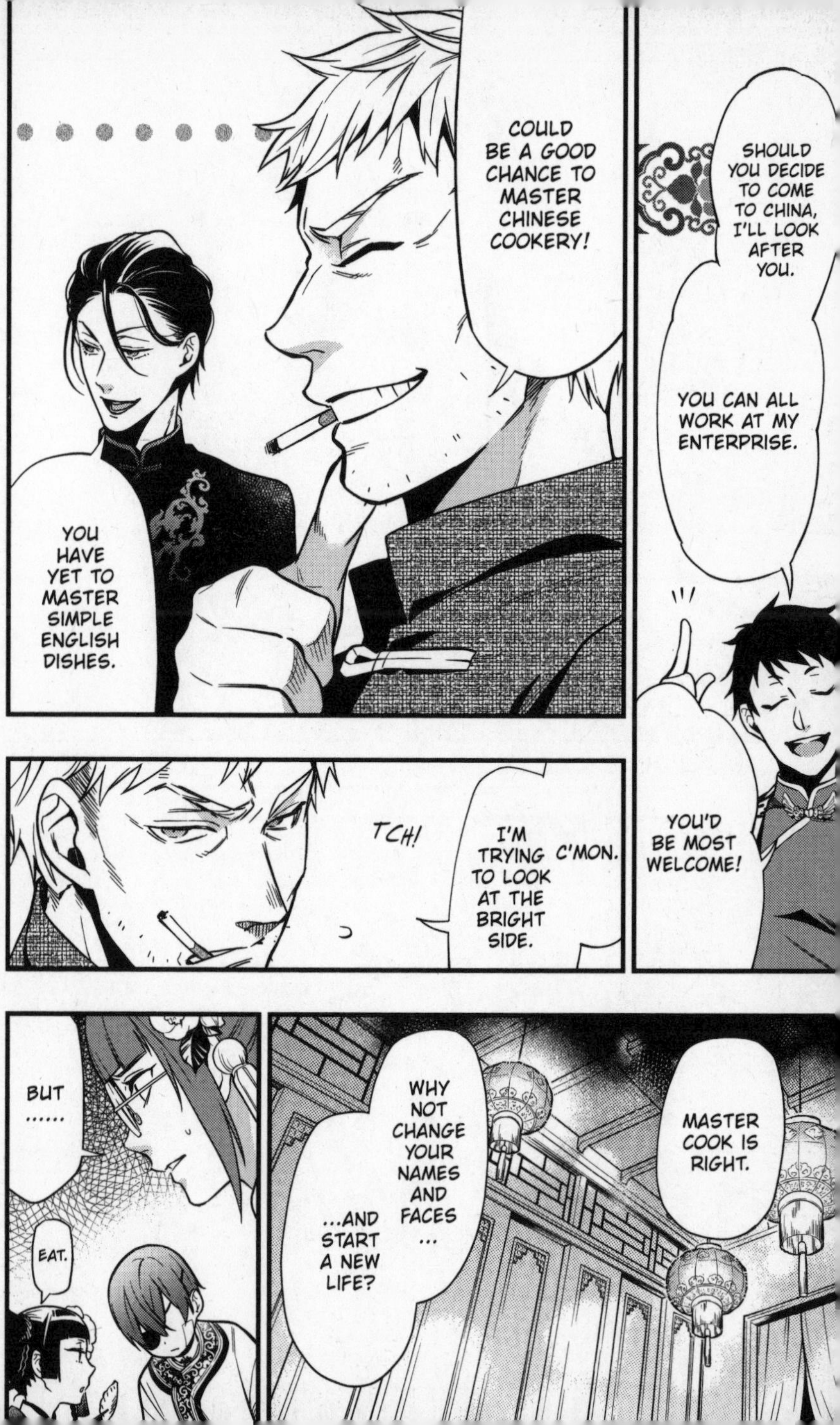
SHOULD YOU DECIDE TO COME TO CHINA, I'LL LOOK AFTER YOU.
YOU CAN ALL WORK AT MY ENTERPRISE.
YOU'D BE MOST WELCOME!
COULD BE A GOOD CHANCE TO MASTER CHINESE COOKERY!
YOU HAVE YET TO MASTER SIMPLE ENGLISH DISHES.
C'MON.
I'M TRYING TO LOOK AT THE BRIGHT SIDE.
TCH!
MASTER COOK IS RIGHT.
WHY NOT CHANGE YOUR NAMES AND FACES ...
...AND START A NEW LIFE?
BUT ......
EAT.

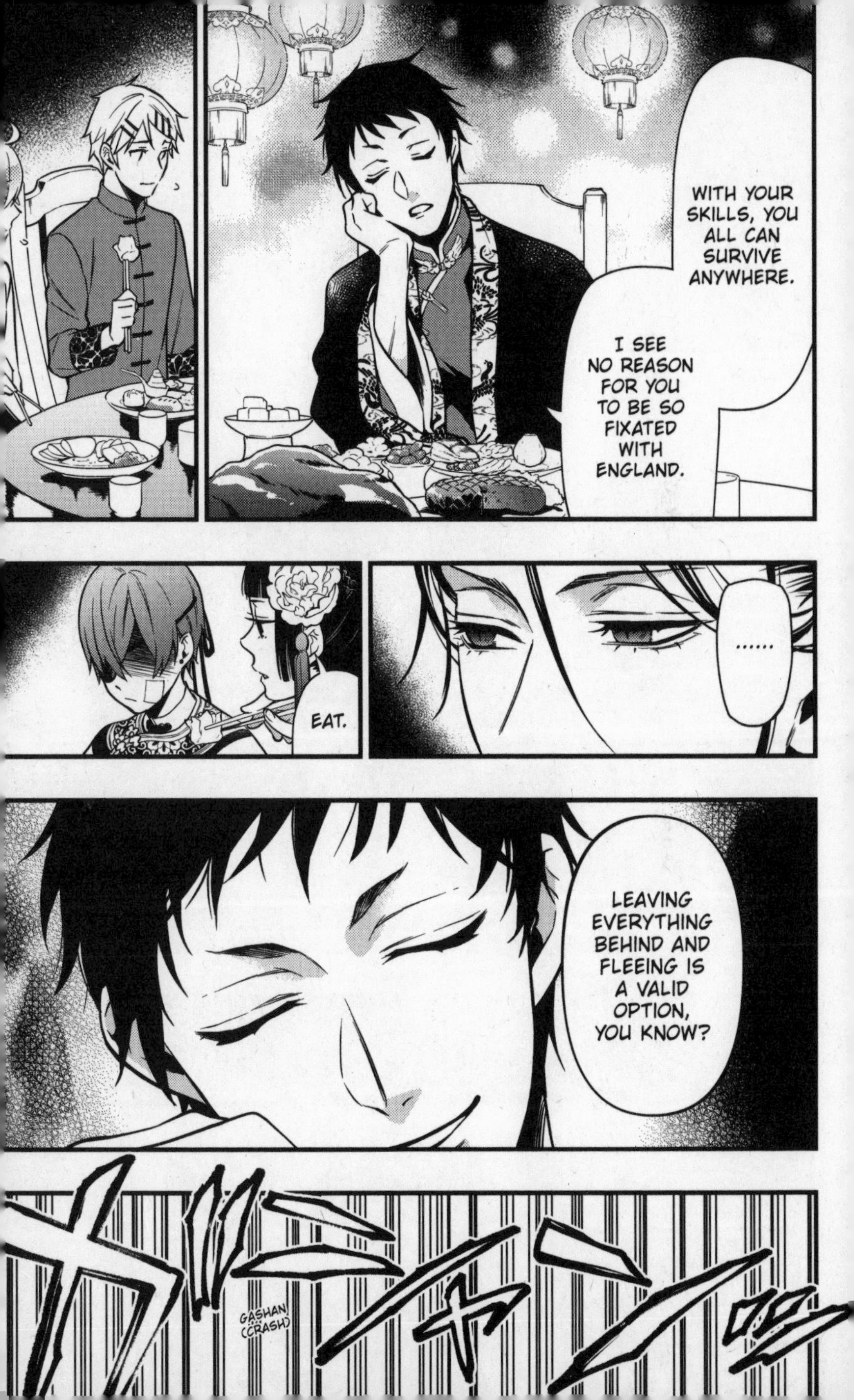
WITH YOUR SKILLS, YOU ALL CAN SURVIVE ANYWHERE.
I SEE NO REASON FOR YOU TO BE SO FIXATED WITH ENGLAND.
......
EAT.
LEAVING EVERYTHING BEHIND AND FLEEING IS A VALID OPTION, YOU KNOW?
GASHAN (CRASH)

НИН…!?

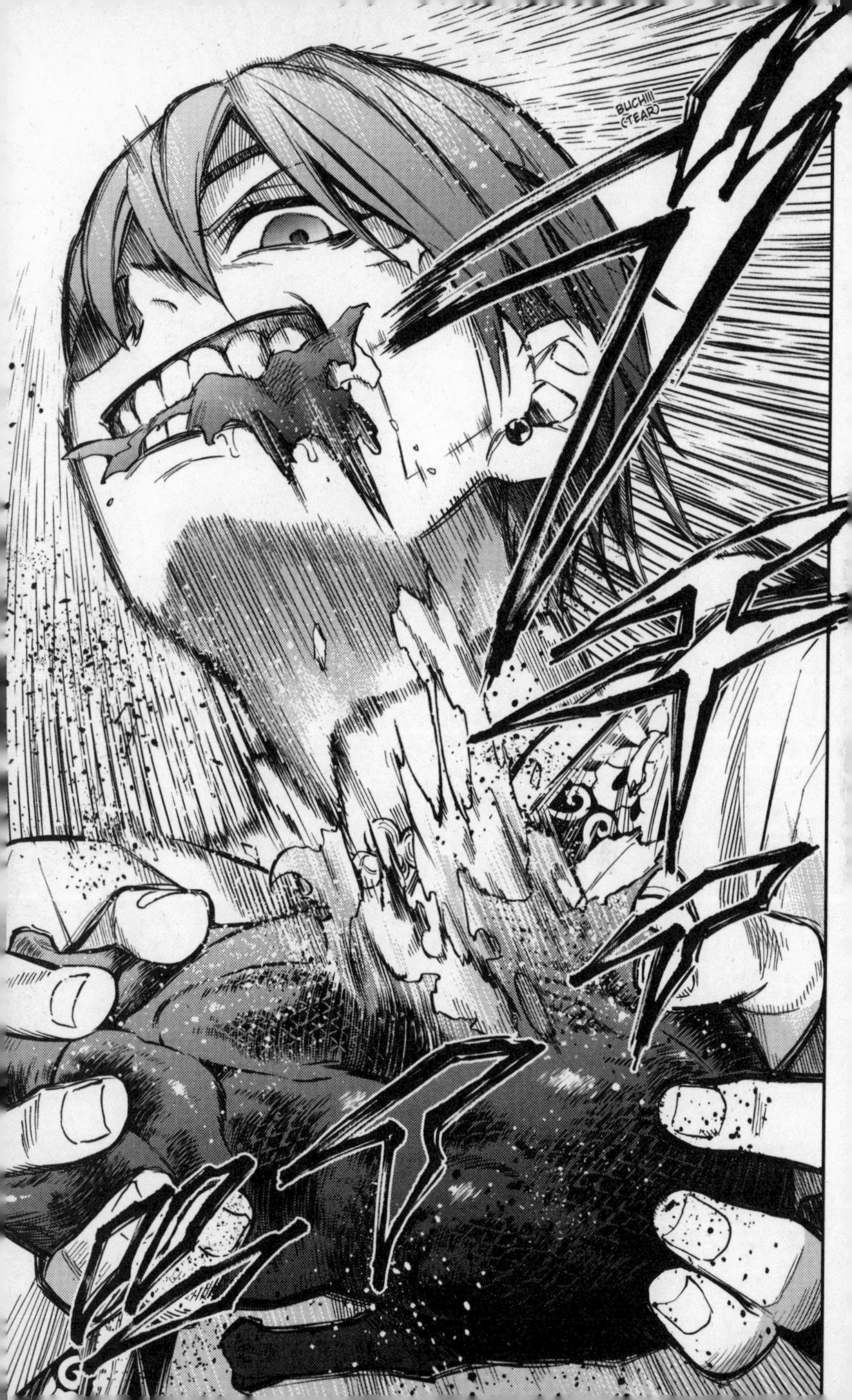
BUCHIII (TEAR)

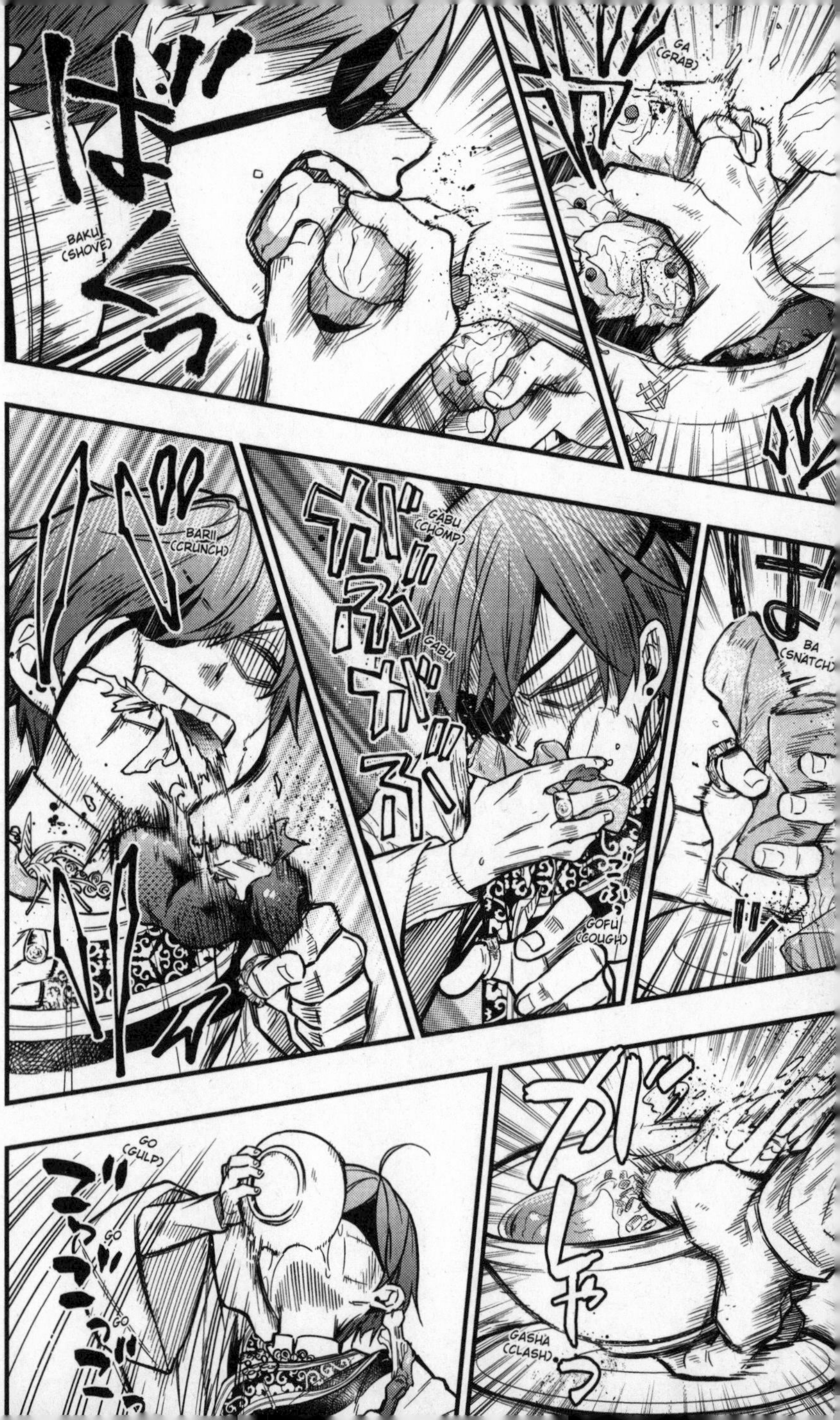
GA (GRAB)
BAKU (SHOVE)
BA (SNATCH)
GABU (CHOMP)
GABU
GOFU (COUGH)
BARII (CRUNCH)
GASHA (CLASH)
GO (GULP)
GO
GO

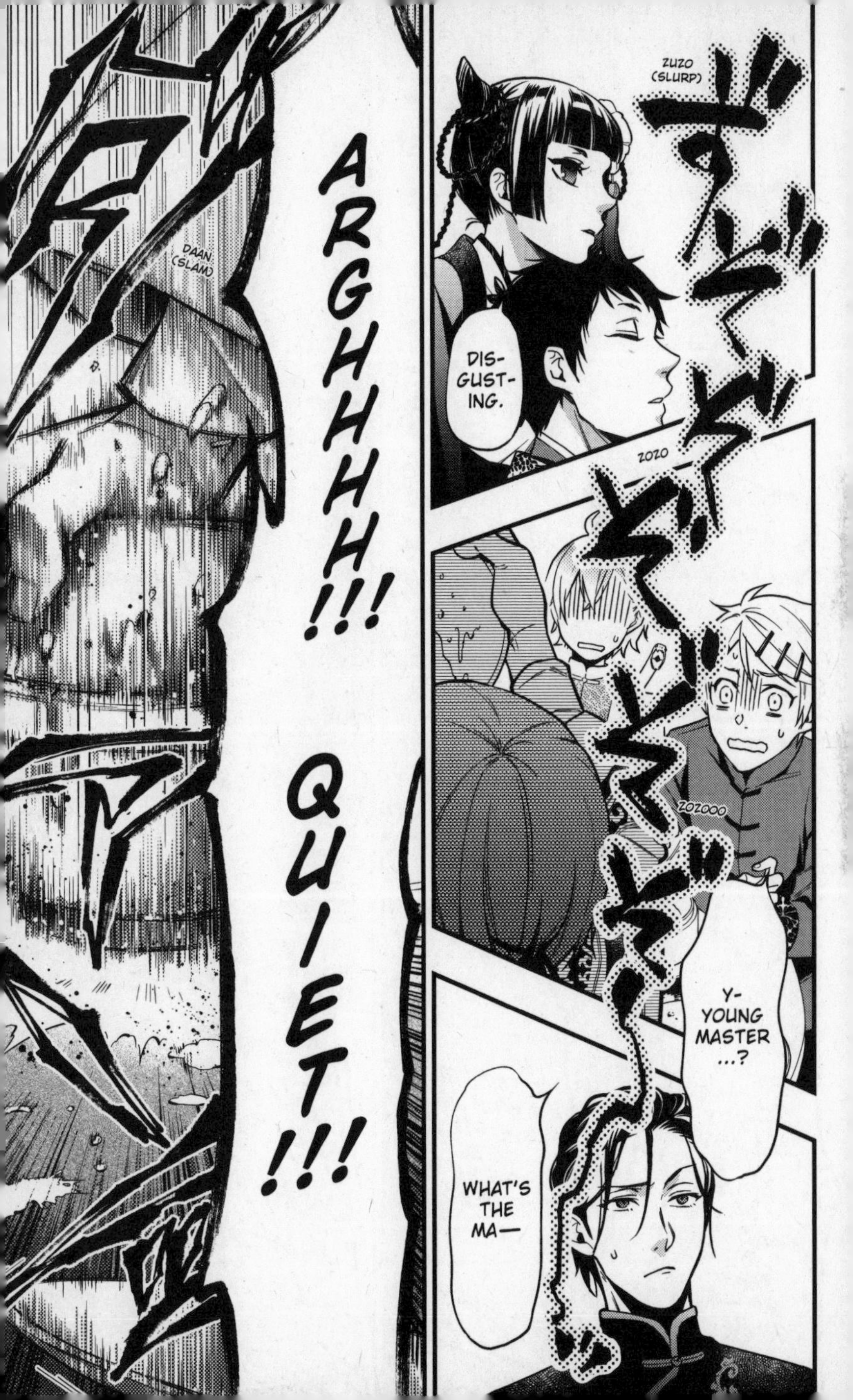
ZUZO (SLURP)
DIS-GUSTING.
ZOZO
ZOZOOO
Y-YOUNG MASTER ...?
WHAT'S THE MA—
ARGHHHH!!! QUIET!!!
DAAN (SLAM)

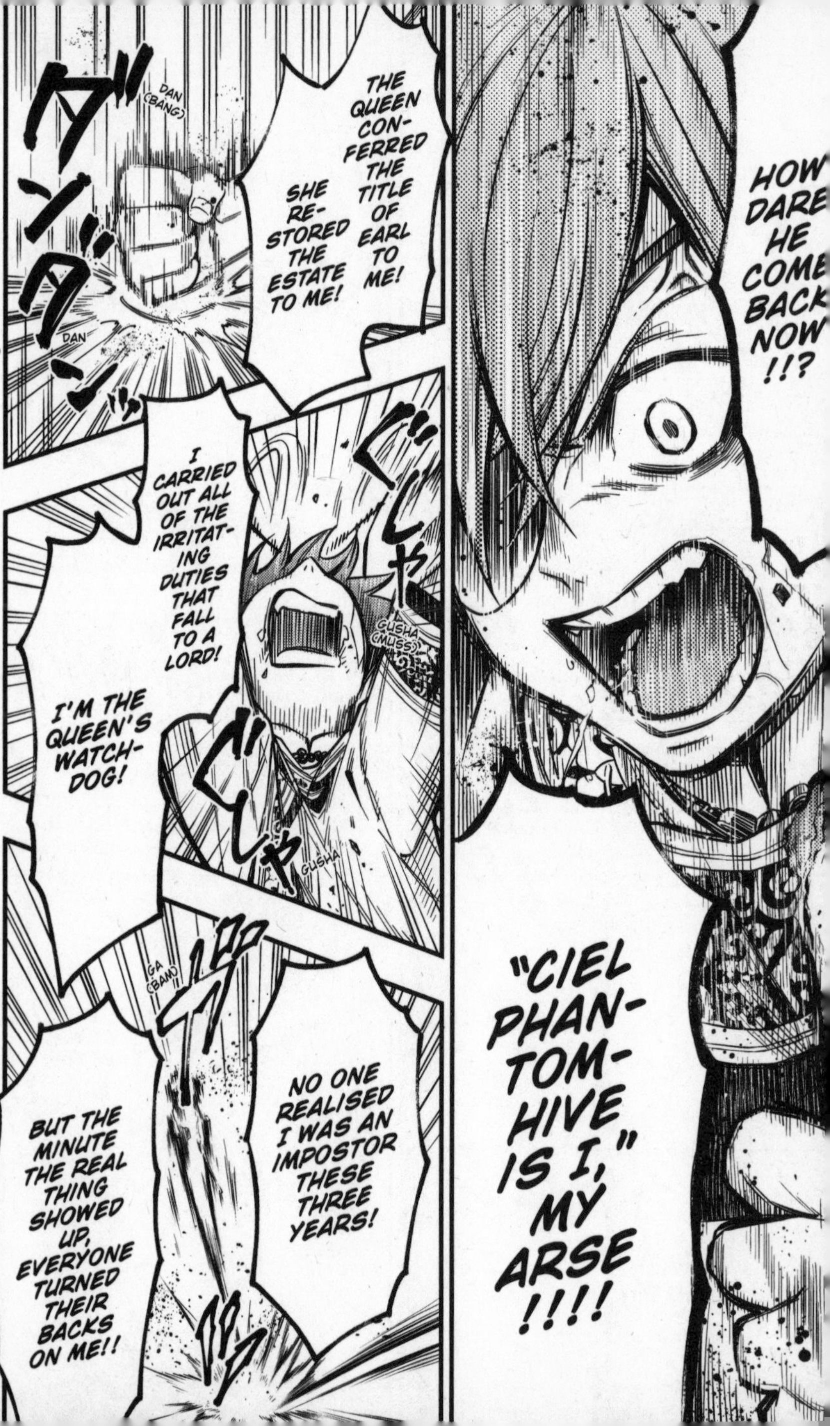
HOW DARE HE COME BACK NOW!!?
"CIEL PHANTOMHIVE IS I," MY ARSE!!!!
DAN (BANG)
DAN
THE QUEEN CONFERRED THE TITLE OF EARL TO ME!
SHE RESTORED THE ESTATE TO ME!
GUSHA (MUSS)
GUSHA
I CARRIED OUT ALL OF THE IRRITATING DUTIES THAT FALL TO A LORD!
I'M THE QUEEN'S WATCHDOG!
GA (BAM)
NO ONE REALISED I WAS AN IMPOSTOR THESE THREE YEARS!
BUT THE MINUTE THE REAL THING SHOWED UP, EVERYONE TURNED THEIR BACKS ON ME!!

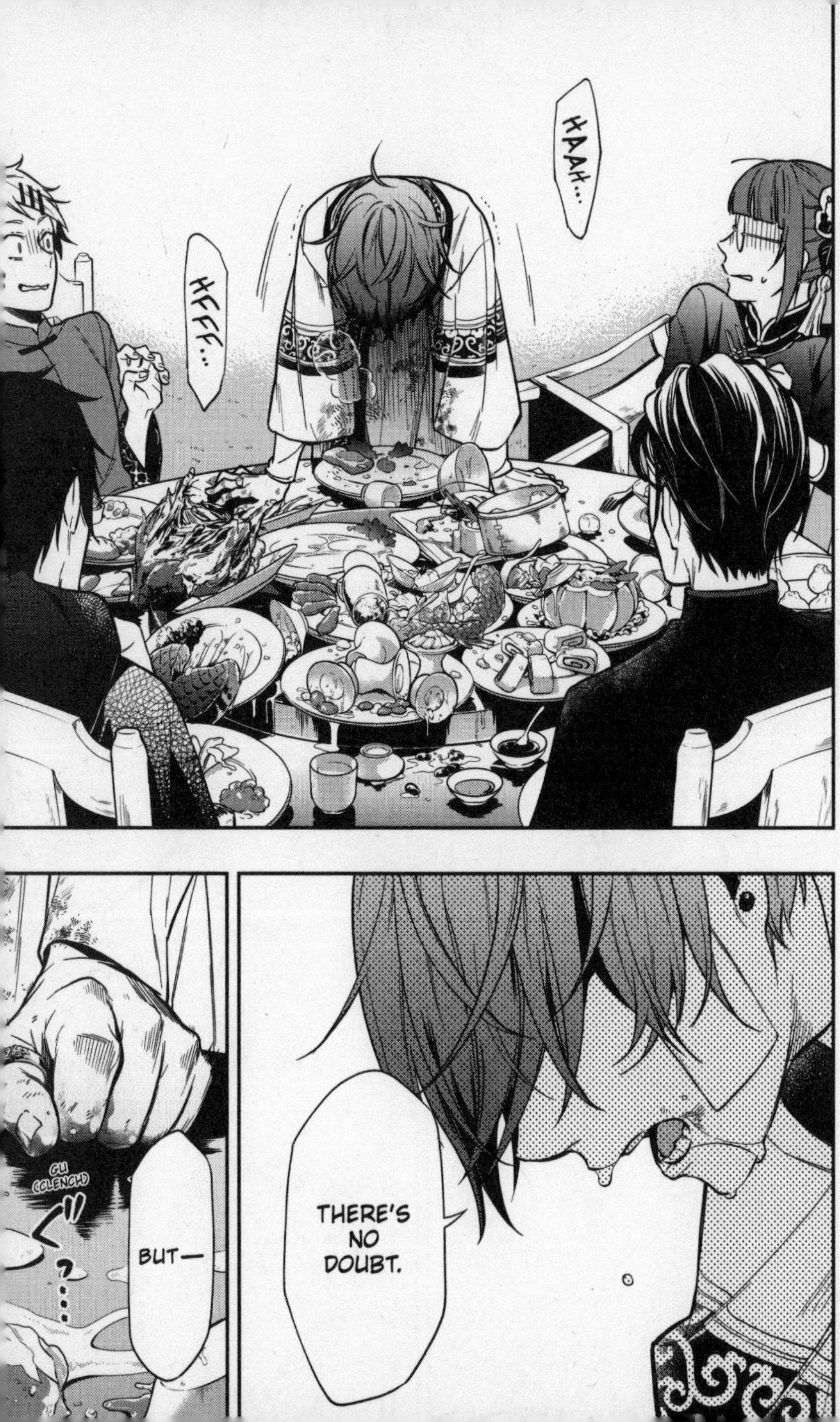
HAAAH...
HFFF...
THERE'S NO DOUBT.
BUT—
GU (CLENCH)

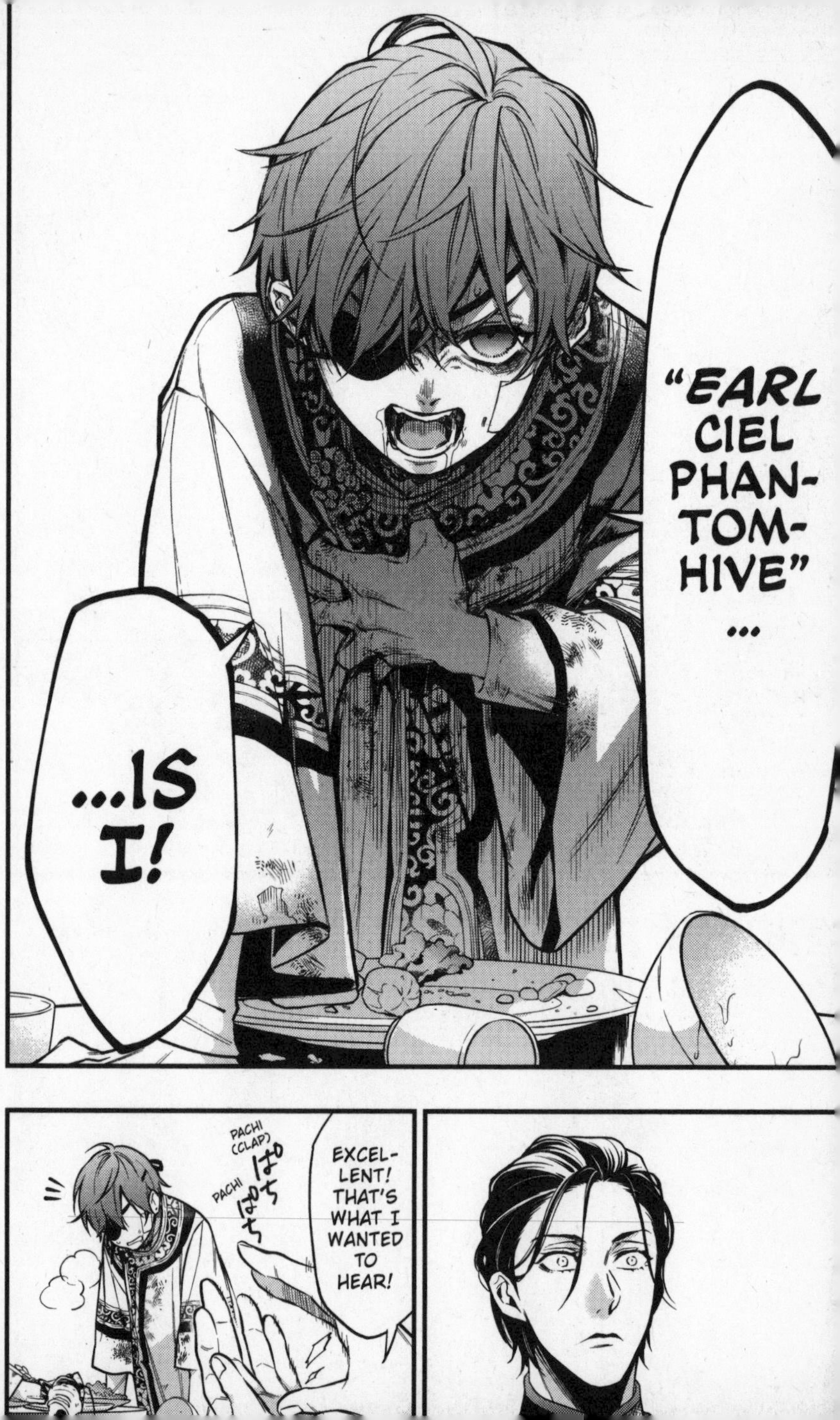
"EARL CIEL PHANTOMHIVE"...
...IS I!
EXCELLENT! THAT'S WHAT I WANTED TO HEAR!
PACHI (CLAP) ぱち
PACHI ぱち

I'LL FIGHT!

I'LL TAKE ON THE GHOST OF MY BROTHER THAT'S ARISEN FROM HIS GRAVE!

THIS IS THE EARL I SIGNED UP TO DO BUSINESS WITH.

LOOKS LIKE I WON'T NEED TO PREPARE AN ESCAPE VESSEL.

LIKE HELL I'LL RUN!

GOSHI (RUB)

...AND THE TITLE OF "EARL CIEL PHANTOMHIVE"... I'LL TAKE IT ALL BACK FOR MYSELF!

AND THEN...

...MY ESTATE, MY MANOR...

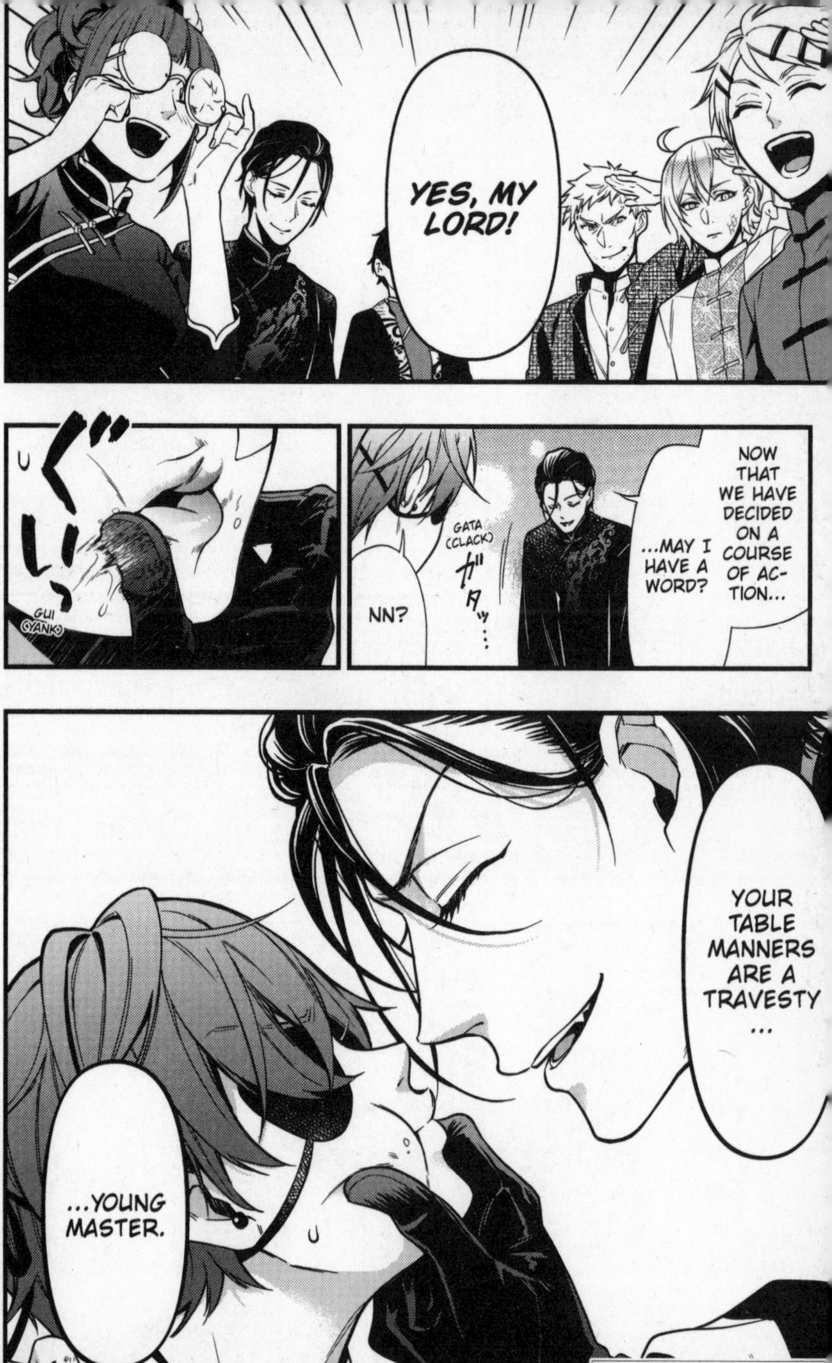
YES, MY LORD!
NOW THAT WE HAVE DECIDED ON A COURSE OF ACTION...
...MAY I HAVE A WORD?
GATA (CLACK)
NN?
GUI (YANK)
YOUR TABLE MANNERS ARE A TRAVESTY...
...YOUNG MASTER.

To be continued in Black Butler 29

⇒ Black Butler ⇐

黒執事

✤

Downstairs

Wakana Haduki
7
Tsuki Sorano
Chiaki Nagaoka
Sanihiko
Seira
Jun Hioki

*

Takeshi Kuma

*

Yana Toboso

✤

Adviser

Rico Murakami

Special thanks to You!

Yana Toboso

AUTHOR'S NOTE

I rented a small studio apartment nearby so I can closet myself to get work done.

I don't have a bed or a futon so I don't succumb to temptation. I use a sleeping bag when I absolutely have to lie down.

But the other day, I suddenly asked myself, "Why...am I sleeping in a sleeping bag when I'm not even camping?" I'll go buy a futon soon.

Sorry to keep you waiting. This is Volume 28.

BLACK BUTLER ㉘

YANA TOBOSO

Translation: Tomo Kimura
Lettering: Bianca Pistillo, Lys Blakeslee

KUROSHITSUJI Vol. 28 © 2019 Yana Toboso / SQUARE ENIX CO., LTD. First published in Japan in 2019 by SQUARE ENIX CO., LTD. English translation rights arranged with SQUARE ENIX CO., LTD. and Yen Press, LLC through Tuttle-Mori Agency, Inc.

English translation © 2019 by SQUARE ENIX CO., LTD.

Yen Press
150 West 30th Street, 19th Floor
New York, NY 10001

Visit us!
† yenpress.com
† facebook.com/yenpress
† twitter.com/yenpress
† yenpress.tumblr.com
† instagram.com/yenpress

First Yen Press Edition: October 2019
The chapters in this volume were originally publi...

Yen Press is an imprint of Yen Press, LLC.
The Yen Press name and logo are trademarks of Yen Press, LLC.

Library of Congress Control Number: 2010525567

ISBNs: 978-1-9753-5855-6 (paperback)
         978-1-9753-5856-3 (ebook)

10 9 8 7 6 5 4 3 2 1

WOR

Printed in the United States of America